THE TRINITY
AND
THE BIBLE
HOW ALL SCRIPTURE
TESTIFIES TO ONE GOD
IN THREE PERSONS

J. Alexander Rutherford

Hardcover ISBN-13: 978-1-989560-53-2
Paperback ISBN-13: 978-1-989560-52-5

To contact Teleioteti publishing for information or to provide feedback, please visit us at **https://teleioteti.ca** or email us at **info@teleioteti.ca**

DEDICATION

This book is dedicated to all the saints, past and present, who have confessed their faith in the Triune God through word and deed, through prayers, confessions, praise, even stories recounting the amazing deeds of our God. To such saints, who have firmly believed in the Triune God revealed in Scripture but could not make heads or tails of the accounts of the Trinitarian mystery developed over the last 2000 years, to these saints I dedicate this book. My prayer is that it would encourage greater confidence in the Triune revelation of our God in Scripture and greater confidence in the practical Trinitarian faith we regularly express in our churches.

ACKNOWLEDGEMENTS

I am indebted to numerous authors—Christians throughout the ages—for my understanding of God and his word. Likewise, among those who I have been privileged to know and learn from, dozens of men and women from my childhood until today have nurtured in me the Christian faith that is expressed in these pages. Among such as these, this book owes itself perhaps most to my friend, Fred Eaton. Fred, I have learned much from your pastoral care and input into my life, but the contribution I have in mind is of another sort. For years, you recounted how Van Til saw the Trinity as the solution to the problem of the "one and the many." For years, I could not wrap my head around what exactly the problem was. I eventually realised my problem: I could discuss many answers to the problem given throughout the ages but couldn't identify what exactly was problematic! When I pressed into that realisation, I came to discover that I indwelt a completely different world than those who wrestled with this problem; in my world, this problem simply didn't exist. I couldn't understand the problem until I stepped out of myself and into their world. When I did this, I reflected on what was different about my perspective that seemed to resolve this problem. It was here that I noticed subtle but significant differences in my understanding and practiced faith in the Trinity than many of those in the ancient church. That discovery led me to rethink the problem of the one and the many in my book *The Gift of Knowledge*, but it also led me to reflect on Van Til's teaching concerning the Trinity, the relation of the Trinity to the one and the many, and how all this related to the biblical teaching. This book is the result of that reflection. Thanks for the many edifying conversations that led me down this road! I have also benefitted greatly from discussing the content of Chapter 8 with Viet Mai; thanks, brother.

CONTENTS

ANALYTICAL OUTLINE

PREFACE

A friend recently asked me, knowing that I was studying and writing in the area of Christology and the Trinity, how to explain the Trinity to his children. The Trinity is a doctrine that confronts and challenges us; even children raise questions about the pattern of language we use in our prayers and churches that attest to our belief in a Triune God—among other things, attributing worship, adoration, and the name "God" to the Father, Son, and Holy Spirit, all the while speaking of "One God" and using "God" without seeming differentiation. Our Triune God breaks the mould of our regular speech conventions and the manner with which we speak about persons and foreign deities. There is an inevitable collision at the worldview level (or the level of interpretive framework) when we learn the Christian faith within a non-Christian world. Such collisions do not only happen between Christian and opposing worldviews; even between prevalent Christian beliefs there can be a similar collision—such as when I began encountering Calvinist literature and teachers as an avowed Arminian (as a result of this collision, I later came to embrace the theology of the Reformed tradition). The philosopher of science Thomas Kuhn popularised (or perhaps stole) Michael Polanyi's account of large-scale transitions in belief systems under the phrase "paradigm shift." A paradigm shift happens when one interpretive framework is exchanged for another; this cannot happen piecemeal, for the former and the latter paradigms offer mutually exclusive interpretations of the same data—to some extent, of all reality. Kuhn describes the gradual accumulation of incongruous data—experience which doesn't fit within the previous paradigm—until there is another paradigm to supplant it, one which takes into account the previous data and the growing collection of incongruities. Michael Polanyi describes this not as a purely inductive process but as a courageous leap of understanding, an almost intuitive realisation of an alternative perception of the entire scope of the matter at hand.

I make no claims to offer the sort of penetrating insight Polanyi attributes to the great intellects in the history of the natural sciences. Yet I have introduced the idea of a paradigm shift because the analysis offered by Polanyi and Kuhn has many parallels to theological developments across the history of the church. The challenges facing the one who seeks a paradigm shift are similar to those that I face as I attempt to commend the vision of the Trinity I have sought to articulate within these pages.

The doctrine of the Trinity, I will contend below, is not a novel invention of the 4th century but a thoroughly biblical doctrine that has been held by God's people since the beginning of Creation. However, there have been several paradigm shifts in the history of the Church that make it hard for any of us raised within Western Christendom to intuitively grasp this doctrine. I will draw your attention to three such shifts: I do so because I am convinced that these paradigm shifts will make the following argument intuitively incredulous, at least at first! These paradigm shifts have so shaped our worldviews that the conclusions I draw in the following pages will seem utterly unnatural, strained, and perhaps ridiculous. By drawing your attention to these shifts, I hope to encourage you to attempt to acquire what missiologists call an *emic* view of my argument—a view from the inside. As your read through this book, do not attempt to evaluate each argument and movement of the argument from within your current interpretive paradigm, but reserve judgment as you move through the argument until you have a grasp of the whole, then weigh that whole-Bible, whole-world vision that I have presented against your current whole-Bible, whole-world understanding. I am not offering merely an argument for the Trinity that fits within the current paradigm of Trinitarian doctrine and biblical exegesis but a reading strategy for the whole of Scripture that sees it as entirely Trinitarian and sees the world as infused with the knowledge of the Trinitarian God. If you find this difficult to believe—if you find it intuitively unlikely—consider the following paradigm shifts and ask whether they or the biblical testimony are shaping your intuition.

The first shift happened around the 3rd and 4th centuries. As Christians multiplied throughout the Roman Empire, there naturally emerged a desire among Christians to engage intellectually with their faith and the surrounding world. In the 4th-century, this engagement was thought to be all the more necessary because of significant errors that had infiltrated the church and because of significant intellectual opposition from the leading pagan thinkers of this time. Part of the answer to the growing threats to the unity of the burgeoning Christendom was an articulation of biblical teaching in the philosophical mode of contemporary discourse, an articulation sufficient to identify those who were threatening the unity of the church and the prevalent understanding of the Lord Jesus Christ. The metaphysical doctrine of the Trinity was elucidated throughout the 4th century until, in the mid-5th century, this teaching began to be considered an infallible and entirely sufficient rule of faith (see Ch. 16-18, 20 below). From this period onward, the Trinitarian faith of the early Christians—which confessed the simultaneous divinity of God the Father, Son, and Spirit without metaphysical elucidation—was no longer sufficient as an orthodox confession of faith; now, the doctrine of the Trinity was, by definition, a metaphysical doctrine. Though I will engage in metaphysics and ontology below, I want to offer a doctrine of the Trinity that is not at first philosophical (though philosophical reflection will enter later in our discussion as a tool to aid us in understanding what we have seen in the Bible). Thus, I want to offer a vision of the Trinity that is not *primarily* philosophical, though it is not *threatened* by philosophical reflection.

The second shift happened at some point in church history, which I will make no effort to identify. Nevertheless, it likewise deeply affects our reading of Scripture and the doctrine of the Trinity. I suspect that what I am treating as a single shift is actually three shifts, but considering them together will simplify the matter. Between the first century and today, I contend, there has been a shift towards treating the terms "Lord" and "God" as primarily titles for Jesus and God the Father, respectively. That is, we treat "Lord" without qualification as a reference to Jesus and "God" without qualification as a reference to God the Father, despite the fact that such a reading is not commended anywhere in the pages of Scripture and is inconsistent with the use of these titles across the Old Testament. "That may be the case," you will say, "but this is clear in the pages of the New Testament!" I would ask that you reserve judgment on this matter, for I will argue below that the New Testament is not in fact employing these titles in such a radically different way than the Old Testament. A related shift has also occurred in the way we perceive our intuitive articulation of our doctrine of God and our technical doctrine of God. That is, if you pay attention to the spontaneous prayers and practical liturgy of Christians across all ages, education levels, and roles in the church, you may observe the startling fluidity in which they move between the persons of the Trinity and the freedom with which they use the term "God" to refer to this or that person, or without specification or, perhaps, differentiation. In my circles, we tend to frown on this "incorrect" use of names and titles for God, instead urging a more rigorously specific invocation of our Lord. Paul's triadic prayers are often used as a model for doing so, yet I will suggest in the following pages that though obviously consistent with the biblical picture, Paul's prayers are not the standard invocation Scripture uses for our God and King. Reserve judgment on this matter as well.

The third and final shift occurred definitively in the Enlightenment, but it built on hermeneutical developments throughout the Middle Ages and the Reformation period. Up to and through the Reformation, it was commonplace for Christians to assume that the whole Bible was Trinitarian and that even Old Testament saints had a Trinitarian faith. However, since the Enlightenment, the Bible has often been treated as non-Trinitarian. Among many Trinitarian Christians, the Bible implies or points to the Trinity, yet the Trinity was first given concrete articulation in the 4th century—thus the subordinationism of Origen, for example, and the crude materialism attributed to Tertullian are excusable errors, for they were grasping after but had not yet arrived at a doctrinal formulation for that which the Scriptures pointed towards. Others will acknowledge that the Trinity is found in the Bible, yet it is the result of progressive revelation; it is unfurled in the New Testament alone. Views such as these are intuitive to many like me who grew up in Bible-believing, Trinitarian, Evangelical churches. Therefore, I beg also your restraint in this matter; entertain with me the possibility that the Church was not wrong when, prior to the Enlightenment, it saw the whole Bible as a Trinitarian document. Entertain the possibility that Henry Bullinger—the famous Reformer—was right to say that the Trinity was a doctrine delivered by God himself to the Patriarchs and that Adam, Noah, and Abraham all would have had a Trinitarian understanding of God.

Each shift, I contend, makes it difficult to perceive what has been before us in Scripture the whole time! For this reason, I am not claiming to be an amazing intellectual with the sort of insight Polanyi finds in the history of science; instead, I happened upon a reading of the Bible such as Augustine and Calvin had—and found the result compelling. I do want to provoke a paradigm shift with this book, but not one of my own, novel creation; I commend to you not my vision of the Trinity but that of Isaiah as he beheld God high and lifted up on his throne, of John as he witnessed the Father on his throne, the Lamb in the midst of the throne, and the sevenfold Spirit sent throughout the earth. I have found the resulting reading strategy for Scripture and the doctrine of God that emerges from it spiritual refreshing and intellectually satisfying. I hope in this book to merely commend this vision to you, with the prayer that you would likewise find it compelling and would see God as simultaneously less mysterious and inaccessible as our technical doctrines make him out to be and also far more complex and incomprehensible than we first believed.

This is my prayer for you the reader.
Sola Deo Goria.
James Rutherford.

J. Alexander Rutherford

INTRODUCTION

In the beginning, He, the Gods, created the heavens and the earth. The earth was formless and void, and darkness was over the face of the deep. The Spirit of the Gods was hovering over the face of the waters. And he, the Gods, said, "Let there be light." And there was light. – Genesis 1:1-3[1]

Hear, O Israel: Yahweh our Gods, Yahweh is one. You shall love Yahweh your Gods with all your heart and with all your soul and with all your might. – Deuteronomy 6:4-5

Coming to them, Jesus spoke to them with these words, "All authority in heaven and upon earth has been given to me. Therefore, go and make disciples of all peoples, baptizing them into the name of the Father, and the Son, and the Holy Spirit, teaching them to keep all of which I have commanded you." – Matthew 28:18-20b

Beginning with translation theory is a wonderful way to lose readers, but here we go. On most counts, the translations I have given above are terrible, but they are not wrong. That is, they are not examples of great English style, nor

---

[1] Unless stated otherwise, all translations are my own.

do they capture the sense of the passage—if you judge translations in such a manner.[2] As for form, they do not woodenly follow the word order and lexical units of the Greek and Hebrew texts. More significantly, the translation of Genesis 1 strikes us as odd if not verging on heretical; as Gregory of Nyssa once insisted, Christians do *not* believe in "three Gods." Predicates like "god" number substances or, perhaps, operations, and Nicaean Christians believe in one *substance* and three persons.[3] We will see later that I disagree with his logic, not his theology—but this is not my point here. The clumsy phrase "He, the Gods, created" is my best attempt in English to capture the Hebrew phrase בָּרָא אֱלֹהִים (*bara' 'elohim*).[4] In this phrase, the verb is singular (hence "He ... created") but the subject, אֱלֹהִים (*'elohim*), is morphologically plural, and implicitly definite, hence, "the Gods." We are told, and not without reason, that the plural-for-singular is a grammatical feature indicating *par excellence;* however, as we will explore later, things are not so clear cut. However, returning to translation, the fact of the matter is that אֱלֹהִים (*'elohim*) is morphologically plural; indeed, its referent is in some regard's plural, though Nyssa would caution us that Yahweh qua *god* (θεός, *theos*) is not plural, only *qua* person (ὑπόστασις, *hypostasis*). Yet translated in this admittedly inadequate way, notice what emerges between these three passages: each proclaims a God who is both more than one yet also one. In Genesis 1, we have God creating and speaking, with "The Spirit of God" over the face of the waters (Chapter 9). As we will consider in Chapter 13, John at least finds a third person here, the Son who is the verbal content of God's speaking. In Deuteronomy 6:4-5, Yahweh who is one is also "the Gods." Finally, in Matthew 28, "the name"—which, echoes if not

---

[2] E.g. Gordon D. Fee and Douglas K. Stuart, *How to Read the Bible for All Its Worth*, 3rd ed. (Grand Rapids: Zondervan, 2003); Gordon D. Fee and Mark L. Strauss, *How to Choose a Translation for All Its Worth: A Guide to Understanding and Using Bible Versions* (Grand Rapids: Zondervan, 2007).

[3] See *Ad Ablabium*, discussed below in Chapter 11.

[4] I will use a simplified transliteration system throughout this book to help the reader unfamiliar with Greek and Hebrew to follow the discussion and catch wordplay or similar phenomena. I am not marking the difference between a short, long, or hataf vowel (and I will transliterate vocal Shewa with a simple "e"). I will mark *Aleph* with an opening quotation mark (') and a *Ayin* with a closing quotation mark (').

refers to *the name* Yahweh—is the name "of" three persons.[5] Is this a figment of my bad translating, or does it reflect the biblical text?

Why have I started on such treacherous ground? The discussion above reveals a plethora of assumptions brought to the table in the contemporary discussion of the Trinity, among which are the Nicaean solution to the Trinity (if it is right to speak of *a* Nicaean solution), the question of the Trinity in the Old Testament, the emergence of Trinitarian beliefs in history, translation theory, Hebrew grammar and lexicon, and probably more. To write on the Trinity to is to enter a minefield of presupposition—presuppositions of theology, exegesis, grammar, logic, and philosophy. However, at the heart of the biblical revelation of God is that God is three, Father, Son, and Holy Spirit. Confessional Christians would identify this claim, that God is Triune, as the *sine qua non* of true Christian faith. To be catholic, to be Christian, is to follow the Christ who is the 2nd person of the Trinity. Yet, does following this Christ mean "following the 2nd ὑπόστασις (*hypostasis*) who eternally proceeds from the Father, sharing with him his οὐσία (*ousia*)"? That, at least for me, is a more difficult question, for many faithful men and women in my life could not make heads or tails of the latter claim while worshipping and following the Christ of the former. So, what does it mean to be Trinitarian?

This question is what this book is about, what does it mean to be a Christian who worships a triune God, to be "Trinitarian"? Is the Trinity a doctrine, arrived at through second-order reflection on the biblical data several hundred years after the canon closed, or is it something different, perhaps a presupposition about the reality of God that has shaped the Christian imagination (the interpretive framework they bring to the world) throughout created history? However, we may have gotten ahead of ourselves. Let's backtrack and lay a little context.

---

[5] I use "person" in the sense of my book *The Gift of Knowledge*: "'persons,' as a concept capturing the relation between humans, spirits, and God, are active, spiritual, communicative, and communal individuals with minds." *God's Gifts for the Christian Life – Part I: The Gift of Knowledge*, "God's Gifts for the Christian Life" (Airdrie, AB; Teleioteti 2021) P. 624.

A. The Trinitarian Centuries

The 20th and 21st centuries could very well be called the Trinitarian centuries—at least they give the 4th century a run for its money. And contemporary scholarship tells us that the 4th century controversies really weren't about the "Trinity"; rather, they were about various concerns related to Christ, the knowledge of God, and the role of the Holy Spirit. These concerns led to a carefully delineated theology of the Trinity. In contrast, the 20th and 21st centuries have witnessed a flourishing explicitly Trinitarian theology.

The flourishing of Trinitarian theology in these centuries is juxtaposed sharply (or ought to be for Reformed Protestantism) with the silence of Biblical Studies on the matter. Sure, theologians appeal to biblical texts, but it often appears they are working with shadows and types. The New Testament does not give us a treatise on the Trinity,[6] and—of course—the Old Testament is silent on the matter.[7] Indeed, theologian Bruce McCormack would argue that the 2nd person of the Trinity didn't exist until the incarnation; before that there was receptivity in God to receive and be united to the human Jesus.[8] It may just appear that the judgment of Hanson and others is correct, "Orthodoxy on the subject of the Christian doctrine of God did not exist at first."[9] It would seem that this is an instance of the development of doctrine or theological trajectories set in the first century finding their fulfilment in the 4th and now 20th and 21st centuries. If only

---

[6] E.g. Hodge writes, "No such doctrine as that of the Trinity can be adequately proved by any citation of Scriptural passages. Its constituent elements are brought into view, some in one place, and some in another." Charles Hodge, *Systematic Theology* (Oak Harbor, WA: Logos Research Systems, Inc., 1997), vol. 1, pg. 446.

[7] E.g. Wayne A. Grudem, *Systematic Theology: An Introduction to Biblical Doctrine* (Leicester; Grand Rapids: IVP; Zondervan, 1994), 226–230; Hodge, *Systematic Theology*, vol. 1, pg. 446. Though, cf. John Calvin, *Institutes of the Christian Religion*, trans. Henry Beveridge (Peabody, Mass: Hendrickson Publishers, 2008), sec. 1.13.9-10, 1.13.14.

[8] Bruce Lindley McCormack, *The Humility of the Eternal Son: Reformed Kenoticism and the Repair of Chalcedon* (Cambridge University Press, 2021).

[9] R. P. C. Hanson, *The Search for the Christian Doctrine of God: The Arian Controversy 318-381* (Edinburgh: T. & T. Clark, 1988), 870.

Paul had read Athanasius, Nyssa, or Barth, he would have understood much more clearly the God he worshipped. Wait a second, does that sound right for one who beheld the risen Lord and (arguably) went to the "third heaven"?

This should give us pause; if we believe in the sufficiency of Scripture, can we really believe that such a defining feature of our God—Tri-unity—is a later development that the New Testament authors could not have anticipated. Would this not be adding to Scripture (Deut 4:2) and the insistence of Trinitarian belief for right faith be "teaching as doctrines the commandments of men," contrary to Jesus' own command (Matt 15:9, cf. Ch. 20)? Is this our only option? If God is fundamentally Triune, if to be God is to be Father, Son, and Holy Spirit, how could this God be worshipped without this knowledge? The early church certainly thought the whole Bible teaches the Trinity. In the NPNF translation of Augustine's *De Trinitate*, William Shedd wrote,

> The trinitarianism of the Old Testament has been lost sight of to some extent in the modern construction of the doctrine. The patristic, mediæval, and reformation theologies worked this vein with thoroughness, and the analysis of Augustin in this reference is worthy of careful study.[10]

Yet even here there is a question, for as Hanson and others have argued, the doctrine of God and the Trinity in the fourth century looks remarkably different than it did in the earlier centuries, and it looked different between the Eastern and Western Church.[11] So even if we accept with the majority of Christians throughout the ages that the whole Bible is Trinitarian, we still

---

[10] NPNF 1.3, p. 47, ftn. 3.

[11] See Hanson, *The Search*; John Behr, *The Way to Nicaea*, The formation of Christian theology v. 1 (Crestwood, N.Y.: St. Vladimir's Seminary Press, 2001); Lewis Ayres, *Nicaea and Its Legacy: An Approach to Fourth-Century Trinitarian Theology*, 1st ed. (Oxford: Oxford University Press, 2004); John Behr, *The Nicene Faith: Vol 2 of Formation of Christian Theology* (Crestwood, N.Y.: St Vladimir's Seminary Press, 2004); John Behr, "Response to Ayres: The Legacies of Nicaea, East and West," *Harvard Theological Review* 100, no. 2 (April 2007): 145–152; John Behr, "Calling upon God as Father: Augustine and the Legacy of Nicaea," in *Orthodox Readings of Augustine*, ed. A. Papanikolaos and Dema Copoulos (Crestwood, N.Y.: St Vladimir's Seminary Press, 2008), 153–165.

need to ask, what does this mean?

What would it mean for the Bible to be "Trinitarian"? I do not think we will find full-blown 4th-century Trinitarian theology in the Bible, that God is three ὑποστάσεις (*hypostaseis*) of one οὐσία (*ousia*) with the Father as the ontological head from which the other two hypostases receive their non-temporal beginning (cf. Chs 16-17). However, I also do not mean the "Trinitarianism" of some modern Evangelicalism, where "pregnant plurals" and divine "'we''s hint at a plurality of persons united as a single God, as discerned in the New Testament. By "Trinitarian" I mean the self-conscious identification of three persons who are God and one God who is three persons. For now, we can call this "the Trinitarian tension," for throughout church history this has been regarded as a tension in need of resolution (cf. Ch. 18). By "persons" I do not intend the modern psychological person, nor the bare hypostasis of the Cappadocians. By "person," I mean an acting, relational, and responsive subject. Acting differentiates a "person" from an inanimate subject. Relational differentiates a "person" from a bacteria: a person engages in relationships (friendship, hostility, acquaintance, love, mercy) with other persons. Responsive reiterates that the subject acts and that the relationship a person has is not a construct imposed upon it by another but involves personal involvement. Humans are of course persons, but biblically, Yahweh, false gods, demons, and angels are all presented as persons in this sense.[12]

In this sense of Trinitarian, a text could be about the Triune God in several ways. A Trinitarian text could either teach that God is one and many, laying forth the fundamental Trinitarian tension; it could explain or resolve the tension between these two, or it could presuppose the Trinity—assuming for another purpose either the tension of the Trinity or its resolution. I think we can agree that the New Testament does not explain or resolve the tension, yet it certainly (from an Evangelical point of view) presents God as one and many and presupposes its resolution, namely, no one seems to be bothered by this fact! We are told that the Spirit, a person (he acts, intercedes, and responds, can be grieved), is the Lord; we are told that Christ is God and Lord and differentiated from the Father, his God; and we are told that the

---

[12] Cf. *The Gift of Seeing* Chapter 5, in *The Gift of Knowledge*.

Father is Lord and God. Alongside statements of plurality, the New Testament also upholds the unity of the Godhead.

Thus, a *doctrine* of the Trinity is an answer, explanation, or resolution to the biblical tension of God as one and many. In this sense, there are many Trinitarian doctrines, though some are clearly false. Modalism or Sabellianism denies the many in favour of the one by explaining Father, Son, and Spirit as different self-presentations of the one God; Arius, the Eusebians, and modern equivalents deny the many by reducing Jesus to a created "god," a mighty being that is like but not identical to God; the Nicaean fathers understood the Father to be the one God and the Spirit and the Son to be truly God, identical in essence and of one substance, because they derived from and were organically connected to the substance of the One God, thereby sharing identity in essence or definition. If we consider a doctrine of the Trinity to be an answer to the Trinitarian tension, then the presence of the tension and the assumption of its coherence leads to the conclusion—however we construe the fact—that the New Testament has an implicit doctrine of the Trinity. Yet if we acknowledge that the New Testament is *implicitly* Trinitarian, we have a glaring problem on our hands.

If, as it is commonly assumed, the Trinity is a New Testament teaching, why is it never taught? Did the authors not *realise* that they were fundamentally overturning all their childhood beliefs by calling Jesus God and associating him with two others called "God"? If they didn't realise it, we have to concede that they were either exceedingly dense or were thinking along totally different lines than we are. We need to revisit that which we assumed was implied. Alternatively, if they were teaching a fundamentally new doctrine, why did they not bother to explain it? The Bible is full of circumstantial documents addressing concerns about Christ's incarnation (1 John), the need for works (James), the unity of God's people through the Gospel (Romans), the nature of the Gospel (Galatians), the superiority of Christ (Colossians, Hebrews), etc. If the apostles were teaching something fundamentally new, would someone not raise a question, as they did with election (Romans 9-11)? Surely something like a total revamp in their doctrine of God deserved a word or two, at least a paragraph. As a Unitarian pastor here in Sydney put it,

> They didn't shy away from controversies and potential
> points of friction.... Of all the conflicts between Christianity

and traditional Judaism, this would have been the biggest of all, overshadowing everything else by far. Any attempt to dismantle or redefine strict monotheism would have been bitterly fought by the Jewish believers. Yet there is no mention of such a controversy anywhere.[13]

In response to the silence, we could conclude with Deuble and many others that the apostles didn't teach the Trinity after all, that it is a delusion that has endured for 1600 years and counting. However, there is another option. We do not conclude from the fact that the New Testament does not teach God's existence (i.e. defend, address, or explain the fact) that the biblical authors did not believe in his existence. Nor do we believe that a lack of explicit teaching concerning the intelligibility of Scripture means it is unintelligible. Instead, we recognise that these are implicit, assumed throughout the New Testament. We accept that many things are implicit in this way, things that would be non-controversial to the early church. Think about that for a moment; theology is left implicit, is assumed, when it is not controversial. This gives us an alternative to rejecting the Trinity:

1. If the New Testament is implicitly Trinitarian
2. and doctrine is implicit when it is not controversial
3. then the Trinity was not a controversial teaching in the First Century.

Let that sink in for a moment. The Trinity was not controversial; it was commonly accepted, easy to swallow. Is that not the picture the New Testament paints? Thomas can cry out "my Lord and my God" without recanting of his former unitarianism. Paul can nonchalantly call Jesus God in a moment of doxology (Rom 9:5). They had no trouble, as Richard Bauckham puts it, including Jesus in the unique divine identity.[14] Consider the Jewish response to Jesus: after he differentiates himself from God his

---

[13] Unitarians are self-proclaimed Christians who deny the Trinity by, among other things, denying that Jesus is truly God. Jeff Deuble, *Christ before Creeds: Rediscovering the Jesus of History* (Living Hope International Ministries, 2021), 49.

[14] Richard Bauckham, *Jesus and the God of Israel: "God Crucified" and Other Studies on the New Testament's Christology of Divine Identity* (Milton Keynes: Paternoster; Eerdmans, 2008).

Father and identifies himself with God, the Pharisees do not charge him with multiplying their God or inventing a son of God. No, "you being a man, make yourself God" (John 19:33). The issue is not divine plurality but that the *human* Jesus would be God. The scandal is the incarnation, not the Trinity.

If the Trinity was an easy pill to swallow for Christians, at least—and apparently the Jews—in the first century, then only one conclusion can be drawn. The New Testament authors are comfortable proclaiming a Triune God and believing in him because the Old Testament is Trinitarian. Such is the thesis of this book, that the whole Bible is Trinitarian, starting with the Old Testament and moving through the New. But this raises more problems than it perhaps solves.

B. Biblical Trinitarianism and Theology

As a Christian, I should be overjoyed at the blooming interest in the Trinity over the last 70 or so years, yet the more I have thought about the growing interest in resourcing the ancient Trinitarian teaching and reformulating contemporary theology in Trinitarian terms, I have come across more and more problems from the various disciplines within which I find myself. On the one hand, my study of linguistics and ontology has led me to reject a realist view of the universal; this means that the standard Nicene formula as interpreted in the 4th century, where the oneness of God is understood on analogy with the universal (one *ousia*, substance/essence) and his plurality with the particular (three *hypostases*), has become philosophically untenable for me. So, my developing ideas of the Trinity in the Bible have led me to question the validity of the 4th-century Trinitarian solution, yet I would recognise continuity between 4th-century Christians and the biblical teaching. This raises questions of right and wrong with reference to doctrine and what it means to be orthodox and stand in line with the Christian tradition (cf. Ch. 20).

A related problem is the manner in which the Trinity appears to be presupposed throughout the Bible and by Christians today who cannot articulate a belief in or doctrine of the Trinity. As such, there appears to be Trinitarian Christianity without Trinitarian doctrine, or at least doctrine as it has been conceived for the last 1000 years. Doctrine is often understood, following Aquinas and, more recently, John Webster, as "universal, necessary truths."[15] However, as I have argued extensively in my book *The Gift of Seeing*, this presupposes a problematic ontology (ontology: a view of the relations between thought and its objects).[16] Instead, I am working with a view of doctrine as a certain subset of "knowledge," understood as the interpretation of things.[17] Doctrine in this context has as its object the characters and events described in the Bible. As a description of "things," namely, persons or events, there is no one-to-one correspondence between doctrine and that which it describes. As a person could be described in dozens of ways from dozens of perspectives, and similarly with events, so doctrine has a certain variability to it.[18] There is a finite set of "right" doctrines, in this sense, for all doctrine must correspond to the reality it seeks to describe, yet no doctrine is hermetically sealed. Like a Venn diagram, three doctrines might enjoy significant overlap as they attempt to describe the same reality. Thus, what one author describes as "immutability" may be captured in another author's definition of God as "simple," or vice versa. There is no one "right" definition of immutability, for various authors may choose to include more or less about God, the object whom they seek to describe, in their doctrine. Doctrine in this way is, as with all other propositional knowledge, an interpretation of things that corresponds, however partially but without error, to God's perfect interpretation of all things.[19] I discuss this view of doctrine

---

[15] John Webster, "What Makes Theology Theological?," in *God Without Measure: Working Papers in Christian Theology*, vol. I, II vols., T&T Clark Theology (London ; New York: Bloomsbury T&T Clark, 2016). Cf. Craig A. Carter, *Contemplating God with the Great Tradition: Recovering Trinitarian Classical Theism* (Grand Rapids: Baker Academic, 2021).

[16] J. Alexander Rutherford, *The Gift of Seeing: A Biblical Perspective on Ontology*, God's Gifts for the Christian Life Part 1 - The Gift of Knowledge III (Airdrie, AB: Teleioteti, 2021).

[17] I follow, very loosely, John Frame's definition of theology as the application of the Bible by persons to the all areas of life. Cf. John M. Frame, *The Doctrine of the Knowledge of God*, A Theology of Lordship (Phillipsburg: P&R Publishing, 1987); John M. Frame, *Systematic Theology: An Introduction to Christian Belief* (Phillipsburg: P&R Publishing, 2013).

[18] Cf. Frame, *The Doctrine of the Knowledge*; Vern S. Poythress, *Symphonic Theology: The Validity of Multiple Perspectives in Theology* (Grand Rapids: Academie Books, 1987).

[19] J. Alexander Rutherford, *The Gift of Knowing: A Biblical Perspective on Knowing and Truth*, 2nd Ed., God's Gifts for the Christian Life - Part 1: The Gift of Knowledge

in several related essays and a coming book, so I will desist.[20]

So what then do we do with "the Doctrine of the Trinity"? I would contend that Origen, Arius, and the Pro-Nicenes—as well as Cornelius Van Til, Wayne Grudem, and Jehovah's Witnesses—all have a "trinitarian" doctrine, though some are clearly right or at least somewhat right and others are clearly wrong. I claim this because each of these men or movements have sought to resolve a problem which confronts them when they read the Bible. They are met there by the claim that God is one, that there is one true God and Lord over all things, yet they are also met by the claim that the Father is God, the Son is God, and the Spirit is God. Wayne Grudem describes these three claims (God is one, three are fully God, each of three is distinct from the other) as a summary of the biblical teaching behind the doctrine of the Trinity.[21] This obviously presents a problem: if God is one, how can three be called God? In what way is each God, and how is this compatible with the initial claim that God is one? This is the *problem* of the Trinity, to which Christians and non-Christian religions dependent on the Bible have sought to answer. If this tension is truly present in the Bible, and I am convinced it is, then this raises an additional problem to be answered: what is the biblical answer to this tension?

That is, if we are faced by this tension, surely the biblical authors and first readers would also be confronted by it. How would Jewish men and women who had been steeped in the claim of God's oneness and Gentile men and women steeped in the belief in a multiplicity of gods reconcile their new belief that Jesus is this one God, alongside of God the Father and God the Holy Spirit? The Gentiles, who would have made no claim that there is one God and no others, would now have to simultaneously renounce polytheism while accepting three who are called God as one God: clearly, they would want a resolution to such a tension. How could they miss it? The Jews who believed in God's oneness would clearly need some resolution to

---

I (Airdrie, AB: Teleioteti, 2021); Rutherford, *The Gift of Seeing: A Biblical Perspective on Ontology*. Both are in *The Gift of Knowledge*.

[20] Cf. Rutherford, *The Gift of Seeing: A Biblical Perspective on Ontology*; J. Alexander Rutherford, *The Gift of Theology*, God's Gifts for the Christian Life - Part 3: The Gift of Wisdom III (Campbell River, BC: Teleioteti, Forthcoming).

[21] Grudem, *Systematic Theology*, 231; Hodge, *Systematic Theology*, vols. 1, §2.A.

the claim that Jesus is likewise God, alongside the Father.

The historical reality of the development of these beliefs is outside of the scope of my interest, yet if Scripture is sufficient, truly it must include a resolution to this evident tension—must it not? Again, reflecting on doctrine, we are back where we concluded our previous reflection: the Bible must teach the Trinity.

Thus is the task before us, to show how the Bible is Trinitarian. The first part of our task is methodological. In Part 1, we will consider the problems with precluding Trinitarian interpretations of Old Testament passages (Chapter 1); we will then consider how we argue for and identify doctrine that is presupposed in Scripture, a different task than building a doctrine on proof texts (Chapter 2). In Chapter 3, we will bring these strands together, outlining the method taken in the body of this book. Part 2 and 3 are the body proper, taking up the exegetical task of illuminating the Trinitarian Bible. Part 2 will consider the Old Testament. Chapter 4 will tackle the vexing problem of "monotheism," or how the Bible freely uses the term "god" for many beings. In Chapter 5, we will look closely at the Great Shema, or Deuteronomy 6:4-5; I will argue that this passage is the key to holding together the biblical doctrine of the Trinity. Chapter 6 will then address supposed defeater texts, or those that would declare an unambiguous unitarian-monotheism, ruling out a Trinitarian interpretation of the Shema and, as such, the Old Testament. Chapter 7, 8, and 9 will then argue that there are several persons called God yet simultaneously differentiated from God in the Old Testament. Chapter 7 will consider the Angel of Yahweh; Chapter 8, the eschatological agent in Isaiah; and Chapter 9, the Spirit of God. Having argued that Yahweh is indeed "one God," with an attendant but not yet clear plurality, Part 3 will explore the complexities of Yahweh's identity across the New Testament. Chapters 10-13 will consider New Testament Christology. Chapter 10 will consider various frameworks employed in contemporary Christology, then the following chapters will consider various aspects of the New Testament picture: Chapter 11 will look at Jesus as Isaiah's eschatological agent in Hebrews 1:13; Chapter 12 will look at Jesus as the Old Testament's Yahweh; and Chapter 13 will look at three texts where Jesus is called God and simultaneously differentiated from him. Chapter 14 will then consider the Spirit, focusing on Paul's claim in 2 Corinthians 3:17-18 that the Spirit is Yahweh. Chapter 15 will close off Part 2 by looking at the unity of

God in the New Testament. Part 4 will then bring together the threads of Part 2 and 3 into the complex task of articulating the biblical Trinity. We will begin in Chapters 16 and 17 by exploring 4th-century Trinitarian doctrine. Chapter 16 will look at the Trinity at Nicaea and Constantinople as interpreted by Athanasius, Basil, and Gregory of Nazianzus. Chapter 17 will then consider the Trinitarian teachings of Gregory of Nyssa and Augustine; in both chapters, we will explore the tensions of tradition, the Bible, and doctrine in the process. Chapter 18 will then articulate the threads of our previous discussion in a positive description of the relation between God's unity and plurality. Chapter 19 will then address the relation of this "doctrine of the Trinity" with the innate knowledge of God in Romans 1 and the intuitive knowledge of God possessed by everyday Christians. Chapter 20 will conclude our discussion by addressing the question of tradition, namely, how we can stand in line with while critiquing tradition and the resultant view of the authority of creeds and their usefulness.

The task before us is far greater than any one person could undertake, so the shortcomings of this study will be evident for many. On the one hand, this is not an academic book, it is at best "semi-technical," rigorously researched and, I hope, methodologically tight, yet built on presuppositions alien to the mainstream academy. So, though I hope to benefit a wide audience, I know the approach adopted will estrange many. The methods of exegesis I employ are those developed in my *The Gift of Knowledge*, which will leave the reader hoping for an interaction with the ins and outs of critical scholarship disappointed.[22] Finally, these theological reflections have been churning within me for over 12 years now, yet they are far from definitive. I am convinced that John Frame is right about the nature of theology, I am convinced that tradition is invaluable, and I am convinced that creeds and doctrine in the formal sense have their place, yet I make no claims to have a definitive answer to how these claims are held together. I make only my best attempt to do so.

May God be glorified by the weak product of my hands, and may you,

---

[22] J. Alexander Rutherford, *God's Gifts for the Christian Life — Part 1: The Gift of Knowledge* (Airdrie, AB: Teleioteti, 2021). Cf. J. Alexander Rutherford, *The Book of Habakkuk: An Exegetical-Theological Commentary on the Hebrew Text*, A Teleioteti Old Testament Commentary 1 (Vancouver, BC: Teleioteti, 2019).

the reader, find something edifying, challenging, and intellectually stimulating in the pages that follow. To the one true God, Father, Son and Holy Spirit, be glory forever and ever, Amen.

—PART 1—
METHODOLOGY

1

AGAINST PRECLUDING THE TRINITY

> In the beginning was the Word, and the Word was with
> God, and the Word was God. He was in the beginning
> with God. – John 1:1-3 (ESV)

However we construe the relevant data, "history" is an important element of biblical interpretation.[1] Our goal is to understand what the text is saying, and the text which is speaking is ancient in its provenance and its content. Put another way, the Bible speaks to us from a different time, so we are confronted with practices and beliefs that do not map readily onto the modern world (though there is much common ground because of the Bible's influence in creating the modern world). We thus make judgments, intuitively and explicitly, as to what the text says, precluding certain readings and entertaining others. We make judgments because not every possible construal of the syntax and lexicon of a text is equally probable; there is a finite set of a meanings that are true for a text (or "applications" if you prefer). So, 2 Peter 3:3-7 is not immediately a rebuke of modern uniformitarian assumptions—however legitimate or illegitimate it may be to use the text in that manner. Our understanding of history (again, however we construe that, as a mere

---

[1] I intend "history" in the sense of implied history, or the world presented implicitly and explicitly by the Bible. But what follows is true for Evangelical grammatical-historical interpretation, where history as it is applicable here is the reality (whatever we make of that) reconstructed from the Bible and extra-biblical data. E.g. Andreas J. Köstenberger and Richard Duane Patterson, *Invitation to Biblical Interpretation: Exploring the Hermeneutical Triad of History, Literature, and Theology* (Grand Rapids: Kregel Publications, 2011). See my, *The Gift of Knowledge*.

biblical history, i.e. the implied historical framework of the Bible, or a reconstructed history to which the Bible attests) informs our judgments as to what a text may or may not mean.

One significant aspect of this history is the broader worldview assumptions that govern our reading of the text: a confessionally Reformed Christian reads the New Testament with categories for incarnation and a fully divine and fully human mediator, categories alien to a text of Platonic provenance. These basic observations lead to two reflections, one on frameworks of interpretation and semantic possibility and one on the reciprocity of history in reading the Old Testament.

A. Reflection 1 - Competing Frameworks of Interpretation

First, a legitimate question in reading the whole Bible is whose worldview or interpretive framework (whose "history") tells us what the text can mean? A developmental view of biblical theology may say that each book is governed by its own frame of reference, such that Genesis cannot be monotheistic because monotheism was not yet developed when the events occurred and/or the book was written (though there are, of course, conservative equivalents of this position).[2] Another approach would be to treat the entire Old Testament as a framework, so that there is a theology of the Old Testament governing the interpretation of its parts.[3] The Old Testament, perhaps, was monotheistic but not Trinitarian, so readings with the former conclusion are possible but not with the latter. Another view would be to treat the whole Bible as the framework, such that because Trinitarian theology is taught in the New Testament, it frames the possibility of the whole.[4] Now, these categories are not mutually exclusive. You could, for

---

[2] E.g. Julius Wellhausen, *Prolegomena to the History of Israel*, reprint of the 1885 ed. (Atlanta: Scholars Press, 1994); Herman Gunkel, *Genesis*, trans. of the 1910 ed. (Macon: Mercer University, 1997).

[3] See many treatments of "Old Testament Theology." E.g. Andrew T. Abernethy and Greg Goswell, *God's Messiah in the Old Testament: Expectations of a Coming King* (Grand Rapids: Baker Academic, 2020).

[4] Calvin, *Institutes of the Christian Religion*, sec. 1.13.9-10, 1.13.14.

example, have three different readings for a text, one for each framework. For example, on the first position, Deuteronomy 6:4, if it dates prior to the 7th century BC, could not express pure monotheism or Trinitarianism, but it may express henotheism (the worship of one god, though others exist). On the second position, Deuteronomy 6:4 cannot express Trinitarianism, but it may express unitarian monotheism. On third position, Deuteronomy 6:4 may teach monotheism, though it cannot teach an exclusively unitarian form, or it could possibly teach Trinitarianism. This is at least permissible; its probability will depend on the textual evidence. Shortly we will argue for taking the third approach, but for now it important only to observe the implications of our decision for any of these frameworks.

B. Reflection 2 – The Reciprocity of History

Second, these observations raise an interesting dilemma for the question of "real" history, as opposed to implied history. Let me clarify the terms: to speak of implied history is not to speak of true vs false (though this could be involved) but interpreted vs open-to-interpretation.[5] By speaking of a reality, a text interprets it: it portrays some aspect of that reality but not the whole.[6] That "some aspect" is the implied history. Therefore, assuming that the implied history is true, this implied history represents a part of a greater whole to which it refers.[7] Here is the dilemma: our choice among the three frameworks discussed above involves different implied histories, and therefore dictates our construal of actual history. That is, if we assume for the sake of argument that the Bible is a window into the life and beliefs of

---

[5] Cf. Jean Louis Ska, *"Our Fathers Have Told Us": Introduction to the Analysis of Hebrew Narratives*, Subsidia Biblica 13 (Roma: Editrice Pontificio Instituto Biblico, 1990), 41; J. Alexander Rutherford, *God's Kingdom through His Priest-King: An Analysis of the Book of Samuel in Light of the Davidic Covenant*, Teleioteti Technical Studies 1 (Vancouver: Teleioteti, 2019), 115–116.

[6] See V. Philips Long, *The Art of Biblical History*, Foundations of Contemporary Interpretation v. 5 (Grand Rapids: Zondervan, 1994); Iain W. Provan, V. Philips Long, and Tremper Longman, *A Biblical History of Israel*, 2nd ed. (Louisville: Westminster John Knox, 2015).

[7] There is an ontological issue of correspondence I will ignore for our purposes. I.e. on an idealist position, the implied is the real; on an idealist position with God as pre-interpreter, all reality is interpretation and the implied is true as it corresponds to God's interpretation. See *The Gift of Seeing* in Rutherford, *The Gift of Knowledge*.

ancient Israel, then the framework of possibility we choose shapes our view of ancient Israel. There is, of course, a chicken and the egg problem here, for our view of ancient Israel may shape our choice of a framework—but I digress. If we choose framework 1 above, from the History of Religions school, then Genesis represents animistic beliefs. If we chose framework 2 above, Genesis represents monotheistic beliefs. If we choose framework 3 above, Genesis may represent Trinitarian beliefs. Now, we may say that by choosing framework 3, we are only committing ourselves to the belief that the implied editor (or author) of the entire canon, so also the implied worldview (or framework of beliefs) for the whole Bible, is Trinitarian, not that any historical party represented in the Bible was. However, to do so, one must make the *a priori* judgment that the whole is different from any of its parts, that the framework of the Canon doesn't represent the historical framework of the original author or audience, that the interpretation of the part is created from the whole and was not just *revealed* by the whole.

Let's consider that from a different perspective. Let's assume for the sake of argument that Isaiah could be interpreted within the entire canon as teaching a messianic king who is also Yahweh himself. Adopting the *a priori* judgment given above, one would say this interpretation is a canonical/theological reading but not a historical one. That is, this is not how Isaiah (or deutero, or trito-Isaiah) or his readers would have understood the prophecies. However, we must recognise that this is an *a priori* judgement, for on the basis of the same evidence, one could argue that Isaiah and his reader's did understand the text this way: their understanding is exactly that revealed by the whole canon. Once again, we make implicit judgments as to what is possible and bring them to bear on our historical and interpretative judgments. So, which is correct (assuming Isaiah's hypothetical teaching), that this is only true canonically or that this represents the historical reality?

At this point, we can only begin to tease out some possible answers. Accepting that the Bible is a valuable historical witness, we do not make much headway in resolving the question. Reading the book of Isaiah isolated from the canon does not help much either, for the canon has revealed one possible textual meaning, the possibility of which we judge from a greater framework. Do we believe that the canon represents Isaiah's worldview? This is at least possible. We recognise that the book of Isaiah is only a slice of Isaiah's worldview, so it cannot decisively rule in either direction. One could, perhaps, appeal to Old Testament foundation texts, arguing that since they are unitarian-monotheistic, Isaiah must also be. However, that raises two problems. First, we have the same interpretative dilemma with reference to these texts. Second, if there were truly texts that were decisively unitarian, then this would revise our entire canonical understanding: the New Testament teaching (that Jesus and the Father are God) would be contrary to the Old Testament. Turning to other historical sources, they are more limited and ambiguous—and more general (about Israel and its neighbours, not Isaiah and his community)—so we are left with no answers here. My preliminary conclusions is, therefore, that we have no *a priori* way of determining whether framework 1, 2, or 3 is correct with regard to the historical Isaiah. One must, therefore, make a judgment about the likelihood of progressive revelation or, conversely, that God's self-revelation over time has been consistent.

I want to suggest at the end of these reflections that it is not so clear cut a question to say that the New Testament is Trinitarian and that the Old Testament is not, that the New reveals something about the Old that was not there in its own time. These judgments are far harder to make than is often accepted. For our purposes, two points have been raised: we must make a decision beforehand as to what frame of reference we will accept in interpreting the text. Second, we have no *a priori* reason against the possibility that Isaiah, for example, is Trinitarian. Furthermore, because our decision concerning the interpretive framework shapes our interpretation of history, such as the beliefs of the historical Isaiah (or Deutero or Trito-Isaiah), we do not yet have an *a posteriori* reason to believe that he could not have been Trinitarian (for the arguments to that effect beg the question, presupposing he could not have been). In Chapter 3, we will bring these considerations together in our positive methodological programme.

2

ARGUING FOR THE ASSUMED

> To them belong the patriarchs, and from their race,
> according to the flesh, is the Christ, who is God over all,
> blessed forever. Amen. – Romans 9:5 (ESV)

How is it that an accomplished Jew and persecutor of the Christian church can reconcile such a claim as Roman 9:5 with his previous beliefs? On one level, he was taught Christ and the Gospel by the Lord himself (Gal 1:11-12), so he would receive this teaching on the highest authority. But there is another "how" question here: what attendant beliefs about God and his world had to change to accommodate the claim that Christ is God over all to the profession of one true God and the deity of the Christ's Father? How did such changes come about? Did Paul's former theology result in a tension between the claims about God and the claims about the Christ? If so, how were those tensions resolved? What did the claim that there was one God look like after the profession of faith in Christ as Lord and God? What did it mean to profess Christ as God while maintaining the profession that there is one God over all, Father, Son, and Spirit?

The problem with this line of questioning is that we have no easy answers. We do not read of Paul struggling with these matters, nor do we find teaching concerning them; instead, as observed above, they are merely assumed. Contrast this with the newness of the Gospel. That the Christ was crucified was contrary to what the 1st-century Jews believed, so it receives much attention (e.g. Luke 24:13-49; 1 Cor 1:18-31). That God could become flesh was untenable, so John's first epistle argues for the physical incarnation (cf. 1 John 1:1-5). That Gentiles could be made right before God apart from the Law and that the Law itself had ended was not intuitive to 1st-century Jews; indeed, it was highly offensive, so the point is laboured at great length (see Acts 10:1-11:18, 15:1-35; Romans, Galatians, and Hebrews). The resurrection was also a stumbling block, so it comes up again and again (Acts 13:13-52; 17:1-9; 1 Cor 15). In each of these cases, some parties in the first century found the teaching to be new and disagreeable, yet Jesus, Paul, and the rest of the Apostles argued that this was indeed the fulfillment of Scripture and taught in the Old Testament. The problem was not that these teachings were new to the Old Testament but that they were new to some 1st-century interpretations of the Old Testament.

In contrast, that the Christ was to be God receives no attention, nor that the Spirit is personal and Yahweh (2 Cor 3:17), nor that Father, Son, and Holy Spirit all share a single name (Matt 28:19). Instead, these claims appear as parts of other arguments, as supporting data, or in doxology. John is comfortable opening his Gospel with claim that the Word was God and with God; he does this without seeing any need to defend himself. John and Mark, as we will see below, are quite comfortable attributing texts about Yahweh or spoken by Yahweh to Jesus, the word "the Lord" justifying the bridge. Not once in the New Testament are these claims at the fore; instead, we are confronted with claims that only make sense if Jesus were God (e.g. Matt 9:1-8), explicit claims to be Yahweh (e.g. John 8:58-59), claims that Jesus is God (e.g. John 1:1; John 20:28; Rom 9:5), and Old Testament allusions that require Jesus to be God (e.g. Matt 3:1-12). In each case cited above, the claims are made in another context, justifying some other point. In the case of John's Gospel, the Jews do recognise what Jesus is saying and treat it as blasphemy, but John finds no need to explain why they are wrong. The contrast with controversial teachings is palpable: there is enough in the Bible for Christian pastors and scholars to argue for the divinity of Christ and the Trinity, yet the New Testament authors never do so. It is as if they were never challenged on the matter—as if it were not controversial. For the 1st-century Christians to freely drop these claims throughout their writings, they were obviously comfortable with them and comfortable with their audience accepting them; thus, such beliefs make up the theological background or presuppositions for the New Testament. This raises the question we are exploring in this chapter, how do identify, elucidate, and argue for the assumed?

In the case of the New Testament teaching, a clear place to start is by looking at the Old Testament. This is how we explain and understand much of what is assumed in the New Testament, beliefs about God, Israel, and redemptive history. What is presupposed in the New Testament is often that which is taught in the Old Testament. If the New Testament appears to presuppose the Trinity (again, the claim that there is one true God and that three are this one true God), then our first course of action is to investigate whether or not Old Testament teaches this. Indeed, given that the Old Testament is the source of the doctrinal presuppositions of the New Testament (as opposed to 1st-century practices that explain and are explained by ancient cultures, such as giving "a holy kiss," e.g. Rom 16:16), then it stands to reason that the Old Testament probably does teach such a thing. This helps us with regard to the frameworks for reading discussed in Chapter 1. Therefore, this is our starting point, to ask if and what the Old Testament teaches about God as Trinity, about the oneness of God and the divinity of the Father, Son, and Holy Spirit.

In addition to exploring the Old Testament in the above manner, we can also read the New Testament to explore its presuppositions. Much (though not all) of the discussion in recent years about the Trinity does not try to understand what *were* the Trinitarian beliefs of the New Testament authors; instead, authors seek to prove the Trinity from the New Testament, or they have treated the Trinity as a "second-order" doctrine that emerged after hundreds of years of reflection on the Bible, not even asking about the nature of the data from which this doctrine is built.[1] If a presupposition is a belief y such that if belief x presupposes y, then y must be held to give an intelligible account of x, it is fair to ask what must that presupposed belief looked like for it to function in this way?[2] Was it explicit, consciously articulated like many doctrines or technical knowledge? Was it tacit, like the

---

[1] In the first case, Grudem and Hodge are fair examples, cited above. In the second case, this is the claim of Carter. In his essay "The Old Testament and the Trinity," Mark Gignilliat presupposes the 4th-century formula in his investigation of the Trinity in the Old Testament, see also the introduction of *The Essential Trinity*. Carter, *Contemplating God*; Mark S. Gignilliat, "The Trinity and the Old Testament," in *The Essential Trinity: New Testament Foundations and Practical Relevance*, ed. Brandon D. Crowe and Carl R. Trueman (London: Apollos, 2016). Se

[2] This definition is adapted from John M. Frame, *Cornelius Van Til: An Analysis of His Thought* (Phillipsburg: P&R Publishing, 1995), 137.

beliefs that make up our "fiduciary framework," to use Polanyi's term? Perhaps it is akin to the knowledge of persons, a particular sort of tacit knowledge?[3] Moreover, what was the content of these beliefs? Did the term "God" function like it was said to in Greek logic? Was it a noun corresponding to an essential, definitional reality? Does the threeness of the persons correspond to the 4th-century understanding of the particular? How were oneness and threeness held together? By exploring how these beliefs are used, by looking at where they are presupposed, the possible justification for their use (such as the middle term "Lord" in the New Testament's use of Old Testament quotations), and the role they play in their contexts, we may just be able to flush out what the New Testament assumes.

---

[3] See Chapter 19 and my book *The Gift of Knowledge*, especially volume 3, *The Gift of Seeing*. Rutherford, *The Gift of Knowledge*. Cf. Michael Polanyi, *Personal Knowledge: Towards a Post-Critical Philosophy*, First Harper Torchbook Edition. (New York: Harper Torchbook, 1964); Michael Polanyi, *The Tacit Dimension* (Chicago; London: University of Chicago Press, 2009).

3

METHODOLOGICAL CONCLUSIONS

O foolish ones, and slow of heart to believe all that the prophets have spoken! Was it not necessary that the Christ should suffer these things and enter into his glory? – Luke 24:25-26 (ESV)

With these important pieces in place, we can now set forth the method we will employ in the following study. First, in Chapter 1, we saw that we have no *a priori* reason to presume that the Old Testament is not Trinitarian, nor do we have an *a posteriori* reason to do so without investigating the matter further. That is, there have been many studies that have flushed out what the Old Testament looks like interpreted as a non-Trinitarian document, yet the ability of such a reading to explain the text does not foreclose a Trinitarian reading. Indeed, to measure the value of each, one must first perform a reading presupposing the Trinity, only then comparing the fruit and asking which better explains the available data. We have already seen significant data left unexplained by the non-Trinitarian readings, namely, the emergence of the Trinity as a presupposition in 1st-century Christianity. Furthermore, if God is actually triune, then those who were in intimate fellowship with him throughout history would be missing something significant if they did not know him as such. If God's trinitarian nature is central to his work in the world, as John's interpretation of the creation narrative in John 1 suggests, then even the intuitive knowledge of God possessed by the unbeliever (Rom

1:18-32) may be Trinitarian.[1] Furthermore, we have no explicit evidence that God's triune nature is a facet of progressive revelation unless we beg the question and assume the Old Testament cannot be Trinitarian. Without explicit teaching on the matter or apparent controversy suggesting this is new and difficult to grasp, it would seem, rather, that it is part of the received revelation in the 1st century. If God is actually triune, and the New Testament assumes the doctrine, then it is apparent those who would show that the Old Testament is *not Trinitarian* share the burden of proof with us who would show *that it is*. That is, no position has the luxury to presume itself to be the right position until proven wrong; one needs to show from the data of the Old Testament that it is not Trinitarian as much as we must show that it is. Indeed, before the modern era, Christians did not seem to blush at interpreting the Old Testament as Trinitarian.[2] Henry Bullinger argued that the Trinity was part of the tradition handed down by the Patriarchs, from Adam through Abraham,

> This is the brief sum of the holy fathers' tradition…. First, therefore, the fathers taught, that the Father, the Son, and the Holy Ghost are one God in the most reverend Trinity, the maker and governor of heaven and earth and all things which are therein.[3]

These are all reasons in favour of a whole-Bible approach to interpreting the Old Testament, or Chapter 1's *framework 3*. To this we can add the explicit evidence of the New Testament.

According to the New Testament, the Old Testament is not primarily a book to "them," to a distant people to be interpreted according to alien presuppositions. On the contrary, the Old Testament is presented as Christian Scriptures, united with the New as a single witness to God and his

---

[1] See my discussion of this knowledge in my book *The Gift of Knowledge*, particularly in Volume 3. Rutherford, *The Gift of Knowledge*.

[2] See Calvin, *Institutes of the Christian Religion*, sec. 1.13.9-10, 1.13.14. Augustine, *On the Trinity*, 2.11. Augustine *Exposition on the book of the Psalms*, 5:2-3; Athanasius, *Four Discourses*, II.XV.

[3] Henry Bullinger, *The Decades of Henry Bullinger: Volume 1* (Grand Rapids: Reformation Heritage Books, 2021), 43.

work in history.[4] On, the one hand, we are told that the Old Testament was written for us (Rom 4:23, 15:4; 1 Cor 10:11). On the other, Jesus and the apostles freely interpret the Old Testament in light of their present understanding, as it concerns Jesus and the coming of the new covenant (e.g. Luke 24:25-27, 44-47; Rom 1:17, 10:5-13; Gal 3:1-9; Heb 2:1-18, 8:1-13; etc.).

Thus, all things considered, reading the Old Testament in light of the New is not only possible but seems to be preferred. Reading it in this way, with no prejudice against Trinitarian readings, is a legitimate avenue of interpretation and, having read it in this way, we can only then judge if the resulting picture produces a more accurate picture of ancient Israel (as argued in Chapter 1). So this is the approach we will take, allowing the Christian framework of beliefs to shape our interpretation of the Old Testament and allowing New Testament readings of Old Testament texts to inform our understanding.[5] Of course, the New Testament readings of the Old Testament are sometimes complex, yet the presence of complex typology in the New Testament does not rule out the presence of simple readings of the Old Testament.[6] In this way, we will approach the Old Testament.

We will do so in Part 2, seeking to identify if the Trinity is taught and/or presupposed in the Old Testament and what the contours of such teaching are. The "Trinity," as we are employing it at this early stage, is merely the teaching of God's unity and/or oneness and his (triune) plurality. We are not looking for "hints" of the Trinity but evidence that the Trinity is presupposed in a way similar to what we have discussed concerning the New Testament or taught, that is, explained or mandated in some way.

In Part 3, we will then turn to the New Testament to investigate the contours of the Trinity presupposed there. Our work here will be shaped by

---

[4] I discuss this extensively in my books *The Gift of Knowledge* and *The Gift of Revelation: A Biblical Perspective on the Bible*, God's Gifts for the Christian Life - Part 2: The Gift of Truth I (Airdrie, AB: Teleioteti, 2022).

[5] See Rutherford, *Habakkuk*.

[6] My work on Habakkuk, cited above, argues for several simple readings. *The Right Doctrine from the Wrong Text* is a helpful introduction to the complexities. G. K. Beale, ed., *The Right Doctrine from the Wrong Texts? Essays on the Use of the Old Testament in the New* (Grand Rapids: Baker Books, 1994).

our interpretation of the Old Testament in Part 2 but will move beyond it, exploring what we can learn in addition to what we saw there. Part 4 will reflect upon our exegesis in dialogue with the Christian tradition.

—PART 2—
GOD IN THE OLD TESTAMENT

YAHWEH AND THE GODS

God stands in the divine council;
he judges in the midst of gods – Psalm 82:1

Our purpose in this Second Part is to explore the contours of the Doctrine of God as it pertains to unity and, if present, plurality within the Old Testament.[1] Our approach in what follows is not "historical" in the sense of historical-criticism or grammatical-historical exegesis; instead of situating the texts in their reconstructed historical setting and identifying diachrony in the development of ideas across the history presented in the text, we are interested in the whole of the Old Testament as the first part of a two-part Covenant document, the Bible. As such, our approach is essentially synchronic, reading the parts in the light of the whole. Though modern scholars largely agree that Israelite religion evolved out of polytheism or animism, the history presented in the Pentateuch indicates continuity between the religion of Adam, Abraham, and the later Israelites. Though the patriarchs were far from perfect, they are presented as followers of Yahweh as he is known to their later descendants. The implied history of the Pentateuch, that Abraham was a worshipper of Yahweh, the God of Israel, is the history we will follow in interpreting Abraham; others can work out

---

[1] Old Testament scholars will be aware that problems abound for such an investigation attempted within the bounds of contemporary biblical scholarship and of the academy. These problems are complex and enduring, which is why I have attempted in prior books to address the sources of these problems and offer an alternative approach. See my books *The Gift of Knowledge, The Gift of Revelation, God's Kingdom through His Priest-King,* and *Habakkuk.*

how close that reading is to the "historical" Abraham. Adopting such a synchronic approach also brackets out legitimate questions and lines of investigation concerning biblical language.

It is common in contemporary Old Testament scholarship to employ the concepts, worldviews, rites, and language of Ancient Near Eastern (ANE) cultures to inform our understanding of both historical Israel and the biblical text. I am persuaded such an approach is riddled with difficulties that are often not acknowledged, yet our approach gives less value to these approaches for other reasons.[2] A comparative study is concerned with the historical situation and historical understanding of the biblical texts, such as looking at 11th and 10th-century Canaan to understand the early Monarchy. However, we are not concerned with the biblical texts as historical products but as a final document intended for Christian readers: we are focused on the redacted whole, not the parts as they were before being integrated into its final form. Comparative studies are also concerned with diachrony, understanding how language and culture develop across time; we are interested in synchrony, understanding how the language and worldview of the whole shape the parts and how the parts shape the whole. As such, our conclusions need to be seen as such: if we conclude that אֱלֹהִים ('elohim) means something in Genesis 1 according to synchronic exegesis, this is not necessarily the case for the same term in the same text understood in terms of diachronic development.[3] However, as we saw in Chapter 1, our synchronic conclusions certainly have a bearing on the diachronic conclusions, though it will take work to move from one to the other.

This Part will be divided into five chapters. Chapter 4 will explore the term אֱלֹהִים, preparing the way for later exegesis. Then, in Chapter 5, we will consider the Great Shema (Deut 6:4-5), a central Old Testament text on God's nature. I will argue that the Shema does not argue for monotheism

---

[2] See Noel Weeks, "Problems with the Comparative Method in Old Testament Studies," *Journal of the Evangelical Theological Society* 62, no. 2 (2019): 287–306. Cf. Rutherford, *The Gift of Knowledge.*

[3] For some of these issues, see John H. Sailhamer, *Introduction to Old Testament Theology: A Canonical Approach* (Grand Rapids: Zondervan, 1995); Peter J. Gentry and Stephen J. Wellum, *Kingdom through Covenant: A Biblical-Theological Understanding of the Covenants*, 2nd Ed. (Wheaton: Crossway, 2018), chap. 3.

over against polytheism, at least not directly, but hedges in the appropriate interpretation of God's unity and plurality. Then, in Chapter 6, we will explore Genesis 1, which flushes out some of what it means for God to be plural, and several defeater texts, texts which, at first, appear to teach unitarian Monotheism. Chapters 7 and 8 will then explore internal differentiation within Yahweh, looking at two figures who are identified and treated as Yahweh. Chapter 9 will conclude this part by looking at the Spirit and the way he is identified with yet differentiated from Yahweh.

A. Approaching אֱלֹהִים

The Hebrew terms translated "God" in the English Bible are אֱלֹוהַ (*eloah*), אֱלֹהִים (*elohim*), and אֵל (*'el*). For several reasons, it is important to begin our investigation with these terms. On the one hand, early Christians often made much of the term "God" as a signifier of the divine essence, as a generic name according to the ontology and logic of the mid-1st millennium AD. This understanding of the term has cast a long shadow over theological readings of the Old Testament, so we need to take the time to understand the term within the Old Testament context.[4] In addition, throughout church history, there has been discussion of the use of the plural אֱלֹהִים for the singular God. As a result of a diachronic and comparative investigation, Joel Burnett argues that the use of the plural has a Canaanite origin and that it is a "concretized abstract plural."[5] Within the biblical corpus, there is extensive use of what Waltke and O'Connor call the "honorific plural," where a singular thing is referred to with a plural noun because it is "so thoroughly characterized by the qualities of the noun."[6] However, a theological approach to the Old Testament reopens the question, for in every other use, the referent is clearly singular and the context makes clear that the referent is singular (e.g. 1 Kgs 1:43; Isa 1:3; Job 40:15, 16, 19). However, God is not simply singular, so the referent of the plural noun as used for God is plural, thus raising the question

---

[4] E.g. Gignilliat, "The Trinity and the Old Testament."

[5] Joel S. Burnett, *A Reassessment of Biblical Elohim*, Dissertation series / Society of Biblical Literature no. 183 (Atlanta, GA: Society of Biblical Literature, 2001), 22.

[6] Bruce K. Waltke and Michael Patrick O'Connor, *An Introduction to Biblical Hebrew Syntax* (Winona Lake, Ind.: Eisenbrauns, 1990), sec. 7.4.3.

within a canonical frame of reference, is the use merely a "honorific plural"?

We will explore the question of the plural in the course of our treatment of texts; the bulk of this chapter will be addressing the scope of the terms for "god." By exploring what these words refer to and what is said about them, we can gain a grasp of the concept signified by these terms.[7] That is, if a concept arises from the relation of particulars, linguistic signs or groups of related signs such as these terms for God create a concept by drawing several particulars into relation.[8] As we will see shortly, the term God is used for a wide variety of things, not only for the one true God and certainly not for a class of things sharing an essence, so in this case, a conceptualist ontology explains the referential range and connotations of the term; each of the terms we translate "god" overlap in the things they signify; together they signify a wide range of beings who, like God himself, possess or are attributed with great power and authority.

אֱלוֹהַ ('eloah; god, God) and אֱלֹהִים ('elohim; God[s], gods), and rarely אֵל ('el; god, God; e.g. Num 12:13), may be used where we would expect a proper name, similar to the English use of "God." אֱלוֹהַ "comes from Teman" in Habakkuk 2:3; אֱלֹהִים creates the heavens and the earth (Genesis 1:1). It is sometimes said that אֱלֹהִים is more like a title than a name because it connotes something about its referent, but it is not evident to me that there is a clear distinction between names and titles in the Hebrew Bible: names often connote something about their referent in addition to mere reference, as is the case with יהוה.[9] Both אֵל and אֱלוֹהַ can also be used in a generic sense, as a title for God (e.g. "the mighty God," Isa 10:21) or to refer to other entities (e.g. Isa 44:8; Deut 32:12).

---

[7] I think the data of the Old Testament supports treating אֱלוֹהַ and אֵל when not used as a title as signifiers of one concept. If I am wrong in this assertion, the main points of this and following chapters stands: these terms are used for various things other than the one true God.

[8] See Rutherford, *The Gift of Knowledge*.

[9] Graham I. Davies, "'God' in Old Testament Theology," in *Congress Volume Leiden 2004*, ed. André Lemaire (Leiden: Brill, 2006), 182.

B. Many Are "God"

In addition to God most high, there are two other sorts of entities referred to as "god" in the Old Testament. There are the supposedly superhuman beings worshipped by other nations and even by Israel itself, and there are humans. I am not convinced that the narrators call Christian "angels" or the constituents of God's heavenly council "gods," though some scholars are. In Job, heavenly beings are called "sons of God [בְּנֵי הָאֱלֹהִים; *beney ha'elohim*]" (Job 1:6, 2:21, 38:7; cf. Gen 6:2, 4). The semantics of the phrase "son of **x**" in Hebrew may indicate that angels are somehow like God, however the text falls short of ever calling them "gods."[10] Some would argue that the form אלים (*'ym*) which occurs in Psalm 29:1 and 89:7 for angels is the plural of אֵל (*'el*), "god." Here the semantics of the phrase would favour "diving beings" or "gods," namely, it is common in Hebrew for the phrase "son of **x**" to embody the characteristics of **x**, where **x** is an abstract noun or a generic name (e.g. a "son of might" is a mighty person, e.g. Jdgs 18:2); this would more clearly be the case here than in Job 1:6, for "אֵלִים" (*'elim*) doesn't function semantically as a name or title as אֱלֹהִים (*'elohim*) does.[11] Job 1:6, in contrast, is "son of **y**," where **y** is a proper name ("son of Edom," an edomite; "son of Abraham," a descendant of Abraham). However, the identification of אלים as a plural of אֵל is not the clear in these Psalms (nor is the conclusion that "sons of gods" would mean in effect "divine beings," for there is ambiguity in this reading on the referent of "gods"). The plural form אֵלִים is found five times in the Old Testament (Exod 36:19; Ps 29:1, 89:7; Job 41:17; Dan 11:36), along with one instance of a defective form (that is, without the expected *mater lectionis*, long vowel marked with a consonant), אֵלִם (*'elim*) in Exodus 15:11. Among these instances, only Daniel 11:36 is clearly from a plural form of אֵל (in the phrase, "God of gods"). Exodus 36:19 is from the word אַיִל (*'ayil*) which here means "ram" but can also be mean a ruler of a nation, or a "mighty one"—perhaps "one with authority" (Exod 15:15; 2 Kgs 24:15; Ezek 17:13, 32:21). Psalm 29:1 has the phrase בְּנֵי אֵלִים (*beney 'elim*),

---

[10] This may be complicated by the fact that אֱלֹהִים regularly functions as a name or title, not a generic noun, so semantically it is more like "son of Abraham" than "a son of humanity" or "a son of might."

[11] Cf. Waltke and O'Connor, *An Introduction to Biblical Hebrew Syntax*, sec. 9.5.3.b. Abbreviated as IBHS from now on.

which is more appropriately "sons of mighty ones," i.e. mighty beings (cf. Deut 3:18, 32:8; Jdgs 18:2, 21:10; 2 Sam 2:7, 7:14; Ezra 4:1, 6:19), than "sons of gods," which is ill suited to the context and the theology of Israel (heavenly beings are identified not as sons of "gods" but as the sons of God, אֱלֹהִים ['elohim']).[12] The same phrase is used in Psalm 89:7; here, a heavenly council assembly is clearly in view (v. 7). However, once again, the phrase "sons of gods" does not seem as fitting as "sons of mighty ones," being an idiom for "mighty beings." The use of this form in Job 41:17 is usually interpreted similarly, as "mighty ones." In light of these instances where "mighty ones" (a plural of אַיִל ['ayil]) is more suitable than "gods" (a plural of אֵל ['el]), we can also suggest that the defective form in Exodus 15:11 is also a plural of אַיִל, "Who is like you, O Lord, among the mighty ones?" This is perhaps confirmed four verses later where the plene (non-defective) form is used, "trembling seizes the leaders of Moab [אֵילֵי מוֹאָב]" (ESV). Thus, there is only one instance where the form אֵלִים clearly means "gods": everywhere else it certainly (Exod 36:19) or probably (Psalm 29:1, 89:7, Job 41:17; cf. Exod 15:11) means "mighty ones" or "rulers." For this reason, I do not think that any of these passages call angels "gods," though they are associated with God as "sons" and are identified as "mighty beings" and heaven-dwelling "holy ones."

There are other instances, however, where the Bible speaks of "gods." The Old Testament refers to these "gods" in two ways: in some passages, they are called "gods" without qualification. In others, usually with reference to "idols," these gods are disparaged as not-gods. The pre-eminent passage in the latter case is Elijah's mockery of Baal in 1 Kings 18:20-40, but the same theme is found elsewhere, such as Psalm 96:5. In the former cases, there are passages that juxtapose the powerlessness of other gods, presupposed to be superhuman, in comparison to Yahweh, God pre-eminent. We will look at Psalm 96:5 and two of the later texts, Deuteronomy 3:24 and Psalm 77:14. Then we will consider the text where humans are called "gods," namely Psalm 82.

---

[12] Cf. Mitchell Dahood, *Psalms II: 51-100*, The Anchor Bible (Garden City: Doubleday, 1968), 57.

a. Psalm 96:5

כִּי כָּל־אֱלֹהֵי הָעַמִּים אֱלִילִים וַיהוָה שָׁמַיִם עָשָׂה:

For all the gods of the peoples are worthless idols,
but Yahweh made the heavens.

Psalm 96:5 is typical of many passages in the Old Testament where the objects of the nations' worship, "gods," are denied reality or power: they are אֱלִילִים ('elilim), "worthless idols." The biblical portrait of the אֱלִילִים is not only something "worthless" but utterly unreal, merely human creations, without any power:

> What benefit is an idol (פֶּסֶל; *pesel*),
>> that its maker would hew it,
>> a cast image (מַסֵּכָה; *massekah*) and a teacher of lies,
> For the maker trust what he has made,
>> enough to craft speechless (אִלְּמִים; *'illemim*) idols (אֱלִילִים; *'elilim*).
> Woe to him who says to wood, 'wake up!'
>> 'awake!' to a dumb stone.
> Is it able to teach?
>> Behold, it is overlaid with gold and silver,
>> but there is no breath at all in it. (Hab 2:18-19)

Such "gods" are not only the physical idols worshipped by the nations but everything in which they put their hope and trust, such as their strength (כֹּח; *koach*, cf. Hab 1:11). In this sense of the term, these "gods" are utterly unreal. However, there are other instances where the terms for "god" are used for beings other than Yahweh and these beings are assumed to be real. Deuteronomy 3:24 and Psalm 77:14 serve as examples of this usage.

b. Deuteronomy 3:24

אֲדֹנָי יְהוִה אַתָּה הַחִלּוֹת לְהַרְאוֹת אֶת־עַבְדְּךָ אֶת־גָּדְלְךָ וְאֶת־יָדְךָ הַחֲזָקָה
אֲשֶׁר מִי־אֵל בַּשָּׁמַיִם וּבָאָרֶץ אֲשֶׁר־יַעֲשֶׂה כְמַעֲשֶׂיךָ וְכִגְבוּרֹתֶךָ:

Oh Lord YHWH,[13] you have begun to show your servant

---

[13] "YHWH" is transliterated from the Hebrew יהוה, God's name as revealed in Exod 3:14-15. Out of reverence, afraid of accidently breaking the 3rd

your greatness and your mighty hand; what god in heaven or on earth can act comparably to your works or mighty deeds?

In response to God's mighty deeds in the Exodus and beyond, it is demonstrated to Moses and the Israelites that God is in a class of his own. The question in the second clause (מִי־אֵל; *mi-el*, "what god?") does not explicitly repudiate the existence of other gods. Instead, it puts them in another category from Yahweh: who among the mighty beings can do anything like Yahweh has done? Like the other statements of God's uniqueness, Deuteronomy 3:24 allows there to be other beings that may be called "gods," yet these beings are nothing in comparison to Yahweh. Passages like Psalm 96:5 decry the unreality of idols; passages like Deuteronomy 3:24 allow that there may be "gods," superhuman beings, yet these "gods" are nothing like God.

c. Psalm 77:14

אֱלֹהִים בַּקֹּדֶשׁ דַּרְכֶּךָ מִי־אֵל גָּדוֹל כֵּאלֹהִים:
O God, holy is your way;
  what god is great like God?

Like Deuteronomy 3:24, אֵל (*'el*) in Psalm 77:14 is referring to superhuman entities and may presuppose their reality. It does not dismiss the reality of other gods, only their comparability with God most high. This once again contrasts with the texts like Psalm 96:5, which dismiss the reality of the objects worshipped by the nations. The sense of reality suggested by Psalm 77:14 may correspond to other passages where the role of idols or "gods" is attributed to "demons" (שֵׁד; *shed*). In Deuteronomy 32:17, apostate Israel sacrificed to שֵׁדִים (*shedim*), "demons," not אֱלֹהַּ (*'eloah*), "God" (rightly NET; not "a god," contra ESV). These "demons" were not God whom they knew

---

commandment and using God's name in vain, ancient scribes would read the Hebrew word "*Adonai*," meaning "lord," in the place of his name Yahweh (the probable pronunciation). This practice was continued by the Greek translation of the Old Testament (the Septuagint) and the New Testament. Among other titles, God, Lord, and Yahweh are the primary ways our God is referred to in the Bible. I will use them interchangeably.

In my translation, I use the transliteration "YHWH" to represent the Hebrew text, where this interplay between "Lord" and the name "Yahweh" is apparent.

intimately through the covenant, they were "gods whom they did not know" (32:17). Similarly, in Psalm 106:37, the idols to whom Israel sacrificed their children are called שֵׁדִים (*shedim*). Being the only two instances of שֵׁד (*shed*) in the Hebrew Bible, the term may be a synonym for an idol, merely a manmade reality, but the LXX translates the term as δαιμόνιον (*daimonion*, "demon"), which refers to superhuman beings. In the New Testament, this Greek word refers to superhuman and malevolent entities (cf. Ps 90:6 in the LXX; in the LXX of Isa 65:3-4, δαιμόνιοις [*daimoniois*, "demons"] is inserted along with the claim that they do not exist). Taken together, this suggests that idols are, in a sense, false realities, for they are powerless to do what they are attributed with and not worthy of worship; yet there may be superhuman powers acting behind these idols, powers that may be called אֱלֹהִים (*'elohim*), "gods" (1 Cor 8:4-6; 10:14-22).

d. Psalm 82:1b-c, 6

אֱלֹהִים נִצָּב בַּעֲדַת־אֵל בְּקֶרֶב אֱלֹהִים יִשְׁפֹּט׃
God stands in the divine council;
He judges in the midst of gods.
אֲנִי־אָמַרְתִּי אֱלֹהִים אַתֶּם וּבְנֵי עֶלְיוֹן כֻּלְּכֶם׃
I said, "You are gods;
All of you are sons of the Most High."

The final text I want to consider is Psalm 82, specifically verse 1b-c and 6. This psalm has engendered no small amount of debate, even being called the "most important text in the Bible."[14] The discussion of this text has been dominated in modern times by the reconstruction of its compositional history and its background in Canaanite religion, namely, the council of El, the most high deity of Canaanite religion.[15] In this context, it is argued that

---

[14] John Dominic Crossan, *Birth of Christianity* (A&C Black, 1999), 575–576; J Clinton Jr. McCann, "The Single Most Important Text in the Entire Bible: Toward a Theology of the Psalms," in *Soundings in the Theology of Psalms: Perspectives and Methods in Contemporary Scholarship* (Minneapolis, 2011), 63.

[15] E.g. M L (Martin Litchfield) West, "Towards Monotheism," in *Pagan Monotheism in Late Antiquity* (Oxford, 1999), 21–40; Peter Machinist, "How Gods Die, Biblically and Otherwise: A Problem of Cosmic Restructuring," in *Reconsidering the Concept of Revolutionary Monotheism*, ed. Beate Pongratz-Leisten (Winona Lake:

the members of the "divine council" are deities, however we might conceive their status (e.g. Moberly sees them as merely phenomenological; Tsevat as "real challenges, emanating from real sources").[16] However, given the literary context and broader canonical context, it is arguable that the reading which dominated in pre-Modern times is correct, namely, that these are merely human rulers.

As preliminary observation, it should be observed that אֵל (*'el;* "God") and עֶלְיוֹן (*'elyon;* "the Most High") as titles are only used for Yahweh in the Bible (together in Gen 14:19-22, separately in Psalm 50:14 and 50:2). As part of the Psalms, Psalm 82 is part of Book III and one of the Psalms of Asaph, among which Psalm 50 is also included.[17] Psalm 50 is a significant instance where Yahweh is referred to as אֵל and עֶלְיוֹן. Considering the theological perspective of the canon (that Yahweh alone is God), Psalm 50 prepares the reader to identify עֶלְיוֹן in Psalm 82 as Yahweh, not the Canaanite deity as is commonly asserted by scholars.[18] As for עֲדַת־אֵל (*'adat-'el;* "council of god"), if read as a title this would be "God's council"; however, the generic use of אֵל may be intended and so, "in (the) divine council." Juxtaposed with the אֱלֹהִים (*'elohim;* "gods") who are gathered, "the divine council" (that is, a council pertaining to divinity or gods) seems appropriate. VanGemeren identifies shared themes uniting the psalms of Asaph (Pss. 50, 73-83), concerning justice in light of the wicked.[19] Gers-Uphaus identifies a similar theme in the psalms of Asaph and a particular affinity between Psalm 50 and

---

Eisenbrauns, 2011), 189–240; James M. Trotter, "Death of the 'lhym in Psalm 82," *Journal of Biblical Literature* 131 (2012): 221–239; Matitiahu Tsevat, "God and the Gods in Assembly: An Interpretation of Psalm 82," *Hebrew Union College Annual* 40 (1969): 123–137; McCann, "The Single."

[16] R. W. L. Moberly, *The God of the Old Testament: Encountering the Divine in Christian Scripture* (Grand Rapids: Baker Academic, 2020), chap. 3; Tsevat, "God and the Gods in Assembly," 124.

[17] Cf. Willem VanGemeren, *Psalms*, ed. Tremper Longman III and David E. Garland, Revised Edition., vol. 5, The Expositor's Bible Commentary: (Grand Rapids: Zondervan, 2008); Christian Gers-Uphaus, "Gott Als Wahrer אלהים Und Retter Der Armen: Psalm 82 Im Korpus Der Asafpsalmen," *Biblische Zeitschrift* 63, no. 1 (2019): 30–48.

[18] See the discussion in Moberly, *The God of the Old Testament.*

[19] VanGemeren, *Psalms*, 5:557–558.

82.[20] Psalm 50 also shares many similarities with 83, where the psalmist calls upon God to judge the nations that they may know that he alone is "the Most High [עֶלְיוֹן, *elyon*] over all the earth" (83:19 MT). Once again, it is Yahweh who is standing in the council.

Verse 1 pictures God taking a position to act among the divine council, populated by אֱלֹהִים (*'elohim*), "gods." The use of this term raises an immediate problem: if these are "gods" in the sense of superhuman beings, it would be unprecedented in the Bible. On the one hand, though prevalent in the ANE and even later Jewish literature, the constituents of God's council elsewhere in the Bible are not called אֱלֹהִים (*'elohim*).[21] That is, God is presented as a holding a heavenly assembly, yet it is unlike the "divine councils" of the Ancient Near East, for these assemblies are "evacuated of the gods" in the Bible.[22] These assemblies are not pictured as a meeting of equals, where God seeks wisdom or collaborates in action, but they are assemblies of the servants of God, summoned to do his bidding (e.g. Job 1:6). The constituents of these councils are never called "gods," but are "the sons of God" (Gen 6:2, 4; Job 1:6, 2:1, 38:7), "mighty beings" (Ps 29:1; Ps. 89:7), or "holy ones" (Job 5:1, 15:15, Zech 14:5). God is often envisioned as holding council in heaven, yet those in the divine council are what Christian theology calls angels, beings that are neither called "gods" nor given godlike status. As Gordon observes, the Divine Council is "evacuated of the gods" which populated the divine council in ANE literature. On the other hand, it would be equally unusual for the term to refer to mere humans. The only other example would be Psalm 45:6: even if the Psalm is read as fully messianic, the figure is still identified as one of "the sons of men."[23] However, the actions attributed to these אֱלֹהִים in the following verses are not those

---

[20] Gers-Uphaus, "Gott."

[21] On the divine council in later Jewish literature, Michael S Heiser, "Monotheism and the Language of Divine Plurality in the Hebrew Bible and the Dead Sea Scrolls," *Tyndale Bulletin* 65, no. 1 (2014): 85–100.

[22] Robert P. Gordon, "Standing in the Council: When Prophets Encounter God," in *The God of Israel*, ed. Robert P. Gordon (Cambridge University Press, 2007), 201.

[23] On the reading of the vocative and how this might be construed, if the figure is not granted identity with God, see Murray J. Harris, *Jesus as God: The New Testament Use of Theos in Reference to Jesus* (Wipf and Stock Publishers, 2008), chap. 8.

practiced by superhuman beings in the Bible, who—when granted reality—are either messengers of Yahweh or the supernatural beings standing behind the false worship of the nations.

The one possible exception is Psalm 58:2 [MT], where we are told that "gods" (אֵלִים; *'elim*) are charged with injustice (cf. ESV).[24] However, this interpretation is not the most likely. As it stands, the MT may be translated, "Do you really speak what is right with your silence?" In the Masoretic text, אֵלֶם (*'elem*) is vocalized as a noun from אלם (*'-l-m*; "to be silent") and appears to have this sense in Psalm 56:1 [MT]. However, many commentators reject this reading of Psalm 58:2, revocalising the word as אֵלִם (*'elim*, "mighty ones" or "gods"), which we discussed above. However, given that the Masoretic pointing makes sense, there is no need for revocalisation, especially not if that vocalisation is "gods," given that there is no contextual evidence for this reading nor precedence elsewhere in Scripture for attributing such a role to the "gods." In favour of the Masoretic reading, we can add that "silence" is readily juxtaposed with injustice and that the contrast of "speaking" with "silence" gives poetic force to these opening lines. Thus, Psalm 58:2 does not give evidence for a judicial role of divine, superhuman beings.

Returning to Psalm 82, the אֱלֹהִים (*'elohim*; "gods") are entrusted with enacting justice (שׁפט; *sh-p-t*, v. 2a-3a) and righteousness (צדק; *ts-d-q*, v. 3b). The charge of injustice towards those in authority is frequent throughout the biblical literature (e.g. Hab 1:1-5), so it is perfectly appropriate for human rulers of all levels. The concern for the "weak and the fatherless" and the "afflicted and destitute" is prominent in the biblical idea of justice and righteousness, with which Israel's leaders were to rule (e.g. Gen 18:19; Exod 22:22, 24-25; 23:3; 30:15; Deut 10:18; 14:29; 16:19; 24:12-17; 1 Kgs 10:9; Isa 1:27; 5:16; 9:7; 16:5; 28:17; 32:1; 32:16; 33:5; Jer 5:28; 10:2; 11:4; 22:3, 16; 2 Chron 9:8).[25] Verse 5 is sometimes taken to refer to the cosmological upset

---

[24] E.g. John Goldingay, *Psalms: Psalms 43-89*, vol. 2, Baker commentary on the Old Testament wisdom and Psalms (Grand Rapids: Baker Academic, 2006), 203.

[25] See Gentry and Wellum, *Kingdom through Covenant (2nd Ed)*; Andrew T. Abernethy, *The Book of Isaiah and God's Kingdom: A Thematic Theological Approach*, New Studies in Biblical Theology 40 (Downers Grove: IVP, 2016), chap. 3 s.v. "Isaiah 56:1".

of the injustice caused by the heavenly אֱלֹהִים ('elohim, "gods").[26] However, it is not immediately clear that verse 5 refers to the אֱלֹהִים. Instead, as Strawn observes, the description in 5a-b is perfectly appropriate for destitute humanity, the "weak, etc." of 3-4.[27] Verse 5 can be read as the result of the behaviour of the אֱלֹהִים recounted in verse 2. Because of the leader's failures, the people walk around ignorant and in darkness. Therefore, verse 5c would not refer to cosmological upheaval but the similar disorientation as envisioned in Psalm 11:13. A similar scene of societal upheaval because of the corruption of power is presented in Habakkuk 1:1-5. Psalm 82:2-5 is thus completely consistent and appropriate if the אֱלֹהִים ('elohim) are human rulers.

However, for many exegetes, the biggest difficulty of this reading is accounting for verse 6. That is, if the "gods" are demoted from immorality because of their behaviour, they could not have been mere humans.[28] This objection is not sound. As argued by Budde, the use of אָמַר ('amar; "to say") followed by אָכֵן ('aken; nevertheless) in verses 6-7 does not indicate a judicial sentence but a re-evaluation.[29] In the uses of this construction elsewhere, the state described by אָמַר is corrected by that given in the clause introduced with אָכֵן. Thus, the original claim that these entities are "gods" is not all that it appeared to be: under the inspiration of the Holy Spirit, the psalmist has called these figures "gods," but their exalted role that esteems them of the title does not eradicate their mortality. Like the "weak" and the "afflicted" from whom they withhold justice, these אֱלֹהִים will die like the rest of "humanity" (אָדָם; 'adam) or "any other ruler" (אַחַד הַשָּׂרִים; 'achad hassarim, 'one of the rulers"). Whether verse 6-7 are the words of God to the "gods" or of the psalmist re-evaluating his initial pronouncement in verse 1 (which seems more likely), these אֱלֹהִים have been found wanting by the "Most High" and will meet their end. The prayer in verse 8 is thus the response of the Psalmist

---

[26] Machinist, "How Gods Die."

[27] Brent A. Strawn, "The Poetics of Psalm 82: Three Critical Notes along with a Plea for the Poetic," *Revue Biblique (1946-)* 121, no. 1 (2014): 25–30.

[28] Machinist, "How Gods Die," 206; Mark S. Smith, *The Origins of Biblical Monotheism: Israel's Polytheistic Background and the Ugaritic Texts* (Oxford University Press, USA, 2003), 156.

[29] K. Budde, "Ps. 82:6 f.," *Journal of Biblical Literature* 40, no. 1/2 (1921): 39–42; Moberly, *The God of the Old Testament*, chap. 3.

J. Alexander Rutherford

to God's judgment pronounced in verse 2-5. That verse 8 calls on God to judge "the earth" only strengthens the argument that these are earthly rulers: as they have failed to give justice upon the earth, so God shall go forth and judge them.

Reading אֱלֹהִים as human rulers thus makes great sense of the Psalm. This reading also finds confirmation in the use our Lord makes of it in John 10:34. There is no precedence for identifying those "to whom the word of God came" as superhuman beings, but if "the word of God" is understood as Scripture (Matt 15:6; Mark 7:13; Luke 5:1; 8:11, 21; 11:28), the rulers of Israel would be natural referents of this description.

The Psalm calls to judgment the unjust rulers of God's people; they must not ignore the fact that though given God's authority on earth and power over their fellow humans, they are not themselves God. They are accountable and will be judged; the song thus ends with a call for God to enact justice against the wicked "gods." The title "god" is not denied to these rulers; indeed, it is given to them by God through the psalmist (v. 1) and appears fitting for them, given their status among their brethren. These rulers who are not God are thus rightfully called "gods," as Jesus' *a minore ad maius* argument presupposes. However, though their authoritative role makes them like God in some way, they are nevertheless mortal like the rest of humanity.

e. Summary

In this section I have only sought to make several observations concerning the use of the terms we translate "god" (אֵל ['el], אֱלוֹהַּ ['eloah], אֱלֹהִים ['elohim]) for entities who are not Yahweh. Considering only a sampling of verses, the term appears to be used for unreal entities, "idols" conceived of us a product of the human imagination. It is also employed for real entities, for humans and spiritual beings who wield power and, at least in the case of the human rulers, authority. That the term is polysemous in referent and sense is no surprise, but this conclusion bears ontological implications for our understanding of the term "god" as used in the phrase "God is one" and our understanding of relationship that obtains between the term and its referent. It is thus possible within the biblical worldview to say that there are many gods, yet none of those who are referred to with the Hebrew terms for "god" are like Yahweh, the true God. He is in a class of his own. Thus, the term

46

"god" does not signify an "essence," something which characterizes Yahweh alone apart from all created reality. Nevertheless, God is distinguished from all other realities, including the gods. In Chapter 6 we will consider the uniqueness of Yahweh the true God, but before this, we must consider the Great Shema.

J. Alexander Rutherford

.

THE GREAT SHEMA

שְׁמַע יִשְׂרָאֵל יְהֹוָה אֱלֹהֵינוּ יְהֹוָה אֶחָד

Hear, O Israel,
    YHWH our God,
        YHWH is one.[1]

The Great Shema (Deut 6:4) is often thought of as the statement of biblical monotheism *par excellence*, yet things become complicated when we consider it more closely. This verse has engendered much discussion, especially the translation of the final four words. These words clearly provide the content of the imperative שְׁמַע (*shemaʿ*), "hear!" (along with verse 5), but scholars are divided over what exactly Israel was to hear. Three main positions are often taken: 1) there may be two predicate clauses describing YHWH ("YHWH is our God; YHWH is one"); 2) there may be one predicate clause with יְהֹוָה אֱלֹהֵינוּ as the subject and יְהֹוָה אֶחָד as the object ("YHWH, our God, is one YHWH"); or 3) יְהֹוָה אֱלֹהֵינוּ may be a pendent nominative (my translation).[2] The first and third translation reflect only a minor difference in emphasis, so the primary opposition is between #1 or #3 and #2. Moberly asserts that #1

---

[1] All translations in this chapter are the author's own unless stated otherwise.

[2] Moberly has a fourth, "Yahweh is our God, Yahweh alone," but this rests on an unlikely use of אֶחָד, as discussed below. R. W. L. Moberly, "'Yahweh Is One': On the Translation of the Shema," in *Studies in the Pentateuch*, ed. John Adney Emerton (E. J. Brill, 1990), 210.

and #3 have a different emphasis, the former indicating Israel's relationship to God and the latter something about Yahweh's "nature or character."[3] Though I agree that there is a difference in emphasis, the specific nuance Moberly identifies is not clear to me. In #1, the emphasis could lay on either predicate ("God" or "one"), with the second predicate clearly saying something *about* God. It could then be argued that both translations say something about God's "nature or character": he is Israel's God, and he is one. Moreover, the distinction between these two translations is more significant in English than in Hebrew. In the first instance, two things are said of God; in the second, the appositional noun אֱלֹהֵינוּ (*'elohenu;* "our God[s]") serves to identify or describe the subject of the predicate clause "YHWH is one." Thus, the focus is Yahweh being one, yet the repetition of יהוה (YHWH) emphasises the role of the clause to identify something about Yahweh; we could paraphrase it as such in this way, "As for YHWH our God, YHWH is one."[4] The repetition also draws attention to the appositional noun, for its inclusion leads to the *pendens* construction I have suggested in my translation, so, "As for YHWH our *God*, YHWH is one." The most significant reason to favour my translation (#3) over #1 is the common use of the phrase יהוה אֱלֹהֵינוּ (*YHWH 'elohenu;* "YHWH our God") in apposition (with or without various pronominal suffixes on אֱלֹהִים); the pair form a complete clause only once (2 Chron 13:10).[5] Thus, taking "YHWH our God" together as the subject is likely. The use of יהוה as a *nominativus pendens* in this manner is not well attested, but the use of the *pendens* construction is. So, translations 1 and 3 are based on common Hebrew syntax and 3 is to be preferred because of the common use of the phrase יהוה אֱלֹהִים. The second reading, on the other hand, does not have much going for it.

Concerning this option, I do not think "one YHWH" makes much sense.[6] So far as I can determine, there is no instance elsewhere in the Hebrew

---

[3] Ibid.

[4] Cf. IBHS 16.3.3.b

[5] Moberly has quantified the use in "Deuteronomic" passages; the pair are in apposition 312/312 times.

[6] Anderson sees אֶחָד (*'echad*) and יהוה (YHWH) as the discontinuous subject and predicate, respectively. There is thus one predicate clause with discontinuous parts,

Bible of a number modifying a name in this way, such that there are several "David"'s or just one. Names in colloquial English can be countable, but it is certainly awkward to do so: it would be more natural to say, "there are four men named Hezekiah" than "there are four 'Hezekiah's." יהוה (YHWH) is treated as a proper noun in Hebrew and so is intrinsically definite.[7] If אֶחָד ('echad;

"one") were an adjective modifying יי, we would expect it to be definite, but it is not.[8] Moreover, it makes little sense for the adjective to function quantitatively with a definite noun, with a name ("a single YHWH"; "one YHWH"). The sense of "one Yahweh" here would need to be that of the English idiom, "There is only one so-and-so," indicating excellence or renown. However, to the best of my knowledge, this idiom is not attested in the Hebrew Bible. Without such an idiom, it is not evident why anyone would need to say that יהוה is not more than one יי. However, many who adopt translation #2 argue that אֶחָד means "alone."

Two problems arise from this reading. On the hand, it is not clear why it is significant to state that Yahweh is "YHWH alone" or "the only YHWH"—as if there were competition for the name. On the other hand, it is not clear that אֶחָד is used in this way.[9] As an adjective, אֶחָד is nearly always treated as a quantitative adjective (one of several possible things). DCH gives several instances where it is apparently an adjective of quality (2 Sam 7:23, 1 Chron 17:21; Ezek 7:5; 1 Kgs 4:19). In each case, the explicit or implicit noun is countable; there is no example of this with an uncountable noun (such as a proper noun), so the use with "Yahweh" would be unprecedented. Instead, if אֶחָד is a qualitative adjective, we would expect it to modify a countable

---

"Our one God is Yahweh, Yahweh." The evidence for this reading appears very strained, as Janzen argues, especially when there are more clear options available (namely, #1 or #3). Francis I. Andersen, *The Hebrew Verbless Clause in the Pentateuch*, Journal of Biblical literature 14 (Nashville: Abingdon Press, 1970), 47; J. Gerald Janzen, "On the Most Important Word in the Shema (Deuteronomy VI 4-5)," *Vetus Testamentum* XXXVII, no. 3 (1987): 295–296.

[7] IBHS 13.4.b; Jouon §137b; Gesenius §125.d

[8] This rule is more consistent in narrative and prose than in poetry, so the article would be expected here, though it is not entirely consistent across the Hebrew Bible.

[9] Moberly, "'Yahweh Is One': On the Translation of the Shema," 211–213; Christopher Wright, *Deuteronomy*, NIBC (Peabody: Hendrickson, 1996), 96.

noun, not the name יהוה. Waltke cites Zechariah 14:9 in this regard, but we will see below that this is not the best reading of that passage (Chapter 6.E). If one wanted to say "alone," as in "Yahweh is our God, Yahweh alone" (unlikely given our considerations above) or, more likely, "Yahweh our God is Yahweh alone," יָחִיד (*yachid*, "only") would be a clearer choice. To the evidence adduced above against reading יהוה אֱלֹהֵינוּ (*YHWH 'elohinu;* YHWH our God) as an independent clause, we could add Moberly's argument that when a predicate is intended (i.e. "Yahweh is our God"), the definite article is used with אֱלֹהִים (*'elohim*) and הוּא (*hu';* "he") is present.[10] However, even if we accept that this means "alone", the sense is still not clear. Usually, Yahweh is said to be the only God; nowhere else is he said to be the only Yahweh, as if others were competing for that title. Thus, interpretations which assume אֶחָד (*'echad*) means "alone" or is an adjective modifying יהוה are unlikely. If no other option availed us, appealing to such a strained reading may be justified, but there are other options available. So, we are left with translations #1 or #3: whether as a predicate or a noun of apposition, YHWH is identified as the Israelites' God. Furthermore, YHWH is identified as "one."[11]

Drawing on Job 23:13, in addition to other evidence, Janzen argues that אֶחָד here means "fidelity" or "integrity."[12] I do not find Janzen's evidence compelling; though steadfastness and fidelity are indeed key themes throughout the Old Testament, the paucity of relevant examples of אֶחָד used in this way is telling. חֶסֶד (*chesed;* "covenant love" or "covenant loyalty") or אֱמוּנָה (*'emunah;* "faithfulness") are used far more frequently and would be more than adequate to express Yahweh's fidelity to his covenant promises if this were the intended meaning (cf. 6:3). Cyrus Gordon argues that "one" should be taken as a name; however, his only biblical evidence for this claim is that Zechariah 14:9 must have this meaning. He gives no contextual argument why this fits Deuteronomy 6, and I have been unable to discern

---

[10] Moberly, "'Yahweh Is One': On the Translation of the Shema," 213–214.

[11] Moberly sees an echo of this claim in Zech 14:9. Ibid., 214.

[12] Janzen, "On the Most Important Word in the Shema (Deuteronomy VI 4-5)," 22. Cf, Patrick D Miller, "The Most Important Word: The Yoke of the Kingdom," *Iliff Review* (1984): 14; IBHS 15.2.1.c.

any (see below on Zechariah, Chapter 6.E).[13] Instead, as in the English phrase "YHWH is one", the statement יהוה אֶחָד (YHWH *'echad*) begs the question, "one what?"[14] In the context of the clause, the clear answer is "one God." That is, YHWH is not a countable term, but אֱלוֹהַ (*eloah*; "a god") is. Therefore, the statement would appear to mean something like, "Hear, O Israel, YHWH our God, YHWH is one god."

But such a rendering engenders an immediate objection; why does it matter that the Israelites proclaim YHWH to be "one god." That is, to declare Yahweh as the *only* (יָחִיד; *yachid*) God would make sense as a polemic against polytheistic worship (though not necessarily the belief in multiple deities), which is usually thought to be the intent of this passage. As McBride puts it, "The verse was read as an oath of allegiance to the suzerainty of Yahweh alone."[15] However, the assertion that God is "one god" does not clearly assert the sole reality of God over against other possible gods. Indeed, to say "YHWH is one god," like saying "Nicole is one human," would most clearly seem to prohibit plurality, or perhaps the wrong sort of plurality, to Yahweh. As we saw, there are several instances where אֶחָד (*'echad*) is used with a countable noun meaning something like "unique." Thus we have two possible readings here, "YHWH is the unique God," perhaps indicating his special status, or "YHWH is one god," over against plurality. However, in the examples cited above, where אֶחָד means "the only something," it is an adjective modifying a countable noun. Here, it is an indefinite, substantive predicate, so I do not think the reading "YHWH is (the) unique (god)" is likely.

At this point, our discussion of frameworks of possibility becomes very important; if our framework presupposes that there is no hint of plurality in

---

[13] Cyrus H. Gordon, "His Name Is 'One,'" *Journal of Near Eastern Studies* 29, no. 3 (July 1970): 198–199.

[14] Christopher Wright suggests that the phrase "John is one" is a statement of his unified conscious or fidelity, yet the only time I can think of in English where we would say anything analogous would be the phrase, "there is only one John," which does not have numerical oneness in mind, as the Hebrew text does, but the sense "unique." Wright, *Deuteronomy*, s.v. 6:4–5.

[15] Samuel Dean McBride, "Yoke of the Kingdom: An Exposition of Deuteronomy 6:4-5," *Interpretation* 27, no. 3 (July 1973): 276.

God at this point, then the reading "YHWH is one god" doesn't make much sense. However, if our framework of interpretation allows us to interpret texts as predicating plurality to God, then there are many texts that imply plurality in God (as we will see in Chapter 6). This is especially the case if we allow a whole-Bible, Trinitarian frame of reference. If one were to permit the possibility of a Trinitarian reading, then a delicate balance of plurality and unity is the crucial tension to be held together in our doctrine of God. Within a Trinitarian framework, the Bible can (and if it is truly Trinitarian, should) posit both plurality in God and true unity. Shortly, I will argue that there are contextual reasons to find both plurality and unity stated in this verse, but for now it is important only to note that our acceptance of Framework 3 makes the sense "YHWH is one god" intelligible, for it is necessary to guard against pure plurality by positing true unity, that the Triune God is one God.

If we return to the first possible reading, "YHWH is the unique God," it fits within a broader pattern of argument in the Old Testament, wherein God is identified as the one and only God, the true God over against those who wrongly claim or attributed with such status. We see this in the first table of the Law and throughout the ministry of the prophets. However, though this theme is very frequent, not once is it expressed in this language (see below on Zech 14:9). Instead, the formula that is regularly used is יְהוָה הוּא הָאֱלֹהִים (YHWH hu' ha'elohim; "YHWH is God"), sometimes with לְבַדֶּךָ (lebaddeka; "alone," e.g. 1 Kgs 8:60; 18:39; 2 Kgs 19:15, 19:19). If Deuteronomy 6:4 were expressing this idea, it is hard to see why its idiom is never used again, especially when this is a crucial polemical claim made throughout the Bible. Furthermore, such a polemic against idolatry appears in verses 13-15 and does not use the language of verse 4.

In contrast, there are contextual reasons for preferring the second reading, "Yahweh is one god," as a hedge against a certain form of plurality. Consider the text of verse 4 more closely,

יהוה אֱלֹהֵינוּ יהוה אֶחָד

Though both pairs in this sentence are not necessarily syntactically parallel (accepting that "יהוה אֱלֹהֵינוּ" is an appositional phrase), the sentence reads like poetic parallelism,

> Yahweh our God
> Yahweh is one

An appositional phrase could be parsed as implying a copulative ("is"), though the whole phrase is functioning as the subject in an independent clause (or, in this case, a *pendens*), so we can imply the copulative in our translation to bring out the parallel construction evident in Hebrew, bearing in mind that this first line is not an independent clause. Given the poetic feel of the text and the "vertical grammar" of Hebrew poetry (where various pieces of a sentence are carried over from one line to another), it is clear that אֶחָד (*'echad,* "one") implies the noun אֱלֹוהַ (*'eloah,* "a god"),[16]

> Yahweh (is) our God,
> Yahweh is one (god).

So, why does this foundational creed make the assertion that "Yahweh is one (god)?" Accepting that יהוה אֶחָד (*YHWH 'echad*) means "Yahweh is one (god)" reveals an inherent tension within the sentence itself. Naturally, the assertion that Yahweh is one god would counter the false belief that Yahweh is many gods, or at least, many gods without fundamental unity. We should ask, is there anything in context that would imply this belief, that Yahweh is plural? Let's look at the text one more time, in Hebrew with an overly literal translation:

יהוה אֱלֹהֵינוּ יהוה אֶחָד

> YHWH (is) our Gods,
> YHWH is one (god).[17]

Translated in this way, there is a sort of balance struck by the two lines: Yahweh is plural; Yahweh is singular. I argued above that יהוה אֱלֹהֵינוּ (*YHWH 'elohenu;* "YHWH our Gods") regularly has an appositional function. Thus, there are not two independent clauses; instead, the phrase in line 1 is the subject of the clause in line 2. Thus, אֱלֹהֵינוּ specifies something about

---

[16] Cf. David Toshio Tsumura, "Vertical Grammar of Parallelism in Hebrew Poetry," *Journal of Biblical Literature* 128, no. 1 (2009): 167–181.

[17] I maintain the capitalisation of "Gods" in the first line because here, as elsewhere, it has not lost its function as a proper noun.

"YHWH" that is pertinent to line 2. We could paraphrase it in this way,

> as for Yahweh who is our Gods,
> that Yahweh is one God.

Elsewhere in the Pentateuch, the emphasis in "YHWH our God" lies on "our," but in contrast with אֶחָד (*'echad*), the emphasis almost appears to fall on "God(s)" (as reinforced by the *pendens* construction, see above). Thus, we would have here, "as for Yahweh who is our *Gods,* that Yahweh is one God."

At this point, someone may cry foul, for we know that the plural is often used for a singular subject, such as when the plural refers to Yahweh and the verb is in the singular (we saw other examples in Chapter 4). On the one hand, we need to be careful not to confuse grammar with ontology; we must not assume real plurality wherever a grammatical plural exists. On the other hand, we cannot assume that language is not adapted and used to indicate a reality. Context must determine which is relevant in each case: is the plural a linguistic phenomenon or one of reference? In the case of many idioms, such as the use of the plural-for-singular, the idiom becomes a frozen form or phrase that a reader immediately registers as idiomatic rather than giving credence to its parts or morphology (e.g. in "straight from the horse's mouth," no one familiar with the idiom ponders the origins of the phrase or the relevance of a horse to the given situation). On the other hand, there is evidence from across the canon that this form, אֱלֹהִים (*'elohim;* "God," gods"), is not treated as such, as a frozen idiom without the connotations of plurality.

For one, this same form is used to speak of plural "gods." When speaking of Yahweh as אֱלֹהִים, the Gentiles sometimes use the singular verb or pronoun, as the biblical narrators do, but at other times they use plurals (Josh 9:9; 1 Sam 4:7-8; 5:7; 6:5, 20). They demonstrate confusion even though they often refer to their own deities with the plural noun and singular verb, or just the plural noun for a single deity (Jdgs 6:31; 8:33; 16:23-24; 1 Kgs 11:33; 1 Kgs 20:10). Thus, the Gentiles are confused whether YHWH who is אֱלֹהִים is one God or many. This is not just a Gentile phenomenon: more significantly, there is at least one incident in the Hebrew Bible where Israelites seem to be caught up on the plurality of the term אֱלֹהִים, perhaps two. In 1 Kings, when Jeroboam makes two calves for Israel to worship, he identifies them as the אֱלֹהִים ("gods") that led Israel out of Egypt (1 Kgs 12:28). In the context of the Exodus, that אֱלֹהִים was clearly the one God, Yahweh. Some confusion has entered the picture by the time of Jeroboam, and whatever the cause or genealogy of that confusion, the term אֱלֹהִים bridges the Pentateuch's account and Jeroboam's error. This incident echoes Exodus 32, where the confusion is even more evident.

The incident with the golden calf occurs in the narrative in Exodus at the same point as the Shema in Deuteronomy, after God delivers the statutes of his covenant to Moses on the mountain (though Exodus also contains the instructions for the cult and its paraphernalia). In Deuteronomy, this event is only mentioned later as part of a warning, not in the narrative (Deut 9:1-29). In Exodus 32, the Israelites ask Aaron to make them "gods" (אֱלֹהִים; *'elohim*) to go before them (יֵלְכוּ; *yelku*; "they will go," pl. verb). Aaron proceeds to make one cast metal calf (מַסֵּכָה עֵגֶל; *massekah 'egel*); this calf is referred to with the singular, masculine pronoun throughout Exodus 32:4-5. Though a single calf is produced, the people proclaim to one another, "these are your gods [אֵלֶּה אֱלֹהֶיךָ; *'eleh 'eloheka*, pl. pronoun and pl. noun], O Israel, who brought you up [הֶעֱלוּךָ, *he'(e)luka*; pl verb] from the land of Egypt." Before and after Aaron makes a *single* calf, the people speak of "gods." Aaron goes on to indicate that the calf is a representation of Yahweh in 32:5; thus, at least for Aaron, the singular calf represents both "the gods" (אֱלֹהִים) and YHWH (יהוה). At this critical moment of covenant failure, the Israelites demonstrate profound confusion not only over how God is to be worshipped but who and how many he actually is. This incident is incredibly instructive for our interpretation of Deuteronomy 6:4, showing us that Israel did indeed have a problem properly identifying their God. For our purposes here, the plurality of אֱלֹהִים is not lost in the plural-for-singular idiom; indeed, it seems to cause confusion on occasion.

Thus, the contrast we have recognised between "your God(s)" and "one (God)" is not imagined: the plurality of אֱלֹהִים is not lost despite the frequent idiomatic use of the plural for a singular object. This raises another question: why continue to use a form that would create such ambiguity if there were not plurality in God? That is, on the evidence I have given thus far, Deuteronomy 6:4 could merely be a grammatical qualification: though Yahweh is "God(s)," he is actually one. אֶחָד ("one") would be rebuking the sort of confusion displayed in Exodus 32, reminding the faithful Israelite that though God is spoken of with a plural term, it is merely a morphological matter; God is actually one. However, in that case, why not stop using the plural altogether? Especially given that the plural-for-singular is used by the Canaanites as well, why not dismiss it as a pagan idiom and use the singular אֱלוֹהַּ (*'eloah*) exclusively (e.g. Deut 32:15)? However, there is further evidence that the statement is not attempting to rule out all plurality, something that would be problematic for the Christian doctrine of the Trinity. Indeed, if אֶחָד (*'echad*) were a statement of absolute unity—unity without plurality—then it would rule out the plurality required by the doctrine of the Trinity; our commitment to a theological framework that includes the New Testament, and so the plurality of God, rules out such a reading.

Instead, this verse could be read as asserting both plurality *and* unity: Yahweh *is the Gods,* but he is also one God. This is ontologically true, God is Father, Son, and Holy Spirit, so this reading makes sense. Not only is this consistent with the whole Bible, but it also makes sense of the context of the Pentateuch. The immediate focus in Deuteronomy 6 is on the right identification of God, as the one who delivered them, and the need for wholehearted allegiance to him (6:1-9). If God is truly Triune, then a statement of unitarian oneness would be out of place. Furthermore, אֱלֹהִים (*'elohim*) is not the only evidence thus far in the Bible that God has plurality; it is one piece of a larger picture.

Consider just the preceding four books, which display the actions of אֱלֹהִים, the God(s) as he has acted for Israel and identify this God(s) as Yahweh. We will briefly introduce several instances here, which we will examine in greater depth in the next three chapters. First, we read of God speaking and the Spirit of God overseeing the act of creation (Gen 1:1-2). The רוּחַ אֱלֹהִים (*ruach 'elohim*; "Spirit of God") or רוּחַ יהוה (*ruach YHWH*; "Spirit of YHWH") is an active agent distinct from Yahweh yet acting with his authority. As confessional Christians, we profess that the Spirit is a person, the third person of the Trinity, so we know that the Spirit is not merely a perspective on God (like the human spirit) but a distinct person of the Godhead. This matches well with the creation narrative, where the Spirit of God is mentioned as acting without being absolutely equated with the God who is creating. We also encounter the enigmatic מַלְאַךְ יהוה (*mal'ak YHWH*; "the Angel of YHWH") who speaks as and is identified as יהוה (Exod 3:1-22). In addition to these passages, there is the cohortative phrase, "let us make them in our likeness" in Genesis 1:26 (cf. 11:7; Fathers like Augustine would add the three men who appear to Abraham in Genesis 18:1-33). If God is a Trinity, then these texts are highly suggestive. Anticipating the conclusions of our later discussion and bringing in the testimony of Scripture after Deuteronomy (Chapter 7-15), there is good reason to believe the plurality indicated by אֱלֹהִים and paired with אֶחָד is true plurality.

Thus, we have reason to believe that אֱלֹהִים (*'elohim*) has plural connotations; it is not a frozen idiom. Furthermore, we have reason to believe that God actually is a plurality; we also have reason to believe that Israelites and Canaanites alike were confused about this matter, whether God was one or many, and that this confusion was related to the term אֱלֹהִים. What would be needed in such a context is a clear statement excluding the wrong sort of plurality, namely, plurality without true unity, and the wrong sort of unity, namely, unity without plurality. Is this not exactly what Deuteronomy 6:4 does?

> Hear, O Israel,
>   YHWH (is) our Gods,
>   YHWH is one (god).

In our first investigation in the Old Testament, we find the Trinity not implied but explicitly taught. Here is a clear statement of God's plurality and God's unity. Israel's encounters with other nations and their pantheons and the danger of successive generations getting muddled with the unity-in-plurality language (cf. 1 Kings 12:25-33) gives a theological necessity for a Trinitarian creed, a statement that the יהוה (YHWH) who is אֱלֹהִים (the Gods) is nevertheless אֶחָד (*'echad*; "one"). In the presence of plurality, stated by אֱלֹהִים, אֶחָד ensures that we do not read God's true plurality as plurality without unity: God is truly plural—Father, Son, and Holy Spirit—yet also truly united, one god. The second line gives a clear qualification to this plurality: Yahweh is one (god). Notice the sort of unity the Shema declares; Yahweh who is three is not one genus, not one abstract substance, not one universal, but *one* thing, one god. He is one particular—one person.

"Yahweh our God, Yahweh is one." Yahweh is a person, an acting, relational, responsive subject. Yet this person is a threefold plurality, a Trinity. Lest we lose Yahweh's personhood in plurality, we are told that this person who is divine plurality is nevertheless one, a *personal* unity. The Shema, therefore, can be read as a guard against detaching the plurality of God from his unity, especially in the polytheistic direction. Though it is a subtle guard against idolatry, it is more significantly a guard against reading polytheism into the Torah. When an Israelite encounters אֱלֹהִים acting as a pluriform of persons, she remembers "Yahweh our God(s), Yahweh is one (god)." Embedded within a narrative that presents a pluriform God as a single personal subject, Yahweh, such a creed is necessary. However, this creed also guards against depersonalising God's unity, for God is one personal thing— not an impersonal unity (whatever that would mean in the Hebrew context). In the biblical context where one God acts to create all things but is seen to act as three persons, such creed is normatively Trinitarian: it teaches the fundamental Trinitarian tension, Yahweh the one God is Gods without losing his personal unity. These Gods—God, the Spirit of God, the Messenger of God—are likewise a single personal subject.

This is, of course, lunacy: how can God be three persons and one person in the same way and in the same manner? Now, it is not purely in the same manner, as in the case of contraries, such that a laptop is wholly black and wholly white. The phrase "wholly white" implies "not black," but there is nothing in our concept of "person" that prevents something from being one and three simultaneously: it is not a simple contradiction. Though the difference between God's unity and plurality is not something we can pin down, this does not mean it is a contradiction. Who are we, his creatures, to reject the fundamental revelation of the God who sustains our logic? We cannot deny on logical grounds the only one who validates our use of logic.[18] We will explore this at length in Chapter 18, but for now, we must concede that we are mere humans, and he is God—rightly beyond us in many ways. To claim that God is three and one in the personal dimension cuts across many interpretations of the Trinity in ancient and modern thought, yet it is not unprecedented; Augustine, Herman Bavinck, A. A. Hodge, Cornelius Van Til, and John Frame are theologians who recognise the personal dimension of God's unity without resolving it into God the Father. But I digress, we will consider these issues more Part 4. For now, we must flush out the Shema by looking more closely at the Old Testament. We will begin

---

[18] Cf. Vern S. Poythress, *Logic: A God-Centered Approach to the Foundation of Western Thought*, Electronic. (Wheaton: Crossway, 2013).

with key texts on God's unity and his plurality in Chapter 6, then we will look at God the Son and God the Spirit as they are revealed in the Old Testament, in Chapters 7 through 9.

J. Alexander Rutherford

6

PLURALITY AND MONOTHEISM IN THE OLD TESTAMENT

Thus far, we have argued that The Great Shema in Deuteronomy 6:4 is a Trinitarian creed that presents personal plurality (אֱלֹהִים; e'lohim) in personal unity (אֶחָד; echad). Looking to the rest of the Old Testament, we are thus asking, does it teach that Yahweh is a personal plurality in personal unity? As a corollary, we are also asking if the Old Testament teaches the contrary, an impersonal unity or unity that excludes plurality. We will begin with Genesis 1, which confirms Yahweh's plurality followed by several possible defeater texts, concerning God's unity. Because we have already discussed the plurality of the term אֱלֹהִים, we will not address it again.

A. Genesis 1

וַיֹּאמֶר אֱלֹהִים נַעֲשֶׂה אָדָם בְּצַלְמֵנוּ כִּדְמוּתֵנוּ

And God said, "let us make man in our image, according to our likeness." – Genesis 1:26a-b

Genesis 1 is an obvious place to start, both because it is at the beginning and because it gives overt attention to God's plurality. We will consider the Spirit mentioned in verse 2 later, in Chapter 9; for now, Genesis 1:26 will be our focus.

If we are reading within a framework of possibility that permits a Trinitarian interpretation, the plural cohortative, "Let *us* make," catches our eye. In light of our discussion thus far, that the cohortative is preceded by אֱלֹהִים (*'elohim*) draws a connection between the plurality of God and the plural verb. Understanding the plural here as a reference to the Trinity is common in Church history; Calvin writes, "Pious readers, however, see how frigidly and absurdly the colloquy were introduced by Moses, if there were not several persons in the Godhead."[1] However, modern commentators prefer to interpret it as a reference to God's heavenly council, the angelic or divine beings who make up his heavenly court.[2]

Thus far, we have agreed that the Bible is comfortable calling beings other than God "god" (a conclusion confirmed in our discussion of texts on God's ontological uniqueness below) but have found that God's council is not that of the ancient world, where divine beings gathered. Instead, hosts of angelic servants are present to do God's bidding. Furthermore, if God were addressing the angelic counsel, it would follow that humanity is created in the likeness of such beings and that they are involved in God's creative activity. However, humanity alone is said to be made in God's image, and never are they said to be made in the image of angels. Humanity's relationship to God as his image-bearers is at the heart of the biblical account of creation and the reason for humanity's significance in redemptive history, so including angels as image bearers would have far-reaching biblical-theological implications. Within a Trinitarian frame of reference, speaking of "our image" makes perfect sense for God creating humanity in his image. We also find the same personal plurality and personal unity we saw in the Shema: humanity is made in "our image," "God created man in his own image" (1:27, ESV). Indeed, if we read the text with the category of divine plurality in mind, we notice that that there is movement from singular to plural in God's statement concerning

---

[1] Calvin, *Institutes of the Christian Religion*, sec. 1.xiii.24.

[2] E.g. Gentry and Wellum in *Kingdom Through Covenant*. Carson dismisses an explicitly Trinitarian reading as anachronistic, though he sees the text as consistent with the fuller revelation of God's Tri-unity. Oseka identifies this reading in the Pseudo-Jonathan Targum on the passage. D. A. Carson, "Genesis 1-3: Not Maximalist, but Seminal," *Trinity Journal* 39, no. 2 (2018): 143–163; Matthew Oseka, "History of the Jewish Interpretation of Genesis 1:26, 3:5, 3:22 in the Middle Ages," *Scriptura* 117, no. 1 (May 2018): 3; Gentry and Wellum, *Kingdom through Covenant (2nd Ed)*.

humanity, as there is such a movement in the description of humanity itself. This passage is often marked as poetry in English translations because of the parallelism present in the passage; treating it as poetry only brings out the movement identified above. I have translated אֱלֹהִים (*'elohim*) according to our discussion in the last chapter, "the God(s)"; as discussed above, the term is used with singular verbs and pronouns to refer to Yahweh, the one God, yet its morphological plurality is not lost. In Genesis 1:27, the plurality of the term is perceptible, following as it does the plural cohortatives and then as part of a parallel structure moving from singularity to plurality.

וַיִּבְרָא אֱלֹהִים אֶת־הָאָדָם בְּצַלְמוֹ
בְּצֶלֶם אֱלֹהִים בָּרָא אֹתוֹ
זָכָר וּנְקֵבָה בָּרָא אֹתָם:

And the God(s) created humanity in his image,
in the image of the God(s) he created him,
male and female he created them.

In the first line, the collective humanity (הָאָדָם; *ha'adam*, see v. 26) is said to be created in God's image (singular); in the second line, humanity or Adam is said to be created in the "image of the God(s)." The singular pronoun ("him") in the second line is ambiguous: it could refer to humanity as a collective entity or to Adam, the first human to be created, אָדָם (*'adam*) referring to either (cf. 1:26, 2:7). For our purposes, it is a singular pronoun echoing "his image" in the previous line. In the final line, we are told God created "them," plural. There is thus a movement from singular to plural in the image, "his image" and "the image of the God(s)," and those who are made in this image, "him" and "them." Seeing "the God(s)" as retaining its plural force is strengthened by the cohortative in the verse 26. So, from the beginning of Scripture, we find the Trinitarian tension of divine plurality and divine unity, as carefully prescribed in Deuteronomy 6:4.

The primary challenge confronting the right worship of God in the ancient context was the competing claims of others to be god, perhaps complicated by God's own plurality (cf. Exod 32). In response, we find testimony through Scripture to God's ontological uniqueness, often accompanied by implicit or explicit testimony to his personal unity. We will now look at four critical texts of this sort. In each text, we will see evidence for God's personal unity but no rejection of his plurality. Furthermore, the main aim of several texts, to rule out ontological parity between God and other so-called gods, will be seen to be compatible with our claims in Chapter 4, that there are many beings called gods.

B. Exodus 20:3

לֹא יִהְיֶה־לְךָ אֱלֹהִים אֲחֵרִים עַל־פָּנָי

There shall not be to you other gods before me.

As with Deuteronomy 6:4, Exodus 20:3 has engendered fierce debate. The nature of the prohibition is more obscure than English translations often reveal. The typical translation, "You shall have no other gods before me" (ESV), invites the reader to interpret "before me" according to conventional English idiom and so take it to mean "You shall not put any gods in my place/as a higher priority." This is itself not a simple command, for it seems to imply a sort of henotheism where Yahweh is to be the preeminent or highest God of Israel though not necessarily the exclusive God.[3] The clarification of Michael Heiser at this point is appropriate. Though the Bible acknowledges other beings called "gods," it does not give them status on par with God nor a ruling or providential role within creation, so it cannot be called "henotheistic."[4] Some argue that the statement is itself monotheistic, excluding the existence of other gods,[5] but this is hard to sustain from the command itself.[6] Rather, it is monotheistic because God alone is sovereign and ruling over all, the creator of all so-called gods. However, the sense of "in my place" or "higher priority" is alien to the idiom used in the Hebrew

---

[3] Cf. Thomas B. Dozeman, *Commentary on Exodus*, The Eerdmans Critical Commentary (Grand Rapids: Eerdmans, 2009), 480.

[4] Heiser, "Monotheism and the Language of Divine Plurality in the Hebrew Bible and the Dead Sea Scrolls."

[5] E.g. Eugene E. Carpenter, *Exodus*, Evangelical Exegetical Commentary (Bellingham: Lexham Press, 2016), 38–39; Douglas K. Stuart, *Exodus*, The New American Commentary v. 2 (Nashville: Broadman & Holman Publishers, 2006), 448–449.

[6] Victor P. Hamilton, *Exodus: An Exegetical Commentary* (Grand Rapids: Baker Academic, 2011), 329; William Henry Propp, ed., *Exodus 19-40: A New Translation with Introduction and Commentary*, 1st ed., The Anchor Bible v. 2A (New York: Doubleday, 2006), 167.

text; this sense would be better rendered by תַּחְתִּי (*tachti*; "in my place"). עַל־
פָּנֵי (*'al-panay*) is literally "before my face"; it is usually used in the spatial sense
"before" and, therefore, "in the presence of...." For this reason, Gentry and
others take the prohibition to be a very literal prohibition of claiming that
any gods are in God's presence. That is, picturing an Ancient Near Eastern
heavenly throne room, the Israelites were not to envision that God held
council with other gods and so shared his power with anyone.[7] However, we
do not have to envision a heavenly throne room to reach a similar
interpretation.

Interpreted in the narrative of Exodus, God is not only covenanting
with the nation Israel but is promising to dwell among them. Though he will
always be God enthroned in heaven, he is also promising to be God
enthroned amid Israel. The seat of his throne would be the ark, located in the
tent of meeting. Because of his presence among the people, they were to
maintain the highest level of holiness: from their garments to their food and
especially their conduct, they were to demonstrate their allegiance to Yahweh
and be wholly committed to him. If the ark and the tent of meeting is his
earthly throne room and the camp of Israel his dwelling place, then Israel is
prohibited from defiling the holy space with other god's.[8] The sense is
immediately spatial, yet allegiance to Yahweh does not only exclude physical
idols (as Israel will break in Exodus 32) but also the condition of their heart.
The exposition in Exodus 24:4-6 forbids making images for worship, thus
legislating the sole worship of Yahweh, along with a brief exposition of his
character. Therefore, though the language is cast as a physical prohibition, it
extends to all worship: as with their physical space, the inner life of the
Israelites was to be dedicated entirely to Yahweh.

Therefore, a good case can be made that "to have no other gods before

---

[7] Following John Walton, Gentry and Wellum, *Kingdom through Covenant (2nd
Ed)*. On the problems of the form of argument employed, Weeks, "Problems with
the Comparative Method in Old Testament Studies."

[8] For an exposition of the sacred space theme see Waltke and Yu; on the
tabernacle as his throne room, see Beale. Bruce K. Waltke and Charles Yu, *An Old
Testament Theology: An Exegetical, Canonical, and Thematic Approach*, 1st ed. (Grand
Rapids: Zondervan, 2007), 445ff; G. K. Beale, *The Temple and the Church's Mission: A
Biblical Theology of the Dwelling Place of God*, New Studies in Biblical Theology 17
(Downers Grove: IVP, 2004).

me" is a prohibition of idolatry cast in terms of Israel as a sacred space, though its implications reach beyond spatiality. For our purposes, Exodus 20:3 does not reject the existence of other gods. Indeed, on the surface, it seems to presuppose that others could be rightfully called "gods." Yahweh is Israel's "God" and, as demonstrated throughout the Exodus narrative, clearly God preeminent and omnipotent, yet he is not declared to be the sole legitimate referent of the term "god." That God can be both ontological unequalled—the sole creator—and share a generic name with others has important implication for our understanding of language, but I digress. Concerning our primary argument in this chapter, this passage does not exclude divine plurality but does suggest a personal unity. Yahweh is the one speaking, and he prohibits worship of any other. As we have seen, and will see again shortly, the divine name refers to God as unity, not any one of the persons in particular (cf. Ch. 18). If the name Yahweh were solely reserved for God the Father or if God the Father were the one God of Israel, then this command would prohibit the worship of God the Son and Spirit (cf. Chs 16-18.

C. Deuteronomy 4:35

אַתָּה הָרְאֵתָ לָדַעַת כִּי יְהוָה הוּא הָאֱלֹהִים אֵין עוֹד מִלְבַדּוֹ

You have been shown [these things] so you would know that YHWH is God; there is no other except him.

Like Exodus 20:3, Deuteronomy 4:35 does not exclude other beings called "god," but it does declare God to be *par excellence* and unmatchable. Like Exodus, this statement would be problematic with reference to God the Father alone, but it is predicated of Yahweh, which signifies God as unity as well as each of the persons (it is an "inclusive term," see Ch. 18).

In this passage, Moses tells the people of Israel that all which God did in Egypt and beyond was meant to exhibit a single truth, that Yahweh alone is God. There are two ways to read the statement of exclusivity. On one hand, the statement of exclusivity could declare that Yahweh alone is God preeminent (אֱלֹהִים; *'elohim*),[9] on the other hand, it could declare that Yahweh is God alone without qualification (אֱלוֹהַ; *'eloah*). The first would be a statement of rank or power, the latter of ontology. If the latter is the case, the former would be implied; if the former is the case, this does not necessarily mean that God is on the same ontological level as other "gods." Instead, it would raise, along with Exodus 20:3, important ontological questions. If biblical authors have no problem putting God in the same "class" as other entities and yet maintaining his sole role as pre-eminent, all-powerful, and the sole creator, this suggests that a class, such as אֱלוֹהַ, does not have the same ontological baggage as the Greek concept of a universal. The use of the article is not decisive in the matter, as Woods suggests;[10] instead of supporting the generic statement, it may be rendering אֱלֹהִים as a title of pre-eminence (usually anarthrous) in an ambiguous context (where an anarthrous noun may be construed as a generic predicate). The first clause seems to suggest pre-eminence with the second indicating that none are like him.

The text does not, therefore, decisively rule out the real existence of other אֱלֹהִים (gods); it does, however, rule out treating such entities, if they exist, as if they were on par with God according to his power and worth. We have seen evidence already that the Bible freely calls others "god" without feeling the need to qualify this claim, so passages like Deuteronomy 4:35 make clear that being called "god" does not equate one with Yahweh, who is alone the true and originating God. All else is his creation, only "god" in so much as they reflected in a creaturely sense some aspect of his glory (which I suggested was God's power and authority). More significantly, as with Deuteronomy 6:4 and Exodus 20:3, "God" in this statement of exclusivity is a statement analogous to the particular, not the universal: Yahweh is one thing, not the sole occupant of a universal class nor the whole of a real substance (on which see Part 4).

---

[9] Taking the plural to be an indicator of pre-eminence, sometimes called an "honorific". Cf. Waltke and O'Connor, *An Introduction to Biblical Hebrew Syntax*, s.v. 7.4.3.b.

[10] Edward J Woods, *Deuteronomy: An Introduction and Commentary* (Downers Grove: IVP Academic, 2011), 114., cf. Waltke and O'Connor, *An Introduction to Biblical Hebrew Syntax*, sec. 13.6.a.

D. Isaiah 44:8f-g

We will now consider Isaiah 44:8f-g. Here we encounter a similar statement of exclusivity as Deuteronomy 4:35, yet here there is no ambiguity as to the sense:

הֲיֵשׁ אֱלוֹהַּ מִבַּלְעָדַי וְאֵין צוּר בַּל־יָדָעְתִּי
Is there a god other than me?
There is no rock, I know not one.

Whether or not Deuteronomy 4:35 declares Yahweh to be God alone, Isaiah 44:8 certainly does so. The obvious answer to the question in 8f is "no," there is no אֱלוֹהַּ (*'eloah;* "god") but Yahweh. The contrasting exclusion of another "rock" focuses on the subjective aspect of אֱלוֹהַּ as a dependable and faithful King and redeemer for his people (Isaiah 44:6). However, that this is the primary force in context does not negate the fact that the positive affirmation of God's dependability and firmness is stated as ontological exclusivity. There is thus no other אֱלוֹהַּ but God; he is truly one of a kind (cf. Isa 43:10). Once again, the oneness of God is stated in terms of *particularity*. There is one thing that is truly God; if we conceptualize a class of אֱלֹהִים (*'elohim*), God is the sole inhabitant. That is, though the term אֱלוֹהַּ may legitimately refer to things other than YHWH, and therefore may signify a concept that includes God alongside of other things, this concept itself is not an ontological class (a statement of shared identity); as it concerns ontological class and identity, God is the sole inhabitant. There is none like him in the heavens above or the on the earth below—to him alone be all glory, honour, and praise forever and ever, amen.

E. Zechariah 14:9

וְהָיָה יהוה לְמֶלֶךְ עַל־כָּל־הָאָרֶץ בַּיּוֹם הַהוּא יִהְיֶה יהוה יהוה אֶחָד וּשְׁמוֹ אֶחָד

And YHWH will be king over all the earth on that day;
YHWH will be one and his name one.

Our next passage comes in the context of the "Day of the Lord," a prominent theme in the Twelve, delineating the day of coming judgment for Israel,

Judah, and the nations and of salvation for the righteous.[11] In Zechariah 14, the day in view is the final day, the end-time judgment and salvation to which the immediate acts point. Zechariah looks to a day when life will pour forth from the holy city and the whole earth will be united under the rule of Yahweh. The final clauses of the verse clearly allude to Deuteronomy 6:4, so our interpretations there will affect our understanding here, and vice versa.

However we interpret "one" here, what is envisaged is the subjective recognition of something about God. The whole earth will recognise that Yahweh is one and his name one. Because "one" is taking its meaning from Deuteronomy 6, our considerations there are pertinent here; our interpretation in Chapter 5 fits well. In the final day, God will be recognised and worshipped as he truly is. He will not be worshipped in various ways, under various names, and as various deities (such as we saw in Exodus 32 and 1 Kgs 12:28). Instead, Yahweh will be one: like Deuteronomy 6:4, the unity or oneness of the Triune God is presented as concrete and personal: Yahweh who is one is a king who rules. Read within a Trinitarian frame of reference, this is not a statement of unity without plurality but of right worship of the one true God, who is seen elsewhere to be plurality alongside of concrete oneness.

F. Conclusion

In Genesis 1, we saw that the plurality of Yahweh is found from the start of the Bible, alongside personal unity. The oneness of God is unanimously presented as oneness in analogy with the particular: God is one *thing* (however we conceive of his thingness). In the following texts, we saw the personal unity of God alongside the exclusion of anyone like him: God is simultaneously in a league of his own and preeminent among other beings that may be called "gods." As we observed in Chapter 4, the statements of God's pre-eminence and oneness do not prevent the Bible from calling other beings "god," but it does require us to reject any interpretation of the term "god" where God and the "gods" are put on the same ontological level. They are created and subservient; he alone is the creator and self-sufficient. In

---

[11] James D. Nogalski, "The Day(s) of YHWH in the Book of the Twelve," in *Thematic Threads in the Book of the Twelve*, ed. Paul L. Redditt and Aaron Schart (Berlin, Germany: Walter de Gruyter GmbH & Co., 2003), 192–213.

these ways, God's uniqueness is predicated not in his relation to a universal term, for there may be other "gods," but in his particularity, to which nothing else compares in power or worth. Therefore, regarding God's plurality, there can be nothing outside of the one true God that is ontologically on par with God, and those who are the one God must be ontologically on par with one another.

7

THE ANGEL OF THE LORD IS YAHWEH

נַיֹּאמֶר אַל־תִּשְׁלַח יָדְךָ אֶל־הַנַּעַר וְאַל־תַּעַשׂ לוֹ מְאוּמָה כִּי עַתָּה יָדַעְתִּי כִּי־יְרֵא
אֱלֹהִים אַתָּה וְלֹא חָשַׂכְתָּ אֶת־בִּנְךָ אֶת־יְחִידְךָ מִמֶּנִּי׃

And he said, "Do not send forth your hand against the
boy nor do anything to him, for now I know that you
fear God, and you have not withheld your son, your
only son, from me." – Genesis 22:12

Thus far, we have dealt with generalities, with the general parameters of the
Trinity in the Old Testament. I have argued that the Shema legislates the
Trinitarian tensions of plurality in unity, and we have seen how this is
reinforced and articulated against the plurality of gods in the polytheistic
milieu of the ANE. We have thus far promised to look at concrete examples
of Yahweh's plurality in the Old Testament, but we have only considered
Genesis 1. To the plurality of God in the Old Testament we will now turn.

In this chapter, we will consider the first of three themes in the Old
Testament that attest to personal differentiation within Yahweh. We will
begin with the Angel of Yahweh. The figure of the מַלְאַךְ יהוה (mal'ak YHWH;
"the Angel of YHWH") has received significant attention, with some
asserting that he is the pre-incarnate Christ.[1] As a construct phrase, the being

---

[1] H Vogel, "The Angel of the Lord," *Wisconsin Lutheran Quarterly* 73, no. 2 (April
1976): 105–118; Gary Simmers, "Who Is 'The Angel of the Lord'?," *Faith and Mission*

identified as מַלְאַךְ יהוה (*mal'ak YHWH*) is often taken to be definite, "The angel of YHWH." However, René Lopez rightly observes that with proper nouns, the construct noun may be indefinite (e.g. בְּתוּלַת יִשְׂרָאֵל; *betulat Yisra'el,* "a virgin of Israel," Deut 22:19).[2] So, the phrase may be indefinite or definite. Douglas Stuart counters that the phrase is actually in apposition, "the angel who is YHWH."[3] This is also a possibility. This reading is thought to be legitimate because this angel is often treated as identical to Yahweh, even when speaking with him.

If we accept that the Angel is identified as Yahweh, there are good reasons to identify the Angel with God the Son. Some would argue that the Angel is the Son because he is Yahweh and his role ceases in the New Testament after Jesus has come; in his place, Gabriel appears. More significantly, Jude 5 indicates that *Jesus* brought Israel up from Egypt. When we look to the Old Testament, the Angel has this role (e.g. Jdgs 2:1-2).[4] These considerations lead many to identify the Angel with Jesus, not the Spirit.

We will consider below a selection of passages that show that the Angel is identified with Yahweh yet simultaneously distinguished from him: this duality is the fundamental tension of the Trinity, unity through identification and plurality through differentiation. In most cases, the Angel is identified with God without differentiation, yet his title, "angel" or a representative/messenger implies differentiation, as one who is sent to represent someone else. That is, even if we follow Stuart in reading the phrase as "the Angel who is YHWH," "angel" nevertheless connotes one sent from another; the sender would have to themselves be Yahweh. Other than the

---

17, no. 3 (2000): 3–16.

[2] René López, "Identifying the 'angel of the Lord' in the Book of Judges: A Model for Reconsidering the Referent in Other Old Testament Loci," *Bulletin for Biblical Research* 20, no. 1 (2010): 1–18. Andrew S Malone, "Distinguishing the Angel of the Lord," *Bulletin for Biblical Research* 21, no. 3 (2011): 297–314.

[3] Stuart, *Exodus,* 111–113.

[4] Wyatt Graham drew my attention to this in Wyatt Graham, "Is Jesus the Angel of Lord?," Wyatt Graham, 2021, https://wyattgraham.com/. Cf. Jarl E Fossum, "Kyrios Jesus as the Angel of the Lord in Jude 5-7," *New Testament Studies* 33, no. 2 (April 1987): 226–243.

name itself, the clearest instance of differentiation is in Zechariah 3:1-2.

A. Exodus 3:2-22

וַיֵּרָא מַלְאַךְ יְהוָה אֵלָיו בְּלַבַּת־אֵשׁ מִתּוֹךְ הַסְּנֶה וַיַּרְא וְהִנֵּה הַסְּנֶה בֹּעֵר
בָּאֵשׁ וְהַסְּנֶה אֵינֶנּוּ אֻכָּל וַיֹּאמֶר מֹשֶׁה אָסֻרָה־נָּא וְאֶרְאֶה אֶת־הַמַּרְאֶה
הַגָּדֹל הַזֶּה מַדּוּעַ לֹא־יִבְעַר הַסְּנֶה וַיַּרְא יְהוָה כִּי סָר לִרְאוֹת וַיִּקְרָא אֵלָיו
אֱלֹהִים מִתּוֹךְ הַסְּנֶה וַיֹּאמֶר מֹשֶׁה מֹשֶׁה וַיֹּאמֶר הִנֵּנִי

²And the Angel of YHWH appeared to him in a flame of fire from the midst of the bush. He looked and behold, the bush was burning with fire, but the bush was not consumed. ³And Moses thought, "I am determined to turn aside to see this great sight, why the bush is not burned." ⁴And YHWH saw that he was turning aside to look, and God called to him from the midst of the bush and said, "Moses, Moses." And he said, "Here I am." – Exodus 3:2-4

One of the most famous events in the Old Testament is the narrative of the burning bush. Many of us learned in Sunday school about the bush that burned with fire and was not consumed, about God revealing himself in a miraculous way to Moses. When we look at this story in Exodus, we discover that it was "the Angel of YHWH" who appears to Moses. In verse 4, the narrative identifies the one speaking from the midst of the bush (מִתּוֹךְ הַסְּנֶה; *mittok hassneh*, same as in v. 2) as "YHWH" and "God." Having been told that it was the Angel who appeared in verse 2, it is clear the narrator is calling the Angel Yahweh. The speaker goes on to identify himself as the God of Moses' ancestors (3:6). Unless we assume the Angel cannot be Yahweh, which we have no reason to do, then it is most obvious to identify him as such.

B. Exodus 23

הִנֵּה אָנֹכִי שֹׁלֵחַ מַלְאָךְ לְפָנֶיךָ לִשְׁמָרְךָ בַּדָּרֶךְ וְלַהֲבִיאֲךָ אֶל־הַמָּקוֹם אֲשֶׁר הֲכִנֹתִי
הִשָּׁמֶר מִפָּנָיו וּשְׁמַע בְּקֹלוֹ אַל־תַּמֵּר בּוֹ כִּי לֹא יִשָּׂא לְפִשְׁעֲכֶם כִּי שְׁמִי בְּקִרְבּוֹ׃

²⁰Behold, I will send an angel before you, to keep you

on the way and to bring you to the place which I have prepared. ²¹Be attentive to him and listen to his voice; do not rebel against him, for he will not pardon your transgression, for my name is in him. – Exodus 23:20-21.

The angel mentioned in this passage is not explicitly identified as "the Angel of YHWH," yet in verse 23 Yahweh calls him "my angel" (מַלְאָכִי; *mal'aki*). In verse 21, not only does God command obedience to his angel, but this angel is also presumed to have the authority to forgive sin (though he will not do so). As Nahum Sarna notes, "rebel" is "overwhelmingly used of rebellion against God."[5] Moreover, Yahweh's name is "within him." This phrase is used nowhere else in the Hebrew Bible; given that God's name signifies his being, presence, and power, Driver and others seem justified when they conclude that this phrase means the Angel is Yahweh.[6]

Yahweh continues speaking of this Angel who goes before the people. The people are not to serve other gods, instead, Yahweh tells them, "You shall serve the LORD your God, and he will bless your bread and your water, and I will take sickness away from among you" (v. 25, ESV). The LXX and Vulgate have the easier reading, "I will bless you," but the Masoretic Text has the more difficult 3ʳᵈ-person reading. Yahweh has thus far been speaking, referring to the activity of the Angel in the 3ʳᵈ person; thus, in verse 25, Yahweh speaks of what Yahweh ("he") does separate from what he will do ("I"). "The LORD your God... he will bless you," would appear to refer to the activity of the Angel; yet Yahweh who is speaking will "take away sickness." Seeing the Angel as the referent of "the LORD your God" and "he will bless you," differentiated from Yahweh who is speaking, is consistent with what we have seen thus far. Yahweh is unity and plurality, so two may

---

[5] Nahum M. Sarna, *Exodus* (Philadelphia: Jewish Publication Society, 1991), 148.

[6] Samuel Rolles Driver, *The Book of Exodus ... With an Introduction and Notes by S.R. Driver*, n.d., 247; Philip Graham Ryken and R. Kent Hughes, *Exodus: Saved for God's Glory*, Preaching the Word Series (Wheaton: Crossway, 2005), 767. Cf. John L Mackay, *Exodus*, A Mentor Commentary (Ross-shire: Christian Focus Publications, 2018), 408.

be identified as Yahweh simultaneously.

C. Genesis 16:10 and 22:9-14

וַיֹּאמֶר לָהּ מַלְאַךְ יְהוָה הַרְבָּה אַרְבֶּה אֶת־זַרְעֵךְ וְלֹא יִסָּפֵר מֵרֹב׃

And the Angel of YHWH spoke to her, "I will certainly multiply your offspring; their number will be too great to number." – Genesis 16:10

וַיִּקְרָא אֵלָיו מַלְאַךְ יְהוָה מִן־הַשָּׁמַיִם וַיֹּאמֶר אַבְרָהָם אַבְרָהָם וַיֹּאמֶר הִנֵּנִי
וַיֹּאמֶר אַל־תִּשְׁלַח יָדְךָ אֶל־הַנַּעַר וְאַל־תַּעַשׂ לוֹ מְאוּמָה כִּי עַתָּה יָדַעְתִּי
כִּי־יְרֵא אֱלֹהִים אַתָּה וְלֹא חָשַׂכְתָּ אֶת־בִּנְךָ אֶת־יְחִידְךָ מִמֶּנִּי׃

And the Angel of YHWH called to him from heaven and said, "Abraham, Abraham!" And he said, "Here I am." And he said, "Do not send forth your hand against the boy nor do anything to him, for now I know that you fear God, and you have not withheld your son, your only son, from me." – Genesis 22:12

The Angel makes numerous appearances in the Genesis narrative. In Genesis 16, after Hagar flees from Sarai, the Angel of the Lord finds her in the wilderness. He promises to bless her with much offspring. The narrator then describes her response, "So she called the name of the LORD who spoke to her, 'You are a God of Seeing.'" (Gen 16:13, ESV); The narrator identifies the Angel as Yahweh, and Hagar calls him God.

Later in the Abraham narrative, when Abraham sets out with Isaac to offer him as a sacrifice to Yahweh (22:1-3), the Angel of YHWH appears to him at the climactic moment of the narrative. Just when Abraham was about to perform the sacrifice, the Angel calls to him from heaven. Instructing Abraham not to harm Isaac, the Angel recognises that Abraham truly fears God, for "you have not withheld your son, your only son from me." We were told in 22:1 that God initiated the sacrifice to test Abraham; the Angel interprets Abraham's actions towards God with reference to himself. Afterwards, the Angel calls out again (v. 15), this time he differentiates himself from Yahweh, "By myself I have sworn, declares the LORD, because

77

you have done this and have not withheld your son, your only son, I will surely bless you…" (vv. 16-17, ESV). Here, the Angel can clearly differentiate his words from Yahweh's, so it once again appears that the Angel is Yahweh somehow distinguished from Yahweh.

D. Judges

וַיַּעַל מַלְאַךְ־יְהוָה מִן־הַגִּלְגָּל אֶל־הַבֹּכִים וַיֹּאמֶר אַעֲלֶה אֶתְכֶם מִמִּצְרַיִם וָאָבִיא אֶתְכֶם אֶל־הָאָרֶץ אֲשֶׁר נִשְׁבַּעְתִּי לַאֲבֹתֵיכֶם וָאֹמַר לֹא־אָפֵר בְּרִיתִי אִתְּכֶם לְעוֹלָם וְאַתֶּם לֹא־תִכְרְתוּ בְרִית לְיוֹשְׁבֵי הָאָרֶץ הַזֹּאת מִזְבְּחוֹתֵיהֶם תִּתֹּצוּן וְלֹא־שְׁמַעְתֶּם בְּקֹלִי מַה־זֹּאת עֲשִׂיתֶם וְגַם אָמַרְתִּי לֹא־אֲגָרֵשׁ אוֹתָם מִפְּנֵיכֶם וְהָיוּ לָכֶם לְצִדִּים וֵאלֹהֵיהֶם יִהְיוּ לָכֶם לְמוֹקֵשׁ וַיְהִי כְּדַבֵּר מַלְאַךְ יְהוָה אֶת־הַדְּבָרִים הָאֵלֶּה אֶל־כָּל־בְּנֵי יִשְׂרָאֵל וַיִּשְׂאוּ הָעָם אֶת־ קוֹלָם וַיִּבְכּוּ׃

[1]And the Angel of YHWH went up from Gilgal to Bochim, and he said, "I brought you up from Egypt and I brought you into the land which I promised by oath to your fathers. I said, 'I will not break my covenant with you forever, [2]but you shall not make a covenant with the inhabitants of this land; you shall break down their altars' — yet you did not listen to my voice; what is this you have done? [3]Yes, I also said, 'I will not dispossess them before you, and they will be to you thorns, and their gods will be snares to you.'" [4]And it happened as soon as the Angel of YHWH had said these words to all the sons of Israel, the people lifted up their voice and wept. – Judges 2:1-4

Jumping ahead in the Old Testament, the Angel makes numerous appearances in the book of Judges. There, the Angel claims to be the one who brought Israel from Egypt; he was faithful to his covenant, though they were not. He had promised with an oath to their fathers; they were guilty of disobeying his voice (Jdgs 2:1, 4).

The Angel later appears to Gideon, who responds to his encounter with the Angel as if he had encountered God himself (Jdgs 6:22). When the Angel reveals himself to Manoah and his wife, the Angel identifies his name as "wonderful" (Jdgs 13:18), suggesting his exalted status; when they realize "the man" was "the angel of YHWH," Manoah fears they will die because they "have seen God" (Jdgs 13:22; cf Zech 12:8). Against this interpretation, López argues that elsewhere in the Old Testament, messengers for both God and man alternate between a 3rd-person perspective and the 1st-person, sometimes speaking about God and other times speaking as God (Deut 29:2-6). This is true; however, as we have seen in instances where the Angel speaks, he speaks as Yahweh in the 1st person and then recounts Yahweh's words in the 3rd person, calling himself Yahweh while also speaking about Yahweh. In contrast, Moses will speak for himself and *then* for Yahweh, never speaking for Yahweh as he talks about Yahweh (e.g. Deut 19:1-21; Deut 29:2-6). Thus, the shift in person doesn't diminish the apparent claims of the Angel and the narrator that the Angel is Yahweh. López also argues that there is a clear indication in the instances in Judges that Yahweh has begun speaking, namely, the shift from the 3rd person to the 1st person and the shift from אֲדֹנִי (*'adoni*; my lord) to אֲדֹנָי (*'adonay*; "my Lord," a plural used for pre-eminence; e.g. Jdgs 6:11-16).[7] However, Deuteronomy 29:2-6 indicates that such a shift in person may happen without a change in speaker (Moses continues to speak, though now he speaks for Yahweh): the same speaker may speak for Yahweh and for themselves. Moreover, the shift to אֲדֹנָי (*'adonay*, "my Lord") in Judges 6 could be read, more probably, as a shift in Gideon's perception of the speaker. At first, he calls the Angel "my lord" (אֲדֹנִי, *'adoni*); then the narrator identifies the Angel as Yahweh (v. 14) and the Angel's own speech suggests a claim to be Yahweh. Gideon then bemoans Yahweh's absence (v. 13), and the Angel responds, "I am with you" (v. 14). At this point, Gideon changes his tone, using אֲדֹנָי (*'adonay*). It is possible there is a change of speaker in these narratives, where the Angel moves from speaking for himself to speaking for Yahweh, indicated when the narrator says Yahweh is speaking. However, in light of what we have already seen from the Pentateuch, that the Angel speaks as a Yahweh and is referred to as such by the narrator, it is more likely that he is presented as Yahweh.

If we were to accept all of the arguments put forth by López, which we have not, Andrew Malone cogently shows that the resulting interpretation of the Angel is compatible with the figure not being Yahweh, a "representative

---

[7] López, "Identifying the 'angel of the Lord' in the Book of Judges," 8–9.

theory," but they cannot rule out that he is Yahweh, an "identity theory." To prove that the latter is false and that these passages teach a "representative theory," argues Malone, one would need to show that Yahweh and his angel are in fact distinct.[8] However, as we have seen, things are not so simple: Yahweh and the Angel are simultaneously distinct and united. So demonstrating distinction neither proves a "representative theory" nor disproves an "identity theory."

E. Zechariah 1:12, 3:1-10

וַיַּרְאֵנִי אֶת־יְהוֹשֻׁעַ הַכֹּהֵן הַגָּדוֹל עֹמֵד לִפְנֵי מַלְאַךְ יְהוָה וְהַשָּׂטָן עֹמֵד עַל־יְמִינוֹ לְשִׂטְנוֹ וַיֹּאמֶר יְהוָה אֶל־הַשָּׂטָן יִגְעַר יְהוָה בְּךָ הַשָּׂטָן וְיִגְעַר יְהוָה בְּךָ הַבֹּחֵר בִּירוּשָׁלָ͏ִם הֲלוֹא זֶה אוּד מֻצָּל מֵאֵשׁ:

I saw Joshua the high priest standing before the Angel of YHWH, and the Adversary [Satan] stood at his right hand to accuse him. [2]And YHWH said to the Adversary [Satan], "YHWH rebuke you, oh Adversary [Satan], YHWH who chose Jerusalem rebuke you; is this not a brand plucked from a fire?" – Zechariah 3:1-2

Malone argues that there is no clear place in Scripture where Yahweh and the Angel are presented as distinct.[9] In one sense, he is correct; the "angel of Yahweh" in the Old Testament is never shown to not be Yahweh. However, in another sense, Malone is wrong, for there are several instances where the angel is both identified as and distinguished from Yahweh. We have already seen patterns of this in the texts above, but we see it twice more in the book of Zechariah In Zechariah 1:12 (cf. 3:1-2; 3:6-10), the angel is distinguished from Yahweh. Here, the Angel calls out to Yahweh, then Yahweh responds to him (v. 13). Other than his title, "the Angel of Yahweh," the Angel is not here identified as Yahweh; he is only distinguished from him.

However, in Zechariah 3:1-10, the narrator appears to call the angel "YHWH" (3:2) even as the Angel invokes Yahweh against the Adversary,

---

[8] López, "Identifying the 'angel of the Lord' in the Book of Judges"; Malone, "Distinguishing the Angel of the Lord."

[9] Malone, "Distinguishing the Angel of the Lord."

that is, Satan (3:2, 3:6-7).[10] We would expect that Joshua and his accuser would stand before Yahweh himself in the vision, such as when Satan stands before God in Job 1:6-12. However, here, Satan stands before the Angel to oppose Joshua. In response to Satan ("the Adversary") the narrator tells us "YHWH said to the Adversary"; in the flow of the narrative, the natural referent for "YHWH" is the Angel of Yahweh. Moreover, Yahweh who speaks invokes Yahweh against Satan, "YHWH rebuke you, O Adversary!" (v. 2.) The one other instance of this invocation in Scripture is attributed to the angel Michael, based on an extra-biblical account (Jude 9); however, this text suggests that the invocation in Zechariah is not self-referential (cf. Exod 22:16-17). Thus, the narrator is, once again, free to identify the Angel as Yahweh (e.g. Exod 3:2-22).

F. The Angel in the New Testament

Thus far, we have painted a compelling picture that the Angel of Yahweh is Yahweh yet not Yahweh alone; the Angel testifies to plurality within the unity of Yahweh. However, the biggest difficulty with identifying "the Angel of YHWH" with Yahweh is the use of the comparable Greek phrase ἄγγελος κυρίου (*angelos kuriou*, an/the angel of the Lord) in the NT (Matt 1:20, 24; 2:13, 19; 28:2; Luke 1:11, 2:9; Acts 5:19, 8:26; 12:7, 23), where the figure is not identified with Yahweh and is distinguished from Jesus (who is usually thought to be the most likely referent of "the angel" if he is Yahweh in the Old Testament).[11] In response, some rightly clam that "ἄγγελος κυρίου" is anarthrous (i.e. it has no definite article) and so, on Greek idiom, indefinite, "an angel of the Lord."[12] However, the matter is not so clear, for the LXX translates the apparently definite Hebrew phrase with and without the article (e.g. Exod 3:2; Jdgs 2:1, 4).[13] Furthermore, in Greek as in Hebrew, both nouns in a construct relationship "usually have the same semantic force,"

---

[10] The name Satan is a transliteration of the Hebrew word for "adversary." Malone argues that only 1:12 distinguishes the Angel from Yahweh. Ibid., 304.

[11] E.g. Fossum, "Kyrios Jesus as the Angel of the Lord in Jude 5-7." Cf. López, "Identifying the 'angel of the Lord' in the Book of Judges."

[12] Simmers, "Who Is 'The Angel of the Lord'?"

[13] Cf. López, "Identifying the 'angel of the Lord' in the Book of Judges."

with the most frequent combination being definite and definite (Wallace draws on evidence from the Paul and Peter's letters and a selection of evidence from the Gospels).[14] This favours taking the phrase to be, "the angel of the Lord," for κυρίου is definite. However, there are exceptions, so it is possible that there is no one figure who is called "the Angel of YHWH." That is, the phrase could be definite or indefinite. Though we have seen evidence that one such figure is identified with Yahweh, Haggai can also be called "(the) angel of YHWH" (Hag 1:13); thus, it is not clear after all that one specific messenger is in view with the use of this phrase. However, we have seen instances where a person referred to as "the Angel of YHWH" is Yahweh himself. Furthermore, as discussed above, Fossum argues that Jude 5-7 identifies Jesus as the "Angel of the Lord."[15] So we are warranted to conclude that on occasion, the phrase מַלְאַךְ יהוה (mal'ak YHWH) is used to refer to Yahweh manifest to his people.

This Yahweh is somehow distinguished from Yahweh who sent him. At times, this divine angel is the 2nd person of the Trinity; we have no reason to presume that he may be the 1st or 3rd persons, so we can tentatively conclude that when the Angel refers to Yahweh, it refers to the 2nd person, God the Son. There are additional instances in the Old Testament where a figure is called Yahweh but apparently distinguished from Yahweh; the next we will examine is Isaiah's eschatological messenger.

---

[14] Daniel B Wallace, *Greek Grammar Beyond the Basics: An Exegetical Syntax of the New Testament with Scripture, Subject, and Greek Word Indexes* (Grand Rapids: Zondervan, 1996), 250–252.

[15] Fossum, "Kyrios Jesus as the Angel of the Lord in Jude 5-7."

8

ISAIAH'S ESCHATOLOGICAL AGENT
IS YAHWEH

In Isaiah, there are three significant passages where Yahweh is differentiated from himself, in addition to several places where Yahweh's eschatological agent is identified as God. In the first instance, Isaiah 8:16-22, "YHWH" who is speaking with Isaiah declares that *he* will "wait for YHWH" (8:17). Shortly thereafter, within the same set of oracles, a seemingly human king is attributed with God's own titles (9:6). Interpreted as a continuation of the promise of a child who will be Immanuel, "God with us" (7:14-17), Isaiah 7:1-11:16 presents a picture of an eschatological agent who may not only be called God, but also Yahweh. Then, in Chapter 53:1, a man is identified as God's very power in action, yet he is "smitten by God" (53:4). Finally, in 61:1-8, a figure often identified as an eschatological messenger is differentiated from Yahweh (vv. 1-2, 10-11) but also identifies himself as Yahweh (v. 8).[1] It is no coincidence that Yahweh is identified with a human agent at these three points, for each of these sections (in Isaiah 1-39, 40-55, and 56-66) highlights the work of an "agent" who will accomplish God's kingdom purpose on earth. Though it is sometimes argued that these agents are distinct in the book of Isaiah, they each find their fulfillment in the one

---

[1] On the Messenger in Isaiah 60-66, see Abernethy, *The Book*, chap. 4; J. Alec Motyer, *The Prophecy of Isaiah: An Introduction & Commentary* (Downers Grove: InterVarsity Press, 1993), 489–490.

person, Jesus Christ.[2]

A. Isaiah 7:10-17

Isaiah 7:14 has long captured the imaginations of Christians, but its significance is somewhat dulled when we realise it is not directly speaking about a coming Messiah, as is the scholarly consensus. Because of the contentious nature of this passage and its importance for our argument that follows, we will spend more time here than we have on most texts.

There are many positions concerning this difficult passage, so it is difficult to speak of a "consensus" interpretation of the whole passage. However, there does appear to be a consensus that it is not directly about an eschatological messiah.[3] Furthermore, there seems to be a broad agreement among scholars that the "sign" must have immediate significance for Ahaz, pertaining to the coming Assyrian invasion and the end of Syria and Israel.[4] Such conclusions are intuitively uncomfortable for those steeped in the Christian tradition, as Abernethy observes,

> Especially for those nurtured within evangelical Christian churches, the impression one can have is that the chief value of prophetic literature resides in its serving as a source of texts for Advent sermons, lyrics for Handel's *Messiah* and Christmas cantatas, slogans for Christmas greeting cards, and proof text for defending that Jesus is the sort of Messiah the OT expected. It is surprising, then, for many to realize that only about 5% of the verses in Isaiah (63 out of 1,292 verses) speak directly about hopes for some sort of

---

[2] On their distinction, cf. Abernethy, *The Book*, chap. 4; Abernethy and Goswell, *God's Messiah*, 85–99.

[3] E.g. the NET study note on 7:25 and Abernethy and Goswell, *God's Messiah*.

[4] E.g. John N. Oswalt, *The Book of Isaiah. Chapters 1-39*, NICOT (Grand Rapids: Eerdmans, 2009), 208; William A. Irwin, "That Troublesome 'Almah and Other Matters," *R&E* 50.3 (1953): 337–60; Paul D Wegner, "How Many Virgin Births Are in the Bible? (Isaiah 7:14): A Prophetic Pattern Approach," *Journal of the Evangelical Theological Society* 54.3 (2011): 467–84.

messianic figure.[5]

However, though perhaps uncomfortable, these conclusions are not theologically problematic. It is evident that the New Testament has no single formula for fulfilment; Matthew in particular employs the fulfilment theme in complex ways.[6] A double or typological fulfilment may appear to lessen the force of our Christmas traditions but need only cause us to re-evaluate our reading of Matthew and Luke.

However, I have continually returned to this passage over the last ten years because though theologically acceptable, this typical exegesis of Isaiah 7:14 and its use in Matthew and Luke has hardly been satisfying. I am now convinced that there are insurmountable contextual problems for the "consensus" view. Indeed, I am now convinced that Isaiah 7 should be read as properly prophetic or messianic, anticipating an eschatological figure. As it contributes to our argument here, this figure is presented as God throughout Isaiah 7-9.

To argue this, we will first consider the sign oracle (7:14-17) and its translation; second, its immediate function in Isaiah's meeting with Ahaz (7:1-25); and third, its function in the broader unit of Isaiah 6-9. We will then reflect on the significance of the sign in its immediate context and its use in the New Testament.

a. Isaiah 7:14-17

---

[5] Andrew T. Abernethy, *The Book of Isaiah and God's Kingdom: A Thematic Theological Approach*, New Studies in Biblical Theology 40 (Downers Grove: IVP, 2016), chap. 4.

[6] See, for example, the essays in *The Right Doctrine from the Wrong Texts?*, Beale's short students handbook, and various commentaries on the Matthew. G. K. Beale, ed., *The Right Doctrine from the Wrong Texts? Essays on the Use of the Old Testament in the New* (Grand Rapids: Baker, 1994); G. K. Beale, *Handbook on the New Testament Use of the Old Testament: Exegesis and Interpretation* (Grand Rapids: Baker, 2012); D. A. Carson, "Matthew," in *The Expositor's Bible Commentary: Matthew, Mark, Luke*, ed. Frank E. Gaebelein, vol. 8 (Grand Rapids: Zondervan, 1984); R. T. France, *Matthew*, Tyndale New Testament Commentary (Grand Rapids: Eerdmans, 1985); Ulrich Luz, *Matthew 1–7: A Commentary on Matthew 1–7*, ed. Helmut Koester, Rev. Ed. (Minneapolis: Fortress, 2007).

לָכֵן יִתֵּן אֲדֹנָי הוּא לָכֶם אוֹת הִנֵּה הָעַלְמָה הָרָה וְיֹלֶדֶת בֵּן וְקָרָאת שְׁמוֹ¹⁴
עִמָּנוּ אֵל ¹⁵חֶמְאָה וּדְבַשׁ יֹאכֵל לְדַעְתּוֹ מָאוֹס בָּרָע וּבָחוֹר בַּטּוֹב ¹⁶כִּי
בְּטֶרֶם יֵדַע הַנַּעַר מָאֹס בָּרָע וּבָחֹר בַּטּוֹב תֵּעָזֵב הָאֲדָמָה אֲשֶׁר אַתָּה קָץ
מִפְּנֵי שְׁנֵי מְלָכֶיהָ ¹⁷יָבִיא יְהוָה עָלֶיךָ וְעַל־עַמְּךָ וְעַל־בֵּית אָבִיךָ יָמִים אֲשֶׁר
לֹא־בָאוּ לְמִיּוֹם סוּר־אֶפְרַיִם מֵעַל יְהוּדָה אֵת מֶלֶךְ אַשּׁוּר

¹⁴Therefore, the Lord himself will give you [pl.] a sign. Behold, the virgin will be pregnant, and she will give birth to a son. You [fs.] will call his name Immanuel.[7] ¹⁵He will eat curds and honey so that he will know to turn from what is evil and choose what is good. ¹⁶Yes, before the boy knows to refuse what is evil and to choose what is good, the land of the two kings before whom you tremble will be forsaken. ¹⁷YHWH will bring upon you, upon your people, and upon the house of your father days such as have not been from the days when Ephraim departed from Judah, namely, the king of Assyria.[8]

Though no significant text-critical problems are present in this passage, there are several issues in the translation. Exploring these issues will allow us to unpack the potential meanings of the sign. First, what God will do is an אוֹת (*'ot;* "sign," 79x in the OT, 11x in Isaiah). It often refers to a miraculous sign, such as God's works in the Exodus, but it may also refer to a "sign" as a memorial or indicator of something. The first instance of the word in Isaiah was in 7:11, anticipating this vision. In the later parts of Isaiah, it regularly refers to a memorial of what God has done (19:20; 55:13), an indicator of what God will do (20:3; 37:30; 38:7), or the signal for the performance of an action (38:22). In his study of the word across the Old Testament, Mark D. Schutzius argues that when God is the one doing the אוֹת, it refers to something that is a miraculous act. From Schutzius' argument and the use of the word across Isaiah, it is not clear to me that the word *must* refer to something miraculous when God performs it, but this should certainly

---

[7] "You" refers to the virgin of the previous sentence.

[8] Unless otherwise indicated, all translations in this chapter are the author's.

present itself to the reader as a possibility.[9] The word does not necessarily have to be used for confirmation or affirmation of something else declared the context, as its use here is often interpreted.[10] Though there are instances where it is used in this manner, there are clear instances where "confirmation" does not fit the word's use (e.g. Exod 7:1-7). The use of this word is not decisive in this regard. The examples of the use of the word for confirmation, to point to Yahweh's character, and the term's use throughout Isaiah all fit a pattern of a sign/signified relationship, with various relationships envisioned between the sign and the signified. The use of the word for a miraculous act also fits withing a broad sense of a sign/signified relationship: in each use, the אוֹת ('ot) is the sign of something; it points the reader through the signifier to that which is signified, whether it is God's power through his miraculous acts or God's past acts and promises through memorials and sign-acts. The use of the word here should, therefore, lead us to look not only for the sign but also the signified. In this and the following three sections, we will consider the sign, then we will consider what it may signify.

The syntax of the following three clauses suggests that the "virgin" is the sign's immediate focus; the focus then shifts to her offspring. The debate over the meaning עַלְמָה ('almah) is extensive, yet five things emerge from the biblical data:[11]

1) the referents of עַלְמָה are young woman, and
2) there is no clear instance where the referent is not a virgin

---

[9] Mark D. Schutzius II, *The Hebrew Word for "Sign" and Its Impact on Isaiah 7:14* (Wipf and Stock, 2015), 54–55, 131–32, 134, 136–37.

[10] Schutzius II, *The Hebrew Word*, 136–37.

[11] Cf. Cuthbert Lattey, "The Term Almah in Is. 7:14," *The Catholic Biblical Quarterly* 9.1 (1947): 89–95; John Joseph Owens, "The Meaning of 'ALMAH in the Old Testament," *Review & Expositor* 50.1 (1953): 56–60; Alfred von Rohr Sauer, "The Almah Translation in Is. 7:14," *Concordia Theological Monthly* 24.8 (1953): 551–59; Irwin, "That Troublesome 'Almah and Other Matters"; Edward J. Young, *The Book of Isaiah* (Grand Rapids: Eerdmans, 1965), 1:286–88; Richard Niessen, "The Virginity of the 'Almah' in Isaiah 7:14," *BSac* 137.546 (1980): 133–50; Wegner, "How Many Virgin Births Are in the Bible?"; Stefan Felber, "The Immanuel Prophecy of Isaiah 7:14 at the Crossroads of Exegesis, Hermeneutics, and Bible Translation," *Unio Cum Christo* 5.1 (2019): 121–36.

(in the English sense).

3) In several contexts, the meaning of the word seems to be "virgin." In Proverbs 30:19, the sexual act of a man with his "virgin" is contrasted with the adulteress and her wanton sexuality. The use of the word elsewhere for unmarried woman and the contrast with the adulteress suggests that this refers the beginning of marital relationships, appropriate and pure sexuality.[12] Furthermore, Song of Songs 6:8 seems to intend a contrast employing this meaning, for if the "virgins" were not virgins in the technical sense, they would be concubines or queens; it would seem that these were young woman prepared for harem life (cf. Esther 2:1-4, using the word בְּתוּלָה; *betulah*).[13]

4) The New Testament authors interpret this sign as referring to and having the meaning of a "virgin" in the English sense.

5) The woman in view is at least young and probably not married, and so most likely a "virgin."[14]

The use of this particular word, over against בְּתוּלָה, which is often synonymous but may refer to a married woman (Joel 1:8), may strengthen the case that virginity is meant. However, Isaiah tends to use rare vocabulary, so the choice of עַלְמָה (*'almah*) over בְּתוּלָה may be stylistic and not meaningful.[15] Nevertheless, given the five points above, it would seem probable that connotations of "virginity" are present.

Returning to the syntax, הִנֵּה (*hinneh*; "behold") introduces the sign that God will perform. The content introduced by הִנֵּה is, first, "the virgin." The use of verbless clauses leaves the question of time open, though the context strongly suggests future, even if it is the very near future (she *will* be pregnant). More significantly, the use of verbless clauses focuses our attention on the virgin and what is said about her. Usually, the use of the

---

[12] Cf. Bruce K Waltke, *The Book of Proverbs: Chapters 15-31*, NICOT (Grand Rapids: Eerdmans, 2004).

[13] Richard S. Hess, *Song of Songs* (Baker Academic, 2005), 51.

[14] Young, *The Book of Isaiah*, 1:287–89; J. A. Motyer, *The Prophecy of Isaiah: An Introduction & Commentary* (Downers Grove: IVP, 1993), 85.

[15] M. McNamara, "The Emmanuel Prophecy and Its Context," *Scripture* 14.28 (1962): 121.

article ("the") is interpreted either to identify a definite, known figure or as an indefinite "generic" use of the article,[16] but these are not the only options. The use of the article may indicate a definite individual known to the prophet and/or the king, or it may have a grammatical function, indicating the definite subject of a verbless clause.[17] The syntax seems to be the focus; we are meant to consider what is said about "the virgin," whomever she may be. Is it coincidental that after a word that often refers to the miraculous, and in a context where the miraculous is expected (more on that below), we find the juxtaposition of "a virgin" with conception and birth? So, even if "virgin" is only one point within the broad semantic range of עַלְמָה ('almah), the context certainly suggests that such a tension is what is intended.

Following the MT as it is most likely to be read, the final clause of verse 14 directly addresses the woman: "you shall call his name Immanuel" (cf. NET). That is, וְקָרָאת (veqara't) in the MT is often assumed to be a 3FS qatal form from קרא (q-r-'), "and she shall call," ESV); Deuteronomy 31:29 is cited as evidence in favour of this reading ("evil will befall you," ESV).[18] However, Deuteronomy 31:29 is an instance of a homonymous verb (קרא; q-r-', to meet, happen). In Genesis 16:11, the same form of קרא meaning "to call" is used and it is a 2FS ("you shall call"); It is used in the same phrase as Isaiah 7:14 (הָרָה וְיֹלַדְתְּ בֵּן וְקָרָאת שְׁמוֹ; harah veyoladte ben veqara't shemo, Gen 16:11; הָרָה וְיֹלֶדֶת בֵּן וְקָרָאת שְׁמוֹ; harah veyoledet ben veqara't shemo, Isa 7:14). The LXX has read the form in this manner (καλέσεις; kaleseis, "you will call") and it is well attested in similar roots, resembling קָטַלְתְּ (qatalt, "you (f.) killed") and its 3rd Aleph form מָצָאת (matsa't, "you (f.) found"). The 3FS form would be קָרְאָה (qar'ah, "she called") as with נָשְׂאָה (nas'ah, "she carried") or מָצְאָה (mats'ah, "she found"). In the three instances where קרא (q-r-') is a 3FS, it is always the expected form, קָרְאָה (Gen 29:35, 30:6; 1 Chron 4:9). Wildberger claims this reading is "impossible" but does not substantiate the claim.[19] The Great

---

[16] E.g. Young, *The Book of Isaiah*, 1:287; Brevard S. Childs, *Isaiah*, 1st ed., The Old Testament Library (Louisville: Westminster John Knox, 2001), s.v. 7:14.

[17] Cf. Paul Joüon and Takamitsu Muraoka, *A Grammar of Biblical Hebrew*, Revised English Edition. (Pontificio Istituto Biblico, 2006), § 137m-o.

[18] Friedrich Wilhelm Gesenius, *Gesenius' Hebrew Grammar*, ed. E. Kautzsch and Sir Arthur Ernest Cowley, 2d English ed. (Clarendon, 1910), § 74.g.

[19] Hans Wildberger, *Isaiah: Isaiah 1-12* (Minneapolis: Fortress, 1991), 286.

Isaiah Scroll from Qumran has neither form; instead; it has a 3rd masculine singular (וקרא; *vqr'*, "and he will call"). The form in the MT explains the versions and would easily be corrupted to Qumran's וקרא, which is the most unlikely reading. The 2nd person may indicate that woman was present to hear the vision, but this is not a necessary conclusion; it may be looking forward to the time of fulfillment (e.g. Isa 53:13-14; 54:1). The focus of the passage shifts to the child at the end of the verse 4, yet the initial focus on the woman and then the content of the following verses, namely details about the child, suggest that the child's name is not the sign. This distinguishes this child from Shear-Jashub and Maher-shalal-hash-baz, whose names have prophetic significance (though neither child nor their names are ever called an אות [*'ot*, "sign"], see below for Isa 8:18).

What, then, is said about the child? The NET is certainly on a better footing than translations such as the ESV when it translates the infinitive with lamed, לְדַעְתּוֹ (*leda'to;* "that he would know"), as a result clause instead of a temporal clause. The point of eating the honey and curds is not temporal (for which בְּ [*be*] would have been more appropriate) but the result, that he would know "to turn from what is evil and choose what is good."[20] This indicates that the sign is not primarily *temporal*, indicating when something will happen. The "curds and honey" focuses on a lifestyle that will result in a sort of righteousness, the knowledge to turn from evil and choose the good. What to make of "curds and honey" is difficult, but I want to suggest it indicates that the child will experience a lowly or travailed life.

חֶמְאָה (*chem'ah;* "curds") and דְּבַשׁ (*debash;* "honey") are not universally used in negative contexts, but they are regularly associated with 1) the wild, 2) the wilderness, and, occasionally, 3) poverty or difficult circumstances. With the first association, the promised land will flow with honey (דְּבַשׁ) and milk (חָלָב; *chalab*, Exod 3:8, 17; 13:5; 33:3; etc.), suggesting its uncultivated fruitfulness (cf. Job 20:17). In 1 Samuel 14, honey is found in abundance in a forest. With the second association, when David is in the wilderness, among the food brought to him is honey and curds (וּדְבַשׁ וְחֶמְאָה; *udbash vechem'ah*) (2 Sam 17:29). On its own, honey is occasionally associated with wealth (Ezek 16:13), but curds are usually associated with herds and the associated lifestyle

---

[20] Cf. Peter Machinist, "How Gods Die," 213; Wildberger, *Isaiah*, 286. Contra Young, *The Book of Isaiah*, 1:291.

(Gen 18:8; Deut 32:14; Jdgs 5:25). With the third association, the only other instance of the phrase used in Isaiah 7:14 is several verses later in 7:22 (cf. 2 Sam 17:29 and Job 20:17, in the reverse order). When the king of Assyria comes, he will settle in the land, including "the pastures" (7:19). The language of verse 21, that a man will *keep alive* (יְחַיֶּה; *yechayyeh*) a "young cow and two sheep" suggests a desperate lifestyle.[21] The negative connotations of such a life are confirmed in verses 23-25, where the land has been rendered hostile to agriculture. From these two animals, the man will eat curds, as will all "left in the land" (7:22). Thus, in the immediate context, "curds and honey" are seen to be an impoverished lifestyle resulting from the devastation wrought by Assyria. Taking into account this immediate use of the phrase and the broader data, it would seem that "Immanuel" will be raised on a lowly diet and, as a result, will know the righteous path. This echoes a significant theme of messianic anticipation seen, for example, in Samuel, where God's king will come from a lowly estate (e.g. 1 Samuel 2:1-10).[22] That this child will also choose what is good and reject what is evil taps into the hope for a righteous king, a theme seen in Samuel and elsewhere (e.g. Deuteronomy 17:14-20). Now, some take "reject what is evil and choose what is good" to be a sort of marker of age, an age of moral accountability or legal responsibility.[23] However, the phrase is not used anywhere else in the Bible, so it is not clear that it indicates a specific age, even if the concept of "an age of responsibility" could be demonstrated in the Bible (which I do not think is possible). The language itself is not that of vague discernment but concrete knowledge: he will not simply know *what* is evil but *to reject it* and *to choose* what is good.[24]

Turning to verse 16, we find the first temporal marker related to the sign. However, it is ambiguous. If כִּי *(ki)* is taken in a strong causal sense

---

[21] Motyer, *The Prophecy of Isaiah*, 86. Cf. John T Willis, "The Meaning of Isaiah 7:14 and Its Application in Matthew 1:23," *Restoration Quarterly* 21.1 (1978): 8; Andrew T. Abernethy, *Eating in Isaiah: Approaching the Role of Food and Drink in Isaiah's Structure and Message*, Biblical Interpretation Series (Leiden: Brill, 2014), 57–58.

[22] Cf. Rutherford, *God's Kingdom*.

[23] Gene M. Tucker, "The Book of Isaiah 1-39," in *The New Interpreter's Bible: A Commentary in Twelve Volumes*, ed. Leander E. Keck (Nashville: Abingdon, 2001), 112; Felber, "The Immanuel Prophecy of Isaiah 7:14 at the Crossroads of Exegesis, Hermeneutics, and Bible Translation," 128.

[24] Machinist, "How Gods Die," 213; Wildberger, *Isaiah*, 286–88, 314–15.

(for/because), then verse 16 would indicate that "Immanuel" will have this diet because, in the time before he learns the righteous way, the land will be desolated by Assyria. However, as argued by Anneli Aejmelaeus, when a כִּי clause has such a conditional sense, its typical placement would be before the "main clause" it modifies. When כִּי follows the "main clause," they are most often causal in the broader sense, often explanatory.[25] Taken in its general explanatory sense, verse 26 may only give a vague temporal reference for Immanuel's appearance. Namely, he will appear after God brings up Assyria; before he has learned the righteous way, they will be destroyed. Such an indefinite but sequential marker is not foreign to Old or New Testament prophecy (e.g. Dan 2:29, 45; Matt 24:30). Because "for" often has strong causal intimations in English, I have chosen to render כִּי here as "Yes, ..." This explanatory clause does not immediately pertain to the Assyrian judgment of Judah but to the judgement of the land of the two threatening kings. The explanatory value is, thus, not to explain why the child will be eating curds and honey; instead, it reinforces the hope of the coming child. God's purpose will be accomplished for the house of David in spite of the threat of Syria and Israel, for these threats will indeed be destroyed, as God has promised earlier (Isa 7:1-9). Verse 17 expands upon this by explaining why the land of Judah's enemies will be desolate and by returning to the broader theme of judgment through Assyria, which dominates this section of Isaiah. In this way, the prophecy begun with וַיּוֹסֶף (vayyoseph, "and again," 7:10) begins on a different note than the previous prophecy; it does not immediately concern the imminent threat but God's promises to Judah and the house of David in particular. The conclusion of the sign-prophecy turns back to the imminent threat, tying these two themes together: that God will fulfill his promises and bring forth a righteous child, who (given his relevance to the Davidic house) will be a Davidic descendant, is not threatened by the present danger.

From what we have seen thus far, we have surfaced several possible interpretations of the text but primarily focused on the tenability of my

---

[25] She uses "main clause" in a slightly idiosyncratic way, "The term 'main clause' will, however, be used in the following discussion to designate the clause to which the כִּי clause is joined, regardless of the distinction between subordination and coordination." Anneli Aejmelaeus, "Function and Interpretation of כִּי in Biblical Hebrew," *JBL* 105.2 (1986): 199–209.

translation. We will now turn to the context to indicate why such a translation is particularly fitting.

b. Isaiah 7:1-25

The sign of Isaiah 7:14 is given in the context of a plot by two kings to wage war on Judah. The use of בֵּית דָּוִד (bet davvid, "the house of David") in verse 2 casts the focus of the following prophecies beyond the individual king Ahaz to the Davidic line. In verse 3, Isaiah is told to bring his son שְׁאָר יָשׁוּב (she'ar yashub), Shear-Jashub, when he goes to meet Ahaz. This child is not mentioned again, but his presence when Isaiah brings his prophecies is significant. However we interpret the emphasis of the subject-verb order, "a remnant will return" is the promise implied by his presence. The presence of the child and so of this promise casts what follows in an eschatological mode: the child's name signifies both coming judgment (שְׁאָר; she'ar, "a remnant") and salvation (יָשׁוּב; yashub, "(it) will return"). In the short prophecy given concerning the two threatening kings, a temporal marker is given, yet it is quite broad: "within sixty-five years Ephraim will be shattered from being a people" (8c-d, ESV). The final two lines of the Shear-Jashub prophecy are important for what follows. In 7:10-11, God tells Ahaz to request a sign. In the immediately preceding lines, we read, אִם לֹא תַאֲמִינוּ כִּי לֹא תֵאָמֵנוּ ('im lo' ta'aminu ki lo' te'amenu). The ESV and NET translate the line as tautology echoing 7:4, "If you are not firm in faith, you will not be firm at all" (7:9, ESV). However, another possibility would be, "If you [pl.] do not believe, you [pl.] will not be firm."[26] The Hiphil often means "to believe something" while the Niphal means "to be steadfast/firm." Currently Ahaz and, presumably, the rest of Judah are not "being firm" (7:2), and this will not change if they "do not believe" what Yahweh is telling them. It is following this that God invites Ahaz to request a sign.

When God invites Ahaz to ask for a sign, I think it is clear that an אוֹת ('ot) of the miraculous sort is intended, "let it be deep as Sheol or high as heaven" (7:11, ESV). It is true that this is a merism, which leads many to deny that it has any miraculous connotations; it merely means, "ask for anything."[27]

---

[26] Cf. Childs, Isaiah, 64.

[27] E.g. Wildberger, Isaiah, s.v. 7:11.

However, the use of these extremes, which elsewhere signify the difficult or impossible (Deut 30:12), along with אוֹת, which regularly connotes the miraculous, orients the reader towards the miraculous. Ahaz refuses to ask, to which Isaiah responds, turning back to the plural with בֵית דָּוִד (*bet davvid*, "the house of David"). God will give the house of David a sign, despite Ahaz's reticence (Isa 7:14). Several important observations emerge from this exchange. First, given its common associations with the miraculous and the invitation cast in miraculous terms, we ought to expect that the sign God gives will be miraculous. Oswalt is right that a miracle does not "necessarily" follow from this terminology, but the terminology certainly sets the stage for one.[28] Second, despite the frequent assertions otherwise, it is not immediately clear what purpose God envisages for this "sign."[29] No purpose is given in 7:10, and the preceding prophecy has already suggested that Ahaz and those with him are unlikely to believe. It is possible that the sign is, as is often supposed, confirmatory, giving Ahaz a solid reason for believing God's prophecy concerning the two nations.[30] However, the text does not specify this. More importantly, verse 10 opens with a commencement formula, וַיּוֹסֶף (*vayyoseph*), suggesting a mild disjunction between the preceding prophecy and the sign (cf. 8:5; Job 27:1, 29:1). Watts recognizes that this marks "a second word and a second occasion," but asserts that "The purpose continues that of the previous episode."[31] Oswalt is right that there is no explicit indication of a shift in location or time, but the presence of an irregular speech commencement must be acknowledged. This marker itself indicates a break in the discourse, even without the markers Oswalt is seeking; elsewhere, when speech is directly continuous, אמר (*'-m-r*, "to say") is employed (e.g. vv. 12, 13). When יסף (*y-s-ph*, "to do again") is used in the midst of someone's speech, as in Isaiah 8:5 and Job 27:1, 29:1, 36:1, it indicates a disjunction within the speaker's continuous discourse (or, in the case of Job 29:1, perhaps a resumption of speech after a break, but here a shift in the discourse from

---

[28] Oswalt, *Isaiah 1-39*, 205.

[29] E.g. Young, *The Book of Isaiah*, 1:281; Tucker, "The Book of Isaiah 1-39," 111.

[30] E.g. Childs, *Isaiah*.

[31] John D. W. Watts, *Isaiah 1-33*, ed. Bruce M. Metzger, David Allan Hubbard, and Glenn W. Barker, Revised ed., Word Biblical Commentary 24 (Nashville: Thomas Nelson, 2005), 134.

27 to 29 is evident, as is 28 to 29 if we see both as Job's speeches). Thus, we do not need to posit a change in time or location to posit that the presence of יסף indicates a disjunction between the preceding prophecy and the one that commences here.[32] Though they are united in a textual unit, it is not clear that they are to be read as sequential, with the sign answering in some way to the prophecy in verses 7-9.

This opens for us several possibilities. Though addressed to Ahaz in the context of the invasion, the "sign" is introduced in a disjunctive way, suggesting that though miraculous, it may not actually be confirmatory. Furthermore, after Ahaz refuses to ask God, God turns from Ahaz (the singular) to the plural house of David.[33] The sign, therefore, is given with significance for the whole house of David, not just Ahaz. It is not clear from the text what, if anything, the sign is supposed to do for Ahaz. Indeed, after Ahaz refuses to ask and Isaiah turns to the house of David as a whole, the next we hear of Ahaz is that he has died (14:28). We are left, then, with the sign itself to tell us what it is pointing to and what its significance in the context of Isaiah is. The contextual clues leading up to the sign indicate a couple things: the sign is for the house of David as a whole and it is to be miraculous. Furthermore, the immediate context of the prophecy concerning the two kings and the presence of Shear-Jashub orient it either towards the present or the future, or perhaps both. The context is replete with connotations of both judgment and salvation, as is commonly recognized.

From these contextual observations, we can revisit our translation. It is now clear that "virgin" is highly likely to be the meaning of עַלְמָה ('almah), for little else would qualify as miraculous in this sign.[34] The timing, like much Old Testament prophecy, is future indefinite. That is, its only temporal marker is oriented to a time after the kings are destroyed, but we have no indication that it is intimately connected with that event. It is not introduced as nor is it uniquely fitting to be a temporal marker of that event. Taking the further resonances of the passage into account, that the boy will come from

---

[32] Cf. Motyer, *The Prophecy of Isaiah*, 83. Contra Oswalt, *Isaiah 1-39*, 204.

[33] Felber, "The Immanuel Prophecy of Isaiah 7:14 at the Crossroads of Exegesis, Hermeneutics, and Bible Translation," 127.

[34] Schutzius II, *The Hebrew Word*, 132.

impoverished life ("curds and honey") and is the subject of such miraculous expectation naturally draws the reader to the broader messianic expectations of the Old Testament. The lowly upbringing resonates particularly with themes of Samuel concerning the ascension of David and, as I have argued elsewhere, a future priest-king who will follow in his line.[35] Turning to the broader context in which this sign falls, the hints that "Immanuel" will be a future Davidic ruler are only strengthened.

c. Isaiah 7:1-9:6 (MT)

In delineating this section, I am loosely following Alec Motyer. Chapter 9, verse 7 (MT) turns from Judah to Israel and so provides a natural break.[36] The unit properly continues until 11:16 (10:5 transitions to another subsection, addressing Assyria). However, 7:1 is a typical transition formula, introducing a new setting, so I believe 7:1 is a more significant section break (7:1-11:16) than Motyer's break at 6:1.[37] Immediately after the sign prophecy, Isaiah 7:18-25 picks up the final line of 7:17, "the king of Assyria." This section shows that Assyria will not only be the means of deliverance from the threat of the two kings but also judgment on Judah. In 8:1-4 we have a short account of Isaiah having another prophetic child, like Shear-Jashub. The birth of this "boy" (cf. 7:16) is clearly a temporal marker for the coming of Assyria. However, there is no suggestion of the miraculous involved in his birth, nor is the word אוֹת ('ot; "sign") employed. Furthermore, given the presence of Shear-Jashub previously, the "prophetess" is clearly not an עַלְמָה ('almah; "virgin") in any sense of the word. Thus, the suggestions that Mahar-shalal-hash-baz is Immanuel are highly unlikely.[38]

Isaiah 8:5 introduces another discourse in the flow of this prophetic unit, a disjunction from the Mahar-shalal-hash-baz story (introduced with וַיֹּסֶף; vayyoseph, "and he again... "). In 8:5-15, Immanuel again enters the scene,

[35] Rutherford, *God's Kingdom*.

[36] 9:2 in English translations is 9:1 in the MT (9:1 in translations is 8:23 in the MT).

[37] Motyer, *The Prophecy of Isaiah*.

[38] Cf. Christopher R. Seitz, *Isaiah 1-39*, Interpretation, a Bible Commentary for Teaching and Preaching (Louisville: Westminster John Knox, 1993), 62–63.

after the brief prophetic narrative concerning Isaiah's child (8:1-4). The re-introduction of Immanuel confirms our earlier observations that he or the sign of which he is a part is significant. Now it is seen that he has significance in the flow of Isaiah's prophecy, not just immediately for the "house of David." First, Judah in the context of an Assyrian invasion is identified as Immanuel's. Motyer is surely right to identify a shift from a national focus to an individual focus by this point (a shift that happens in Jeremiah's prophecies and is at the heart of the book of Habakkuk).[39] Thus, though Assyria is poised to bring judgment on the nation as a whole, their plans will not be fully realized. Instead, God will ultimately triumph over them, for he is with his people for their salvation (8:10). Verses 12-15 confirm this reading, for they juxtapose Isaiah as a righteous remnant with rest of the nation. Turning to the following verses, things get interesting.

In verse 16, Yahweh is clearly the speaker (cf. v. 11), addressing Isaiah. The content of the imperative is as follows, "seal the teaching among *my disciples*" (ESV, emphasis added). Yahweh is speaking, so "my disciples" are his disciples, not Isaiah's.[40] Verse 17 continues the same speech from Yahweh, with no apparent disjunctive and the use of *veqatalti* construction indicating the continuation of a discourse:

> [16]Tie up the teaching
>   seal the instruction among my disciples,
> [17]And I will wait for YHWH,
>   who is hiding his face from the house of Jacob;
>   yes, I will hope in him.
> [18]Behold, I and the children
>   whom YHWH has given me
>   as signs and miracles among Israel,
>   from YHWH of hosts,
>   who dwells on Mount Zion (Isa 8:16-18)

Who, then, "waits" for Yahweh? It is none other than Yahweh, who commanded Isaiah to "seal the teaching among *my disciples*." This is how the author of Hebrews interprets these verses (following the LXX), taking the speaker of the discourse, Yahweh[1], to be Jesus (Heb 2:13, see Ch. 11 below).

---

[39] Motyer, *The Prophecy of Isaiah*. On Habakkuk, see Rutherford, *Habakkuk*.

[40] Motyer, *The Prophecy of Isaiah*, 96.

Thus, Yahweh[1] is somehow distinguished from Yahweh[2].[41] Though it is, to the best of my knowledge, not commonly recognized, this dynamic is not unheard of in the Old Testament (see our discussion of the Angel above). We will consider this passage in greater depth below.

Continuing in Isaiah 8, in verse 18, Yahweh[1] has solidarity with "the children whom YHWH" has given him. Hebrews once again takes the speaker to be Jesus (Heb 2:13). It is often assumed that the speaker here is Isaiah and "the children" refer to Shear-Jashub and Mahar-shalal-hash-baz.[42] However, though הִנֵּה (hinneh) may indicate a change in perspective and so speaker, it could also invite the reader to take up the speaker's perspective; therefore, it does not necessarily indicate a change in subject. We already have a distinction between Yahweh[1] and Yahweh[2] in verse 17, so it is not nonsensical to see children given to Yahweh by Yahweh. Furthermore, Isaiah's two children are never called "signs" or "miracles" and these words are not appropriate for these children. That is, the immediate use of "sign" in 7:14 is most likely miraculous. מוֹפֵת (mophet; "miracle") has even more miraculous connotations, hardly fitting for the offhand mention given to Shear-Jashub in 7:3 and normal birth assigned to Mahar-Shalal-Hash-Baz in 8:1-4.[43] Without a clear indication of a speaker change and the poor fit between "the children" and Isaiah's own children, it seems the author of Hebrews is on a good footing to see the speaker here as the same person in verse 17, Yahweh[1]. The children, if they are Yahweh[1]'s, would be the righteous remnant, which is appropriate for our interpretation of verses 5-15. Though we usually do not think of a "remnant" or God's people as "miraculous," their preservation among the apostate nation is a sign of God's power (1 King 19:8) and the implied heart of faithfulness is elsewhere identified as the result of God's own power (e.g. Deut 30:6; Isa 53:1; 54:13;

---

[41] See Chapter 18 for a discussion of the relationship between the name Yahweh and three persons. In the terminology of that chapter, "Yahweh[1]" and "Yahweh[2]" are functioning as non-exhaustive referents, such that what I am labelling "Yahweh[1]" is an instance of {"YHWH" → Son (Yahweh, Spirit, Father)} and "Yahweh[2]" {"YHWH" → Father (Yahweh, Spirit, Son)} or, perhaps, an inclusive term, so {"YHWH" → Yahweh (Father, Son, Spirit)}

[42] E.g. Young, The Book of Isaiah, 1:316–17; Oswalt, Isaiah 1-39, 236; Motyer, The Prophecy of Isaiah, 96; Willis, "The Meaning of Isaiah 7," 6.

[43] Cf. Schutzius II, The Hebrew Word.

Jer 31:31-34; Ezekiel 36-37).[44] Yahweh[1], by identifying the righteous remnant as his own children and his disciples, closely identifies himself with them. This would be highly appropriate if this figure were Immanuel, "God with us." The possibility of this identification is not left to the context alone, for it is indicated by the following prophetic oracle.

Isaiah 9:1 turns from the gloom of judgment in 8:19-22 to hope. It is cast in an eschatological light, evoking the expectations implied by the presence of Shear-Jashub and attached to Immanuel. Salvation has come (vv. 2-5)! Why? "For to us a child is born, to us a son is given" (v. 6a-b). Here we apparently find the fulfillment of the Immanuel prophecy. The arrival of Mahar-Shalal-Hash-Baz was anticlimactic, yet he was followed by another Immanuel oracle oriented towards the salvation of God's righteous amid the judgment on the unrighteous. Here we find the climactic introduction of a child in the context of salvation, which is appropriate for what we have seen thus far. However, lines 6a-b do not suggest the miraculous, at least not yet. 6c invokes the expectation for a messianic ruler; this child will be king. This suits the Immanuel sign, which was given to the "house of David." The mundane is turned to the miraculous in 6e-7g. This child will be called "Mighty God," a title God himself bears (10:21). A child identified with God is surely miraculous, and not out of sorts for the context in which Immanuel seems to be strongly associated with Yahweh[1], who is differentiated from Yahweh[2]. This God-child will receive an everlasting kingdom ruling on the throne of David; he is, therefore, the fulfillment of Davidic expectation. This is another point of contact with the Immanuel sign, which was given to the house of David. Indeed, this association of an earthly ruler who is God himself gives new significance to "Immanuel"; it is not a child who represents God with his people but is indeed "God with us." There is thus significant contextual evidence not only for identifying the Immanuel sign as a future, miraculous birth of a Davidic king but as the future, miraculous birth of a Davidic king who is Yahweh himself somehow distinguished from Yahweh.

d. What Does the Sign Signify?

---

[44] See further J. Alexander Rutherford, *Prevenient Grace: An Investigation into Arminianism*, 2nd Revised Ed., Teleioteti Technical Studies 2 (Vancouver: Teleioteti, 2020).

Earlier, we suggested that אוֹת (*'ot*, "sign") indicates a reality which points beyond itself: it is a "sign" that signifies something. We have argued thus far that the sign is the miraculous birth of a Davidic king who is also God, and so "God with us." What, then, is the significance of the sign?

As already observed, we have no clear statement concerning the sign's significance. Given the nature of the sign, one possibility comes to the forefront. The presence of Shear Jashub has given the context an eschatological mode. We are not far from the "later days" when God would bring judgment on the earth and send his people into far off lands, only to turn a remnant back to himself and restore them with a Davidic king (e.g. Deut 29:1-30:14; Isaiah 53:1-54:17; Jer 31-33 ; Ezek 36:22-37:28).[45] For those to whom the vision will be realized, the "sign" signifies the faithfulness of God to fulfill his promises, to uphold them, give them a Davidic ruler, and be with them as he promised in Exodus (33:12-23). Like the miraculous signs of the Exodus and elsewhere (e.g. Exod 7:1-7), this sign points beyond itself to Yahweh and his character. For those who heard it in Isaiah's day and for those who read the prophecy when it was written, the promise of this sign has a similar force to the presence of Shear-Jashub and the similar promises made throughout the Old Testament: they remind God's people that imminent judgment does not have the final say. For the righteous who draw near to Yahweh, there is salvation.[46] God is faithful to uphold his promises to those who trust in him; corporate sin and his righteous response will not have the final word; a remnant will return and God himself will be present among them in association with or even as their Davidic king. If Ahaz were to hear this sign and believe, he would not need to fear; judgment will not have the final word. This significance also, as I suggested above, ties the sign into its literary context concerning as it does the Assyrian judgment. God's promises will be fulfilled despite the present threat and, presumably, any future threats; God would bring Assyria against these two kings, so they are not an ultimate threat to God's promises. This application may have relevance in its original context and present literary context because the plot

---

[45] On the connection between Deut 30:11-14 and what precedes see Appendix 1 in Ibid.

[46] A similar focus on God's purpose for the righteous amidst judgment is found in Habakkuk, see Rutherford, *Habakkuk*.

of these two kings was directly addressed to Ahaz's throne and so the Davidic dynasty. By reiterating his commitment to the Davidic house through a miraculous fulfilment, God reiterates the promise that these kings would be defeated and that their plan would not come to fruition. As observed above, verse 16 relates the sign to the present threat, indicating that the threat would not affect God's fulfilment of his promise.

e. The New Testament Revisited

The sign as we have interpreted it has significant resonance with how the New Testament understands not only the coming of the messiah but the specific fulfilment of Isaiah 7:14. In addition to the "Immanuel" prophecy fulfilment themes in Matthew and Luke, Hebrews 2:10-18 interprets Isaiah 8:17-18 as a reference to Jesus Christ, specifically as God incarnate. Though prophetic fulfilment in the New Testament is complex, there are clear instances where Jesus fulfils a future-oriented prophecy. This sort of fulfilment is certainly appropriate for the context of Matthew 1:22-23. In this context, Matthew is focused on the miraculous expectation of the Davidic messiah, themes which we found in Isaiah 7:14. This would also give the immediate purpose for the "virgin birth." The Bible is mum concerning the sorts of explanations made by latter theologians, but if 7:14 is a forward-looking prophecy that anticipates the miraculous birth of a divine Davidic king from a literal virgin, then Mary's virginity is at least God's intentional fulfilment of this prophecy. This may very well be all that is intended by the virgin birth. Though Luke does not explicitly quote this prophecy, he repeatedly identifies Mary as a virgin and the birth as miraculous, indicating he has this prophecy at the back of his mind (1:26-27; 34-38). He makes sure to mention that Joseph was "of the house of David" (1:27), which when combined with "virgin," clearly echoes Isaiah 7:14 in its context. Though he overstates the matter, Felber is right to identify similarities between Isaiah 7:14 and Luke 1:31.[47] Reading these texts in conversation with Isaiah 7:14 and its context, we can see that the authors of the New Testament had good reason to identify messianic and even divine themes in Isaiah's prophecy. Reading the other way, we are alerted to these features by the New

---

[47] Felber, "The Immanuel Prophecy of Isaiah 7:14 at the Crossroads of Exegesis, Hermeneutics, and Bible Translation," 123.

Testament's use of the passage, and once alerted, we cannot deny that they were present all along.

d. Conclusion

I have argued that the interpreting Isaiah 7:14 in its context does not allow us to relegate it to a local, non-miraculous fulfilment for Ahaz. The sign's contents and context point us far beyond Ahaz and his present struggles to God's ultimate plan for Judah and Israel as a whole, to come as a child for his people, to be "God with us." In the process, we were also alerted to a phenomenon that is all too often ignored in the Old Testament: God is repeatedly differentiated from himself. In Isaiah 8:17-18, we are confronted with two figures identified as Yahweh speaking with and acting towards one another. This phenomenon is not relegated to this passage alone, for Isaiah 53:1 identifies the Arm of Yahweh as a suffering human who would be smitten by God (v. 4). Again, God is differentiated from himself in a similar manner as in 8:17-18. We will now look closers at Isaiah 8, 9 and 53, as well as 61, where we find a similar occurrence of God differentiated from himself.

B. Isaiah 8:16-9:6

צוּר תְּעוּדָה חֲתוֹם תּוֹרָה בְּלִמֻּדָי: וְחִכִּיתִי לַיהוָה הַמַּסְתִּיר פָּנָיו מִבֵּית
יַעֲקֹב וְקִוֵּיתִי־לוֹ: הִנֵּה אָנֹכִי וְהַיְלָדִים אֲשֶׁר נָתַן־לִי יְהוָה לְאֹתוֹת
וּלְמוֹפְתִים בְּיִשְׂרָאֵל מֵעִם יְהוָה צְבָאוֹת הַשֹּׁכֵן בְּהַר צִיּוֹן:

[16]Tie up the teaching
   seal the instruction among my disciples,
[17]And I will wait for YHWH,
   who is hiding his face from the house of Jacob;
   yes, I will hope for him.
[18]Behold, I and the children
   whom YHWH has given me
   as signs and miracles in Israel
   from YHWH of hosts
   who dwells on Mount Zion. – Isaiah 8:16-18

Though not betrayed by the commentators, there is a subtle but important ambiguity in Isaiah 8:16-18 that draws our attention. Though usually delineated as prose (ESV), each verse bears the marks of poetic parallelism (NET; BHS)—even if verse 18 needs to be rendered as a cumbersome pentacolon. The ambiguity lies in the questions, who is the speaker? and, to whom is this addressed? Wildberger dismisses the imperative in verse 16 because he identifies the speaker in verse 17 as Isaiah.[48] However, this is too easy of a solution: can we make sense of the text as at stands? The problem is that the speaker leading into verse 16 is Yahweh addressing Isaiah; thus, "bind!" is a command to Isaiah. Following the logic of the passage, Yahweh would be the antecedent for the 1st person suffix on לִמֻּד (limmud; "disciple"),[49] and the speaker in verse 17 would not be Isaiah, as Wildberger assumes, but Yahweh.

The trouble, of course, is that in verse 17, the speaker says he "will wait for YHWH." Verse 18b-d likewise indicates that the speaker's "children" are given him by Yahweh. It could be argued that הִנֵּה (hinneh; "behold!") in verse 18a indicates a shift in speaker, but this would not solve the initial problem of Yahweh apparently addressing Yahweh in verse 17. Furthermore, הִנֵּה need not indicate a change in speaker, only in perspective (cf. 7:14): it orients the reader's "gaze" in a new direction. It is often assumed that the speaker in verse 18 is Isaiah, "children" referring to Shear-Jashub (7:3) and Maher-Shalal-Hash-Baz (8:1-4). However, these children are not elsewhere referred to as "signs" (אוֹת; 'ot),[50] let alone "signs and miracles" (אֹתוֹת וּמוֹפְתִים; 'otot vemophetim), with the phrase's distinct connotations of the miraculous.[51] "Children" in this context is parallel with "disciples" (cf. 54:13), suggesting that the speaker is the same in both passages. "Children" would then refer to Yahweh's faithful remnant, a miraculous fact indeed given the widespread apostasy, attested so clearly by Ahaz in 7:1-13 and again in 8:11-15. Indeed, the root למד (l-m-d; "to teach") is used with בֵּן (ben; "son"), which has semantic overlap with יֶלֶד (yeled; "child"), in Isaiah 54:13, within a context that suggests the miraculous change in the condition of Israel as envisioned in

[48] Hans Wildberger, *Isaiah: Isaiah 1-12* (Fortress Press, 1991), 364, 368.

[49] Motyer, *The Prophecy of Isaiah*, 96.

[50] Against the identification of Maher-shalal-hash-baz with the Immanuel sign, see above.

[51] Cf. Mark D. Schutzius II, *The Hebrew Word for "Sign" and Its Impact on Isaiah 7:14* (Wipf and Stock, 2015).

Deuteronomy 30:1-14, Jeremiah 31:31-34, and Ezekiel 36-37. Taking the MT at face value, the speaker throughout 8:16-18 appears to be Yahweh even as he addresses Yahweh. Looking several verses earlier, we find a similar phenomenon: Yahweh begins speaking to Isaiah in verse 11 and commands Isaiah and the faithful, "YHWH of hosts, it is he whom you [pl.] must honour." Verse 14 and 15 continue to refer to Yahweh in the 3rd person. The use of the plural in these verses introduces a possible antecedent for "my disciples": Yahweh had been instructing Isaiah as part of a larger group; when God turns to command Isaiah personally (צוֹר; *tsor*, "bind!"), the broader group is the natural antecedent of the "disciples" for whom Isaiah must "bind… and seal…." Indeed, this is apparently the interpretation of these verses adopted by the author of Hebrews. Though usually explained as a sort of typology base on the prophet Isaiah or prosopological exegesis, Hebrews 2:13 (cf. Isaiah 8:17 LXX) can also be read as direct exegesis of the Isaiah passage with Jesus as the speaker.[52] Through Jesus' identity with the singular Yahweh, this fits perfectly with the exegesis offered above.

If we accept this interpretation, there is an issue that we must hold back on resolving. Though Yahweh is distinguished from himself in various passages, in effect as Yahweh[1] and Yahweh[2], there is no direct correspondence between one of these persons called "Yahweh" and the Father or the Son. Some passages suit one or the other, perhaps neither. We will return to this issue at the conclusion of this chapter (see also, Chapters 15 and 18).

C. Isaiah 9:1-7

כִּי־יֶ֣לֶד יֻלַּד־לָ֗נוּ בֵּ֚ן נִתַּן־לָ֔נוּ וַתְּהִ֥י הַמִּשְׂרָ֖ה עַל־שִׁכְמ֑וֹ וַיִּקְרָ֨א שְׁמ֜וֹ פֶּ֠לֶא
יוֹעֵץ֙ אֵ֣ל גִּבּ֔וֹר אֲבִיעַ֖ד שַׂר־שָׁלֽוֹם׃

For a child is born to us;
    a son will be given to us.
    The government will be upon his shoulders.
His name will be called,

---

[52] See the discussion of Hebrews below (Ch. 11). Against prosopological exegesis, see Peter J Gentry, "A Preliminary Evaluation and Critique of Prosopological Exegesis," *Southern Baptist Journal of Theology* 23, no. 2 (2019): 105–122.

> Wonderful Counsellor,
> Mighty God,
> Everlasting Father
> Prince of Peace. – Isaiah 9:6

Given what we have seen thus far in Isaiah, it is hardly surprising to read the exalted epitaphs given to this son of promise. Above I argued that this child is "Immanuel," and that context has aligned Immanuel with God himself, perhaps calling him Yahweh. If this child is God himself, the epitaphs given are perfectly appropriate; if not, it is hardly fitting to call a mere human not only "Mighty God" but "Everlasting Father." As noted above, the former is God's own title in Isaiah 10:21. The latter is fitting only for the creator of all things, who has no beginning or end and is like a father to his creatures (e.g. James 1:17, cf. Chapter 15), especially to his people (Isa 63:16-17; Isa 64:8-9; Deut 14:1-2; Ps 103:13; Jer 31:20). As a man, this child is our brother (Heb 2:10-18); as Yahweh the creator and redeeming God, he is our Father.

D. Isaiah 53:1-2

מִי הֶאֱמִין לִשְׁמֻעָתֵנוּ וּזְרוֹעַ יְהֹוָה עַל־מִי נִגְלָתָה: וַיַּעַל כַּיּוֹנֵק לְפָנָיו וְכַשֹּׁרֶשׁ מֵאֶרֶץ צִיָּה לֹא־תֹאַר לוֹ וְלֹא הָדָר וְנִרְאֵהוּ וְלֹא־מַרְאֶה וְנֶחְמְדֵהוּ: נִבְזֶה וַחֲדַל אִישִׁים אִישׁ מַכְאֹבוֹת וִידוּעַ חֹלִי וּכְמַסְתֵּר פָּנִים מִמֶּנּוּ נִבְזֶה וְלֹא חֲשַׁבְנֻהוּ:

¹Who has believed what we have heard?
  To whom has the Arm of YHWH been revealed?
²Yes, he rose up as a nursing babe before him,
  like a root from the parched ground.
He had no beautiful form nor honour,
  that we should look at him;
And no appearance,
  that we should desire him.

Though closely related to the previous stanza, 53:1ff should be treated as a separate stanza (an argument could be made for the next break at verse 4,

11c, or 54:1).[53] For one, the situation envisaged in 53:1 is the opposite of that in 52:15: the servant's priestly work (נזה; *n-z-h*) and ministry received a positive response in 52:15, but in 53:1 the situation is dire. Few believe what they have heard, for few have received a revelation of the Arm.[54] A strong contextual case is made by many commentators for the objective suffix in verse 1, "what we have heard,"[55] but the use of the subjective suffix cannot be ruled out, which would make this the word of the believing community. ("our report"). The line articulates a lament over unbelief, consistent with either reading. However, we will not linger on this point, for either interpretation is compatible with the following argument.

This shift in situation between 52:15 and 53:1 mirrors a shift in the perspective of the speaker. No longer is Yahweh speaking about and to his servant (52:13, עַבְדִּי; *'abdi*, "my servant"; 52:14, עָלֶיךָ; *'aleka*, "upon you"). Now, there is a corporate outcry (v. 1) and the servant is referred to in the 3rd person (53:1, זְרוֹעַ יהוה; *zeroa' YHWH*, "the arm of YHWH"; 53:2, וַיַּעַל; *vayya'al*, "... he grew up"). The use of a *vayyiqtol* verb in verse 2 closely ties the situation described in verses 2-3 with that described in verse 1; this close connection suggests that the subject of וַיַּעַל is the Arm of the Lord as personified in 53:1.[56] Given the broader context, this figure is to be equated with the servant of Yahweh. Now, the phrase זְרוֹעַ יהוה (*zeroa' YHWH*) is not simple, yet Alec Motyer has persuasively argued that "The 'arm of Yahweh'... is no mere metaphor or literary flourish; it is Yahweh's alter ego."[57]

---

[53] Cf. Peter Wilcox and David Paton-Williams, "The Servant Songs in Deutero-Isaiah," *Journal for the Study of the Old Testament* 13, no. 42 (October 1988): 95. As I will use the term, a stanza refers to the next level of textual cohesion above that of the colon: a colon is constituted by lines; a stanza is constituted by one or more cola.

[54] Motyer, *The Prophecy of Isaiah*, 426–427; Edward J. Young, *The Book of Isaiah*, vol. 1 (Grand Rapids: Eerdmans, 1965), s.v. 53:1.

[55] John Goldingay, *A Critical and Exegetical Commentary on Isaiah 56 - 66*, The International Critical Commentary on the Holy Scriptures of the Old and New Testaments (London: Bloomsbury, 2014), 297; John Oswalt, *The Book of Isaiah. Chapters 40-66*, NICOT (Grand Rapids, MI: Eerdmans, 1998), 381.

[56] Motyer, *The Prophecy of Isaiah*, 426–428; Goldingay, *A Critical and Exegetical Commentary on Isaiah 56 - 66*, 298.

[57] J. Alec Motyer, "Stricken for the Trangression of My People," in *From Heaven He Came and Sought Her*, ed. David Gibson and Jonathan Gibson (Wheaton: Crossway

Goldingay writes, "YHWH's arm is virtually hypostatized and is the subject of a verb…. The revelation is indeed a revelation of Yhwh, but it is a revelation of a part of Yhwh in some sense representing Yhwh and distinguishable from Yhwh."[58] Outside of 53:1 and 51:9-10, this or a comparable phrase refers to "the way the Lord himself acts in power (cf. 51:5)," "God's strength in action."[59] This parallels the use of the term throughout the Old Testament, where "arm" is a frequent metonym for God's power (e.g. Exod 15:16; Ps 89:14) and God's salvific acts are described as God acting "with an outstretched arm" (בִּזְרֹעַ נְטוּיָה; *bizroa' netuyah*, Exod 6:6; Deut 4:34; 5:15; Jer 32:21). In each case, God's arm is a metonym for his power and often is used in contexts where God acts mightily on behalf of his people. Isaiah 51:9-10, where the same phrase as 53:1 appears, "the arm" is personified. Similarly, God's "arm" is personified in 40:10. Without exception, in the nine places where the phrase בִּזְרֹעַ נְטוּיָה, "with an outstretched arm" (once, וְהַזְּרֹעַ הַנְּטוּיָה; *vehazzeroa' hannetuyah*), occurs, God has or promises to personally act in a miraculous manner to save his people. Seven times, it refers explicitly to the Exodus (Exod 6:6; Deut 4:34; 5:15; 7:19; 26:8; 2 Kgs 17:36; Ps 136:12); twice, it refers to God's future deliverance of his people (Ezek 20:33, 34). It is no surprise, therefore, that 51:9 reflects on the Exodus as the action of the Arm "in days of old" (vv. 9-10). The shout in verse 9, "awake, awake, put on strength, O arm of the Lord" (ESV), is thus a call for Yahweh himself to intercede and act as he has in the past. Thus, "the arm" refers to God via his power, as Motyer puts it, his "alter ego."

Therefore, when we get to 53:1, we have two options before us for interpreting זְרֹעַ יהוה (*zeroa' YHWH*); either God's power or the personified Arm. In favour of the latter option, the only other occurrence of this phrase is in 51:9, where the Arm is personified. In addition, the close connection between verses 53:1 and 2 suggests that we should find the subject for the verb in verse 2 in verse 1, for which "the Arm" is the only possible candidate.[60] (For what it's worth, I have argued elsewhere that the use of this

---

Books, 2013), 251.

[58] Goldingay, *A Critical and Exegetical Commentary on Isaiah 56 - 66*, 298.

[59] Motyer, "Stricken," 251.

[60] So Goldingay, *A Critical and Exegetical Commentary on Isaiah 56 - 66*, 298.

verse in John 12:38 identifies "the arm of the Lord" with Jesus.)[61] So, minimally, there is a strong contextual case for identifying God's servant with Yahweh himself, his personified strength.[62] However, as in 8:16-17, though identified with Yahweh, the servant is nevertheless distinguished from him: in verse 2, "before him" (לְפָנָיו; *lephanayv*) is usually interpreted as a reference to God, which makes great sense; additionally, in verse 4, he is said "to be struck by God" (מֻכֵּה אֱלֹהִים; *mukkeh 'elohim*) (cf. 53:10).

E. Isaiah 61:1-8

Isaiah 56-66, or a comparable division, is commonly recognized as a literary whole in the contemporary discussion of Isaiah. The flow of thought, especially as we approach Isaiah 61, is not always easy to follow, almost like a "stream of consciousness," so closely following the syntax and flow as we have in Isaiah 8 – 9 and 53:1-2 is not as easy here.[63] However, I nevertheless want to argue that it is plausible to identify the figure speaking in Isaiah 61:1-3 with Yahweh, again in a way that is simultaneously distinguished from Yahweh.

Alec Motyer begins a similar argument at 59:21, where God turns from his "covenant with them" (בְּרִיתִי אוֹתָם; *beriti 'otam*, "my covenant with them") to "you" (עָלֶיךָ; *'aleka;* "upon you"). A similar turn to an individual occurs throughout the Servant songs in 40-55 (42:6, 49:8, 54:10, 55:3). There is also a parallel between 59:21 and 8:17-18, where Yahweh speaks of his children (יְלָדִים; *yeladim*), which has significant semantic overlap with זֶרַע (*zera';* "offspring"). Motyer argues that we find a comparable figure to the Servant and the Davidic king introduced here.[64] Others who see a specific eschatological agent in Isaiah 61:1ff highlight the thematic parallels between this figure, the Davidic king, and the Servant, such as the language of

---

[61] Rutherford, *Prevenient Grace*, 27–30.

[62] In support of this conclusion, Dekker argues that the Servant is later granted the divine glory. Jaap Dekker, "The High and Lofty One Dwelling in the Heights and with His Servants: Intertextual Connections of Theological Significance between Isaiah 6, 53 and 57," *Journal for the Study of the Old Testament* 41, no. 4 (2017): 475–491.

[63] Cf. Goldingay, *A Critical and Exegetical Commentary on Isaiah 56 - 66*, 289.

[64] Motyer, *The Prophecy of Isaiah*, 493.

"anointing" and the explicit presence of the Spirit, along with kingly themes.[65] Drawing on the argument of W. W. Cannon and others, Richard Schultz suggests that Isaiah 61 may actually be another servant song, such that the figure is identical with the suffering servant and, therefore, the Davidic king.[66] Several authors argue that there is an eschatological figure here, but that he is distinct from the previous two.[67] Given the parallels with the preceding eschatological figures, the extraordinary presence of the Spirit, and the way the figure in 61:1-3 fulfils the surrounding eschatological expectations, there seems to be sufficient reason to identify this figure as an eschatological agent.[68] The evidence that this passages is a call of the prophet, of Isaiah, is wanting.[69] Goldingay claims that the presence of 1st person discourse in prophetic texts is indicative of either the prophet or Yahweh; however, at least in Isaiah, an eschatological figure or another figure distinguished from the prophet and Yahweh begins to speak (e.g. 8:17-18; throughout the so-called servant songs), so this cannot be a hard or fast rule.[70] If this is an eschatological figure, the next question is, where does his speech stop?

Goldingay defends the traditional MT division between verses 9 and 10, identifying 61:1-9 as a single unit.[71] For our purposes, it does not matter if this unit goes further, only that it is not closed off earlier. There is no clear indication that it should be. 6:1-3 are a syntactical unit, so the first candidate for an earlier break would be between verses 3 and 4. However, verse 4 is

---

[65] E.g. Goldingay, *A Critical and Exegetical Commentary on Isaiah 56 - 66*, 291. Cf. Randall Heskett, *Messianism within the Scriptural Scroll of Isaiah*, Library of Hebrew Bible / Old Testament Studies 456 (New York: T & T Clark, 2007), 252–263; Oswalt, *The Book of Isaiah. Chapters 40-66*, 562–563.

[66] Richard Schultz, "The King in the Book of Isaiah," in *The Lord's Anointed: Interpretation of Old Testament Messianic Texts*, ed. P. E. Satterthwaite, Richard S. Hess, and Gordon J. Wenham, Tyndale House studies (Carlisle: Paternoster Press, 1995), 160. W. W. Cannon, "Isaiah 61 1—3 an Ebed-Jahweb Poem.," *Zeitschrift für die Alttestamentliche Wissenschaft* 47, no. 1 (1929): 284–288.

[67] E.g. Abernethy, *The Book*, chap. 4.

[68] Cf. Heskett, *Messianism within the Scriptural Scroll of Isaiah*, 252–264; Abernethy, *The Book*, chap. 4.

[69] Contra Goldingay, *A Critical and Exegetical Commentary on Isaiah 56 - 66*, 290.

[70] Ibid., 295.

[71] Ibid., 289. Cf. Motyer, *The Prophecy of Isaiah*, 499–504.

connected to the preceding speech both by the initial verb with *vav* and the implied subject וּבָנוּ ("and they will build"), namely, those described in verse 3. The same can be said of verses 5-7, where the same speaker describes the same subjects. Verse 8 is logically connected to what precedes it, giving the reason why Yahweh will accomplish this.[72] So, given the flow of the passage, the "I" of 61:8 is naturally taken to be the "I" of 61:1.

We have already seen instances where Yahweh can be distinguished from himself, so it should not be difficult to accept that this figure may be anointed by Yahweh while being Yahweh himself. The other two instances were in passages concerning the Davidic king and the Suffering Servant; taken with the similar themes surrounding all three figures, it is plausible that the book of Isaiah identifies these figures with one another and, as a single eschatological figure, with Yahweh himself. Goldingay argues that despite the continuity expressed by the syntax, Yahweh who has begun speaking in v. 8 is to be distinguished from the preceding figure.[73] However, there is no contextual reason to demarcate the two. Therefore, Isaiah 61:1-8 appears to distinguish Yahweh from himself, as in 8:16-18, 53:1-2, and in several appearances of the Angel of YHWH.

F. Conclusion

Before we turn to the New Testament, there is one more set of Old Testament passages that we must consider that portray Yahweh as one and many. Now, as we read of our God acting in distinction from himself, it is not always clear that we can demarcate every instance of his acting with one person of the Trinity. In some cases, it appears that "Yahweh" could be any person or all three. This fits remarkably well with our exposition of the Shema, where God's unity is a *personal* unity such that all the actions of the persons can be attributed to God as one and that God as one is presented as a person like the Father, Son, and Spirit. This view is neither unprecedented nor pervasive in Church history, as we will consider in Part 4.

---

[72] Goldingay, *A Critical and Exegetical Commentary on Isaiah 56 - 66*, 289.

[73] Ibid.

9

GOD THE SPIRIT IS YAHWEH

Daniel I. Block claims that "Few branches of theology suffer from neglect of the OT like the doctrine of the Spirit."[1] Though only a few occurrences of the phrase "the Holy Spirit" (רוּחַ קֹדֶשׁ; *ruach qodesh*) occur, the figure of the "Spirit of YHWH" (רוּחַ יהוה; *ruach YHWH*) or "Spirit of God" (רוּחַ אֱלֹהִים; *ruach 'elohim*) is prevalent in the Old Testament (45 instances of either phrase). References to this Spirit beyond these phrases are replete. Like the similar phrase, מַלְאַךְ יהוה (*mal'ak YHWH*; "the Angel of YHWH"), these phrases could be appositional, "The Spirit who is YHWH," or as a genitive, probably "YHWH's Spirit." The difference between these two renderings may only be slight, for when related to a person, רוּחַ (*ruach*) may refer to someone's breath, often with connotations of life; it may also refer to the whole person as alive or specifically to their life (along with other possible connotations). Unlike רוּחַ as it is used of human persons, when used in relation to Yahweh, the רוּחַ seems to be an acting subject. So, like the מַלְאַךְ יהוה, the רוּחַ יהוה is closely identified with Yahweh and yet distinguished from him.

We will consider several key instances where the Spirit seems to be treated as a distinct individual or person. In these passages, he appears to be

---

[1] Daniel I Block, "The View from the Top: The Holy Spirit in the Prophets," in *Presence, Power and Promise: The Role of the Spirit of God in the Old Testament* (Downers Grove, 2011), 175.

111

distinguished from while identified with Yahweh, as we witnessed with the Angel and the Servant.

A. Genesis 1:2

וְהָאָרֶץ הָיְתָה תֹהוּ וָבֹהוּ וְחֹשֶׁךְ עַל־פְּנֵי תְהוֹם וְרוּחַ אֱלֹהִים מְרַחֶפֶת עַל־
פְּנֵי הַמָּיִם

Now, the earth was formless and void, darkness was over the face of the deep, and the Spirit of God was hovering over the face of the waters. – Genesis 1:2

We first encounter the Spirit of God in the very beginning, at the moment of creation. It is possible that the רוּחַ אֱלֹהִים (*ruach 'elohim*) is not "the Spirit of God," as the phrase is regularly used; instead, it could mean a "mighty wind," with אֱלֹהִים (*'elohim*) indicating the superlative. Bediako makes the argument proficiently.[2] רוּחַ (*ruach*) clearly means "breath" or "wind" regularly. Though it is never used this way with אֱלֹהִים, the related phrase רוּחַ יהוה (*ruach YHWH*) is used for "the wind/breath of YHWH" (Isa 40:7; Hos 13:15). However, given the predominant use of these phrases for Yahweh the Spirit (or YHWH's Spirit), an alternate interpretation for both passages, as well as Genesis 1:2, presents itself. Instead of merely speaking of a wind from Yahweh, indicating his sovereign control over the creation, both of these passages may speak of God's Spirit. Though in Isaiah 40:7 the withering of the grass is accomplished by the wind, the prophet's point with the use of the phrase רוּחַ יהוה (with its common use for God himself present or acting) may be that God is intimately involved in even such apparently natural phenomenon. The focus is, of course, on the fleeting nature of human life like that of grass, but God's intimate involvement in both passages appears to be stressed. This is also the case in Hosea. Perhaps it is no coincidence that Isaiah 40:7 uses this illustration in contrast with the enduring word of God: as in creation the רוּחַ is accompanied by God's speaking activities. The point is, Isaiah 40:7 and Hosea 13:15 may be speaking of the Spirit of God

---

[2] Daniel Kwame Bediako, "A Note on Rûaḥ 'Spirit/Wind' in Genesis 1:2," *Valley View University Journal of Theology* 4 (2017): 78–84.

as is regularly the case with this phrase.

Returning to Genesis 1:2, Bediako's most persuasive evidence is the parallelism between חֹשֶׁךְ (*choshek;* "darkness"), תְהוֹם (*tehom; "the deep"*), מַיִם (*mayyim;* "water"), and רוּחַ as natural phenomenon not accounted for in the six days of creation. However, the parallelism breaks down on examination. First, he argues that "Clauses 2 and 3 are parallel ... which further describe the condition of the earth [given in Clause 1]."[3] However, this is not clear; instead, all three clauses seem to be parallel, for the deep, waters, and "formless and void" are all parallel descriptions of the same thing, the earth. Instead of giving the "component parts" of the earth, this verse sets the scene for the acts of creation delineated in the six days.[4] The darkness and the water are parallel as that which will be shaped in opposition to something God creates, the light and land respectively. Whereas both are featured throughout the six days, the רוּחַ does not. Nor is the רוּחַ opposed to anything in the creation account. Furthermore, the creation of the wind hardly needs to be accounted for, for like waves it merely describes an aspect of something explicitly created, in this case, the heavens beneath the expanse. Thus, I think this is indeed the "Spirit of God" here in Genesis 1.

In the context of the creation where God "speaks" creation into being, it is fitting for his "breath" to be attending over the creation. The word "hovering" only occurs twice in the Piel stem, here and Deuteronomy 32:11. In Deuteronomy, the word is used for an eagle's care of their young, "hovering" over them, attending to them. For now, what we see is that the Spirit acts; the word "hover" is not the regular word for the movement of the wind. Moreover, the Spirit's action is presented within God's creative act but alongside his speaking, which appears to differentiate the Spirit of God from God.

B. The Spirit Upon God's People

In the Old Testament, the Spirit of God repeatedly descends upon specific people, empowering them for a wide variety of tasks. The Spirit is frequently

---

[3] Ibid. 83.

[4] Ibid.

said to "come upon" or "rush upon" certain persons, giving them the ability to fulfill God's purposes. In Exodus 31:3, Yahweh tells Moses that he has filled Bezalel with "the Spirit of God," differentiating himself from the Spirit (cf. Num 24:2, Jdgs 3:10; 6:34; 11:29; 13:25; 14:6; Isa 44:3; Ezek 37:14; 39:29). In none of these instances is it clear that the Spirit is Yahweh, though this empowering work is not incompatible with the personal action of the Spirit who is Yahweh. Whether the Spirit is God or is the instrument of God, this empowering work is God's work.

C. The Spirit and Other Spirits

However, there are several texts where the Spirit is juxtaposed with other spirits that the Bible regards as personal beings, supporting the broader reading of the Spirit of God as a personal agent who is Yahweh. Specifically, in 1 Samuel 16:14 we are told, "Now, the Spirit of the Lord departed from Saul, and a harmful spirit from the Lord tormented him" (ESV; cf 18:10). In 1 Samuel 18:10, the "harmful spirit from God" (רוּחַ אֱלֹהִים רָעָה; *ruach 'elohim ra'ah*) is the same construction as "the Spirit of the Lord" in 16:14 but modified with the indefinite רָעָה (*ra'ah*; calamitous/harmful). That both verses juxtapose the work of a spiritual being with the Spirit of the Lord suggests that the Lord's Spirit is also personal.

D. Other Instances where the Spirit Acts or Is Acted Upon

וְהֵמָּה מָרוּ וְעִצְּבוּ אֶת־רוּחַ קָדְשׁוֹ וַיֵּהָפֵךְ לָהֶם לְאוֹיֵב הוּא נִלְחַם־בָּם וַיִּזְכֹּר יְמֵי־
עוֹלָם מֹשֶׁה עַמּוֹ אַיֵּה הַמַּעֲלֵם מִיָּם אֵת רֹעֵי צֹאנוֹ אַיֵּה הַשָּׂם בְּקִרְבּוֹ אֶת־רוּחַ
קָדְשׁוֹ

[10]They rebelled,
 they grieved his Holy Spirit,
And he became their enemy;
 he made war against them.
[11]And he remembered the ancient days,
 of Moses and his people.
Where is he who bought them up from the sea,
 with the shepherds of his sheep?

Where is he who set in their midst
his Holy Spirit? – Isaiah 63:10-11

Elsewhere, the Spirit is said to speak through a person, for example, through David in 2 Samuel 23:2. Though, on occasion, inanimate, non-personal things are said to speak (e.g. Num. 22:28; Hab 2:11; Luke 19:40), these are clearly exceptions (the first results from supernatural intervention, the second and third [?] are non-literal) to the general rule that *persons* speak (God, humans, spiritual beings); thus, we can safely say that metaphors and supernatural intervention otherwise, speaking is a personal action. Therefore, the frequent statement that the Spirit speaks—even if a human person is the agent of communication—suggests that the Spirit is a person. 2 Samuel 23:3 suggests that the Spirit's speaking through David in 23:1 is God's speech, identifying the Spirit with God. More importantly for our purposes, on several occasions, the Spirit is equated with Yahweh's presence (e.g. Hag 2:5; Isaiah 42:1, 44:3; Psalm 139:7; 143:10).[5] In Isaiah 63:11, the Spirit represents God's presence among the Israelites; verse 10 tells us that they grieved the Spirit through their actions, so Yahweh became their enemy. The word "grieved" (עָצַב; *'itstseb*) is regularly used of persons (1 Kgs 1:6; 1 Sam 20:34; 2 Sam 19:3). Only once is the verb used with רוּחַ meaning "grieved in spirit" (Isa 54:6), where "spirit" appears to refer to some aspect of the human constitution (a well-attested use of רוּחַ). The uncommon use of the phrase "Holy Spirit" may be interpreted as "the spirit of his holiness," along the lines of the use of spirit for an aspect of the human constitution, yet the use of the phrase in 63:11 does not yield such an interpretation readily. As in Psalm 51:11, the "Holy Spirit" refers to God's presence with his people. Interpreted this way, "grieving the Holy Spirit" seems more like the use of the word "grieve" with persons rather than a person's spirit.

Thus, in these and other passages, the Spirit's presence is the presence of Yahweh or is interchangeable with Yahweh.[6] The "Spirit of Yahweh" thus

---

[5] On the Spirit and God's presence, see Meredith G Kline, *Images of the Spirit* (Eugene, OR: Wipf and Stock, 1999). However Kline envisaged the relationship of the Glory-cloud to the Trinitarian Holy Spirit, he does make the connection between various instantiations of the Holy Spirit and the fiery presence of God in the tabernacle.

[6] On Isa 40:13 and 63:7-14, see Block, "The View from the Top," 180–181.

seems to be equated with Yahweh himself and seen to be an acting agent, able to speak through, speak to, be grieved (Isa 63:10), and fill God's people. The most significant instance of the Spirit acting is Ezekiel 11:5.

E. Ezekiel 8:1-4 and Ezekiel 11:1-5

In Ezekiel 11:1-5, I will argue that the "the Spirit" (רוּחַ; *ruach*) first brings Ezekiel to the temple, then *speaks* with him (v. 2). In verse 5, the Spirit "falls" on Ezekiel and then speaks with him again. This text is significant, for throughout the Ezekiel, the Spirit acts alongside the "the glory of YHWH," or Yahweh on his throne. For instance, after describing the one seated on the throne (Ezek 1:26-28), Ezekiel identifies this one as the "likeness of the glory of YHWH" (דְּמוּת כְּבוֹד־יְהֹוָה; *demut kebod-YHWH*) (v. 28). Ezekiel falls on his face and hears "a voice speaking" (קוֹל מְדַבֵּר; *qol medabber*). The one speaking identifies himself as Yahweh (cf. 2:3-3:11; 5:17). After commanding Ezekiel to get up, the Spirit picks Ezekiel up (Ezek 2:2). When the glory of the Lord appears again and stands before Ezekiel (3:22-23), Ezekiel falls on his face and the Spirit again lifts him up (v. 24). In 8:1-3, a Form appears, the manifestation of God's control over Ezekiel (v. 1); his description is that of the "likeness of the glory of God" in 1:26-28, though Ezekiel does not identify him as such. Indeed, in 8:4, Ezekiel once again beholds the glory theophany; if the "Form" is the "he" speaking throughout the vision, the form is differentiated from the glory theophany. This "Form" grabs Ezekiel and "the Spirit lifted me up between earth and heaven and brought me in visions of God to Jerusalem" (ESV, 8:3). If this figure is to be identified with the theophany of Yahweh who speaks to Ezekiel throughout the book, then he is differentiated from the Spirit, which would contribute to our argument. However, because the action of grabbing seems to anticipate the action of movement performed by the Spirit, and because Ezekiel does not explicitly associate this figure with the glory of Yahweh (cf. 1:28; 3:12, 23; 10:4; 43:5), another reading presents itself (contrast the Spirit lifting Ezekiel in 3:12; 11:1, 24; 43:5). The syntactical flow of 8:3 suggests that this Form is the same as the Spirit who moves Ezekiel. As the Form speaks to Ezekiel, he identifies himself as the object of Israel's sinful behaviour and speaks of his own wrath against them (8:17-18). Given the close association of the Spirit with Yahweh, it would not be surprising that the Spirit manifest in the likeness of man has an appearance similar to "the likeness of the glory of YHWH" (cf. 1:28).[7] This figure is further differentiated from the glory theophany in 9:3, when Ezekiel speaks of "glory of the God of Israel" (the figure from 1:27) rising from among the cherubim. Later, the "Form" of chapter 8 disappears from sight, but in 11:1, we read that the Spirit continues to move Ezekiel, and the speaker referred to with the 3rd masculine singular verb resumes speaking in 11:2.

To the identification of the "Form" with the Spirit it may be objected that the first two verbs in 8:3 are masculine singular, where the third, with the "Spirit" as the subject, is feminine. In response, this shift does not make this interpretation impossible. First, grammatical gender pertains to words and not referents, that is, a male figure could be, for textual reasons, referred to with a feminine verbal form. In this case, the figure in verse 2 is identified with the masculine pronouns, suitable for his human-like appearance, but if "Spirit" (רוּחַ; *ruach*) is then used to refer to the same figure, the gender of the verb changes not because a new referent is in view but because a new way of speaking about the same figure emerges (cf. Jonah 2:1-2). רוּחַ is itself either feminine or masculine and my survey of the use of different verbal and nominal genders with this noun demonstrates no discernible pattern. In at least two instances, masculine and feminine forms are interchanged (1 Sam 16:14-16; Prov 18:14). Moreover, Ezekiel has already demonstrated a tendency to alternate gender without apparent significance. In Chapter 1:8-11, for example, feminine and masculine grammatical forms are used interchangeably with no clear difference in referent or sense. Thus, the shift in gender found in 8:1-3 does not prevent us from interpreting the Spirit here portrayed as a divine, theophanic figure. Nevertheless, the Spirit is distinguished from the "the glory of the God of Israel" in 8:4, as he was in previous appearances. After the Spirit brings Ezekiel to the temple, "the glory of the God of Israel" (כְּבוֹד אֱלֹהֵי יִשְׂרָאֵל; *kebod 'elohe yisr'ael*) was there already (8:4). In 8:4, this "glory" is equated with the theophanic figure Ezekiel saw in Chapter 3:22-27, which itself referred back to the vision in 1:4-28. In verse 5, the "Form" of 8:2 speaks to Ezekiel. So, minimally, the "Spirit" as he moves

---

[7] De Vries sees the figure as "inseparably linked with the Spirit" and identifies him with the theophanic figure described earlier. Pieter de Vries, *The Kābôd of YHWH in the Old Testament: With Particular Reference to the Book of Ezekiel*, Studia Semitica Neerlandica volume 65 (Leiden: Brill, 2016), 268–269.

Ezekiel around and fills him is distinguished from the theophanic Yahweh who was first seen on the throne (1:26-28); the Spirit is also potentially identified with the "Form," whose appearance is like Yahweh enthroned upon the cherubim.

Before turning to Ezekiel 11, it is important to observe that up to this point, and until Chapter 11, the speaker or source of the divine words Ezekiel receives is indicated everywhere but in 8:4-5. In addition to the times when the "likeness of the glory of YHWH" is the speaker (2:1, 3:24, 9:1), 3:22 implies that Yahweh whose hand is heavy upon Ezekiel is speaking. This is apparent when Yahweh appears to Ezekiel in 3:24 as the glory theophany. The most ambiguous speech introductions of Ezekiel's first part are found in 3:16, 6:1, and 11:14, for no speaker is indicated.[8] However, these three passages share a form distinct from all the other speech introductions: we are told that the "word of YHWH came" (דְּבַר־יְהנָה וַיְהִי; *debar-YHWH vayhi*) "saying" (לֵאמֹר; *le'mor*). The means by which the word came is not made explicit, yet it is clear that Yahweh speaks in these instances. In 8:5, the speaker is the Form of 8:2, for 8:4 (where the Glory of Yahweh is introduced) stands outside of the mainline narrative indicated by the *vayyiqtol* forms; these verbs in the mainline narrative refer to the form in 8:1-3, except perhaps the use of the feminine in verse 3 (discussed above). Following the mainline narrative, the speaker is clearly introduced at the beginning of his actions in 8:1-3. For these reasons, when we get to Chapter 11, where Ezekiel will again get a divine word, we expect that the speaker will be indicated.

By the end of Chapter 10, we are told that Yahweh is again (as in chapter 1) standing enthroned among the Cherubim and that the cherubim are standing at the east gate of the temple (10:19). Pieter DeVries argues that Ezekiel's movement to the East Gate is a "flashback" or vision taking place before the appearance of God's glory at the East Gate recounted in Chapter 10; if this is accurate, our interpretation below would receive further support, namely, that Yahweh does not speak to Ezekiel from his throne in the following verses.[9] Returning to Chapters 10-11, the Spirit then takes Ezekiel to this East Gate (11:1). After seeing some men, "princes of the people"

---

[8] De Vries identifies this as a marker of key section breaks. Ibid., 234.

[9] Ibid., 280.

(ESV, v. 1), someone starts speaking to Ezekiel (11:2).

This speech introduction, a *vayyiqtol* form, would naturally pick up the subject of the last mainline narrative action (the notice of the men who were seen being a parenthesis introduced by וְהִנֵּה [*vehinneh*, "and behold"], v.1). The one performing this previous action is the רוּחַ (*ruach*, "the Spirit"). As was observed above, it is possible for רוּחַ to be grammatically masculine or feminine, and there are several instances (perhaps Ezekiel 8) where this interchange happens within the same verse or textual unit. Robson asserts that this does not happen, but I have adduced two instances and argued for a third where it does (1 Sam 16:14-16; Prov 18:14; perhaps Ezek 8:1-4; cf. Jonah 2:1-2, Ezek 1:8-11).[10] Given the pattern of speech introduction earlier in Ezekiel, the Spirit is presented as the speaker at this point. This is strengthened by verse 5.

In previous mentions of the Spirit, he has always acted to do something relevant to the context: he has moved or picked up the prophet Ezekiel. In Ezekiel 11:5, the Spirit of Yahweh "fell" (נָפַל; *naphal*) on Ezekiel. This is the only instance of this collocation in the Old Testament. We would expect that the Spirit falling would precede or be accompanied by some action, either by the Spirit or by Ezekiel as empowered by the Spirit. What we find is that the Spirit falls, then "he speaks." Given the previous pattern of speech introduction, where the speaker is indicated and is often the subject of the previous mainline action, the Spirit would be the speaker here.[11] Now, we were told in Chapter 10 that the glory-theophany was located at the East Gate, but we are not given any indication here in Chapter 11 that God enthroned on the Cherubim is now speaking. As noted above, de Vries argues that God's theophanic throne is at the Gate *after* the events recounted here in Chapter 11. Even if God is at the East Gate with Ezekiel, we have no indication that he is the one speaking here.

Thus, Ezekiel 11:1-5 is one of few instances in the Old Testament where

---

[10] James Robson, *Word and Spirit in Ezekiel*, Library of Hebrew Bible/Old Testament studies 447 (New York: T & T Clark, 2006), 121.

[11] Contra Pieter de Vries, "The Relationship between the Glory of YHWH and the Spirit of YHWH in the Book of Ezekiel Part One," *Journal of Biblical and Pneumatological Research* 5 (2013): 124–125.

the Spirit can be compelling argued to be the speaker, which fits with the rare use of "the Spirit fell." Understood in this way, we could posit that the Spirit falling is similar to previous verses where the "hand of YHWH" is said to be upon Ezekiel, indicating his power over and presence with Ezekiel (e.g. 1:3; 3:14, 22; 8:1). If we accept that the Spirit speaks here, referred to with the 3rd masculine verb, then our argument concerning Ezekiel 8 is strengthened, giving us a second instance where the Spirit speaks and is revealed in the terms used to describe Yahweh yet is distinguished from Yahweh. Unlike 3:22, where the phrase "the hand of YHWH" introduces the glory theophany of Yahweh as the speaker, in Ezekiel 11:1-5, the Spirit has already been acting and continues to do so, now speaking.[12] Therefore, within the book of Ezekiel, the Spirit is an acting, speaking subject who is equated with yet nevertheless differentiated from Yahweh, similar to the angel of Yahweh and the eschatological agent of Yahweh in Isaiah.

F. Conclusion

As we saw in the last two chapters, we once again find a personal figure who is Yahweh yet differentiated from Yahweh. In Chapter 7, we saw that the Angel of Yahweh is Yahweh but not exclusively. In Chapter 8, we saw that Isaiah's eschatological agent is God, identified as Yahweh, but may also trust in YHWH (Isa 8:16-18). Here, in Chapter 9, we saw that the Spirit is also differentiated from Yahweh and identified with him. If Yahweh who sends is the Father, as the New Testament attests, we then have three divine figures delineated in the Old Testament, each of whom is God and Yahweh. Furthermore, there are instances where Yahweh acts, yet he cannot be easily identified with any one of the Trinitarian persons, so we have suggested that Augustine and Van Til are right to assert that God's unity is a personal unity. We saw this in the Great Shema, where God's oneness is in analogy with the particular: he is one God, one being, a person. Therefore, the Shema provides a foundational Trinitarian Creed, our God(s) are one (God), which is consistent with the testimony of the rest of the Old Testament that three are God, that three are Yahweh, but also that Yahweh alone is God, the unique and unmatchable creator and sustainer of all things.

---

[12] Cf. Block, "The View from the Top," 181–183.

—PART 3—
GOD IN THE NEW TESTAMENT

10

A CANONICAL CHRISTOLOGY AND NEW TESTAMENT TRINITARIANISM

In the previous chapters, we considered the Old Testament doctrine of God within a Trinitarian theological framework. We saw pervasive evidence of Trinitarian theology in the Old Testament, namely, that God is simultaneously plural and one. We identified three figures differentiated from Yahweh yet simultaneously identified with him, surmising that the Angel and Isaiah's eschatological agent probably both refer to God the Son. Guided by the New Testament fulfilment of these passages, we find three divine figures who are united as Yahweh, the one true God. Significantly, the unity of God is not presented as a nature or universal. Indeed, the Bible recognises many beings as "god," though the use of this term by no means sets such beings on ontological parity with Yahweh. Yahweh is alone unique and unmatchable, creator and sustainer of all things. The unity of God is presented on analogy with the particular, not the universal: he is one God, one personal being, Yahweh. Yet Yahweh who is one is also Yahweh, our God(s). We of course find the clear statement of God's threeness in the New Testament, but we have found a foundation for it in the Old Testament. Thus, the Old Testament teaches the Trinity in terms of the foundational tension of personal plurality (many who are God) in personal unity (one God, Yahweh); the New Testament clearly delineates that God's plurality is three, not more or less.

As in the previous chapter, our exegetical approach could be broadly identified as "theological interpretation," a reading that is open about its confessional presuppositions, particularly as they concern the nature of Scripture.[1] That is, we will approach the Bible as a canonical whole, oriented towards the text as it is currently found in a whole-Bible context. Such an approach is closely related to yet nevertheless distinct from the dominant approaches to the question of Christ's divinity in the New Testament. For this reason, we will briefly survey several of these approaches before turning to the texts that we will investigate. Many of these approaches arrive at complementary conclusions as I have yet not necessarily in compatible ways.

A. Christologies of the Divine Identity

There have been many studies concerning Christ's divinity in the New Testament (or lack thereof) in recent years; I do not intend to offer a comprehensive survey of these developments. Instead, by drawing attention to three different methodological approaches, we can situate this Part within the broader literature. Of the approaches that could be highlighted, I have chosen to focus on those New Testament Christologies that could broadly be defined as Christologies of the divine identity and Daniel Kirk's study of the "exalted man" Christology, along with an Old Testament Christology. It will become apparent that among these studies there is a contrast between exegetically focused and historically focused approaches; this contrast will help situated my study on the former side of this divide (all the authors are concerned with exegesis, but certain studies ask what the Bible says and others what we can learn about history through what the Bible says).[2]

Through this survey, several features of this book will become clear. First, the approach in this book is not concerned with the development of Christology within the historical Church or across the New Testament but as is communicated by the New Testament texts interpreted within their canonical context; in this way, our approach is more like that of Nina Henrichs-Tarasenkova and the volume by Andrew Abernethy and Gregory Goswell than the studies of Richard Bauckham or Kirk. However, by looking

---

[1] Cf. Kevin J. Vanhoozer et al., eds., *Dictionary for Theological Interpretation of the Bible* (Baker Academic, 2005), 21.

[2] This corresponds to Sailhamer's "text-centred" and "event-centred" biblical theologies, respectively. Sailhamer, *Introduction to Old Testament Theology*.

at how Jesus is presented in relation to Yahweh, our approach closely approximates the "Christology of the Divine identity" developed by Bauckham and later authors.

a. Jesus and the God of Israel – Richard Bauckham

In the background of Bauckham's ground-breaking monograph *God Crucified* lies the 20th-century debate between "ontic" and "functional" Christologies. Last century, some biblical scholars argued (or were supposed to have argued) that the metaphysical approach to Christology expressed in Conciliar Christology and its adherents is incompatible with or at variance with the Hebraic, functional interpretation of Jesus. On this later view, for Jesus to be God would say nothing about his being—that he possessed a "divine nature"—but only that he functioned in a divine manner.[3] Cullman, for example, argued that in the New Testament the question was never exclusively, "what is his nature?" but primarily "what is his function?"[4] The ontic question of natures was, argues Cullman, a Greek problem, not Jewish or biblical one.[5] The Bible identifies Jesus' uniqueness by titles, titles which indicate his function and work.[6] Cullman argues that the Bible only ever identifies Jesus as God in this functional way, as part of *Heilgeschichte* (Redemptive history), never in the manner of "later Greek speculations about substance and nature."[7] Put strongly, "The New Testament neither is able nor intends to give information about how we are to conceive the being of

---

[3] This was often argued, along with other aspects of the Biblical Theology Movement, with lexical arguments. The lexical arguments employed by proponents of the Biblical Theology Movement were thoroughly addressed by James Barr in his *Lexical Semantics* and *Biblical Words for Time*. James Barr, *The Semantics of Biblical Language* (Oxford: Oxford University Press, 1961); James Barr, *Biblical Words for Time* (London: SCM Press, 2005).

[4] Oscar Cullmann, *The Christology of the New Testament*, trans. Shirley C. Guthrie and Charles A. M. Hall, 2nd English Edition. (London: SCM Press LTD, 1963), 3–4.

[5] Ibid., 4.

[6] Ibid., 5.

[7] Ibid., 206. This seems to lead Cullman to a modalistic interpretation of the Father / Son distinction in John. Ibid., 309–311.

God beyond the history of revelation,"[8] and "in light of the New Testament witness, all mere speculation about his natures is an absurdity. Function Christology is the only kind which exists."[9]

This is the general stance found among proponents of a functional ontology, however in the case of Cullman's book in its 2nd edition, his concluding comments may suggest that he intends only to outline what can be said about *New Testament* Christology, that is, as a responsible exegete and not a dogmatician.[10] Even if the language of the New Testament were purely *functional*, this would not preclude the questions of ontology raised by the Fathers. For example, if Christ spoke with the authority of God, it must be asked *what* authorizes or makes legitimate that function (over against, say, me claiming to speak with God's authority). If Christ functions as God in healing sickness and knowing the inner thoughts of humans, it must be asked what enables him to do so over against the normal capacities of a human. Functions imply capacities, properties, and identity: functions have ontological implications—as has been recognised by the critics of functional Christology past and present. As D. A. Carson writes, "it is far from clear that absolute distinctions between what is 'functional' and what is 'ontological' can legitimately be made."[11] Furthermore, the method of argument adopted is highly problematic. It cannot be easily argued that language in its structure indicates a certain form of thought, as argued (though perhaps overstated) by James Barr,

> [The difference between Deuteronomy or Amos and Plato or Euripides] lies in the *content*, in the literary style, in the type of argument, in the things that they say: it cannot be tied to the language as such, as if no Hebrew speaker could think other than Amos and no Greek speaker other than Plato. The difference or similarity does not correlate exactly with the difference or similarity of their linguistic structures. It was quite possible to convey much of Hebrew thought

---

[8] Cullmann, *Christology*, 327.

[9] Ibid., 326.

[10] Ibid., 327-330.

[11] D. A. Carson, *Divine Sovereignty and Human Responsibility* (Eugene, OR: Wipf and Stock Publishers, 2002), 149. Cf. Bauckham, *Jesus and the God of Israel*, 30–31.

adequately—though with some stylistic loss—in Greek, as the Septuagint shows, and to convey some Greek thought adequately in Hebrew, as Maimonides later showed.[12]

The approach of the biblical theological movement and the resulting functional Christology reveals a significant methodological issue. We cannot assume that the presence of a certain sort of language implies a certain ontology, such that the use of φύσις (*phusis*; "nature") or μορφή (*morphe*; "form") in the Bible requires a certain ontology. Instead, as Barr and others have made clear, words avail themselves of many uses, so we must attend to the use of a word in its context to understand its meaning and, therefore, its implication.[13]

It was within the debate over the propriety of "ontic" questions and whether a "functional" interpretation might be better, or at least more "biblical," that Richard Bauckham released *God Crucified*. In this 1998 monograph and the expanded argument in *Jesus and the God of Israel* (2009), Bauckham argued that reading the New Testament in light of the monotheism characterizing 2nd Temple Judaism moves us beyond the ontic-functional debate in New Testament Christology.[14] Jesus is identified as God in the New Testament primarily by association with the unique identity-markers Jewish Monotheism attributed to God. [15] When we read the New

---

[12] James Barr, *The Concept of Biblical Theology: An Old Testament Perspective* (London: SCM Press, 1999), 165. However, for a mild corrective on Barr's structuralism see Nicholas J. Ellis, "Biblical Exegesis and Linguistics: A Prodigal History," in *Linguistics and New Testament Greek: Key Issues in the Current Debate*, ed. David Alan Black and Benjamin L Merkle (Grand Rapids: Baker Publishing Group, 2020). Cf. Vern S. Poythress, *In the Beginning Was the Word: Language: A God-Centered Approach* (Wheaton: Crossway Books, 2009).

[13] Cf. Barr, *The Semantics of Biblical Language*; Moisés Silva, *Biblical Words and Their Meaning: An Introduction to Lexical Semantics*, rev. and expanded ed. (Grand Rapids: Zondervan, 1994); Poythress, *In the Beginning Was the Word*; Ellis, "Biblical Exegesis and Linguistics: A Prodigal History."

[14] Bauckham, *Jesus and the God of Israel*, 30. Cf. the criticism of this thesis in, J. R. Daniel Kirk, *A Man Attested by God: The Human Jesus of the Synoptic Gospels* (Grand Rapids: Eerdmans, 2016), 17–21.

[15] Bauckham, *Jesus and the God of Israel*, 18. An outline of these identifiers can be found on pgs. 233-234.

Testament, we do not find a definition of the divine nature attributed to Jesus but that he is included in the overall characterization of the divine identity.

Read as an attempt at theology, giving a reasoned account of the Incarnation (the sort of approach characterizing the "ontic" Conciliar Christology), Bauckham's thesis fails to impress.[16] Furthermore, to say merely that the New Testament authors "included Jesus in the unique divine identity" does not tell us much about what it means for Jesus to be identified as God, how we reconcile the humanity of Christ with this deity, and how Jesus relates to God the Father if both are included in the divine identity. However, this is not what Bauckham appears to be attempting, and it is not where his thesis is most provocative. Instead, Bauckham argues that Jesus' deity is asserted throughout the entire New Testament and that the New Testament authors identify Jesus as God by attributing to him the unique identity markers Jewish monotheism associated with God. Within 2nd Temple Judaism, monotheism was consistent yet permitted diversity in the unity of God, a tension which Bauckham makes no attempt to resolve.

Bauckham's thesis contributes to our understanding of Christ's deity as is it is presented in the New Testament and it reasserts what dogmatic Christology has long recognized, that the functions Jesus performs cannot be separated from who and even what he is.[17] Bauckham's proposal has been criticized most heavily on his interpretation of 2nd temple Judaism vis-à-vis the "unique divine identity" and the way he applies this framework to the New Testament portrayal of Christ.[18] Similar but more extensive studies have been performed by Larry Hurtado.[19] Two more recent proposals along these

---

[16] One reviewer takes Bauckham to task for this very reason, however, Bauckham can hardly be faulted for failing a task he never attempted. Dale Truggy, "On Bauckham's Bargain," *Theology Today* 70, no. 2 (2013): 128–43.

[17] Bauckham, *Jesus and the God of Israel*, 30, 235.

[18] Crispin H. T. Fletcher-Louis, *Jesus Monotheism: Volume 1: Christological Origins: The Emerging Consensus and Beyond* (Eugene, Ore: Wipf & Stock, 2015), 101–127, 182–205; Kirk, *A Man Attested by God*, 17–21.

[19] Larry W. Hurtado, *One God, One Lord: Early Christian Devotion and Ancient Jewish Monotheism*, Third edition., Cornerstones Series (London: Bloomsbury T & T Clark, 2015); Larry W. Hurtado, *Lord Jesus Christ: Devotion to Jesus in Earliest Christianity* (Grand Rapids: Eerdmans, 2003); Larry W. Hurtado, "'Monotheism' in the New

lines will serve to situate our argument in line with the "divine identity" approach before contrasting it with Kirk's analysis of the Synoptics.

B. Jesus Monotheism – Crispin Fletcher-Louis[20]

Jesus Monotheism is the first volume in Fletcher-Louis four-volume series on "Christological Origins." He takes as his starting point the "emerging consensus" concerning an early divine Christology. His proposal in Jesus Monotheism concerns two thesis, 1) "that in Israel's Scriptures (and for first-century Judaism) the one God has already revealed himself to be an incarnational and scandalously humanity-focused God"; and 2)

> that, within the context of a fresh understanding of the shape of Jewish monotheism, a straightforward explanation of Christological origins is now available: the historical Jesus believed himself to be uniquely included—as one who served as Israel's royal and priestly Messiah and as a fully divine person—within the identity of the one god (as the 'Son' of the 'Father'). Jesus' own monotheism was this new, radically fashioned 'Jesus monotheism.'[21]

In this volume, Fletcher-Louis attempts to lay out the groundwork of contemporary scholarship in which his proposal for Christological origins would be presented in the latter three volumes of the series. As with Bauckham's work, Fletcher-Louis takes up a historical thesis and so focuses intently on Jewish precedence for "Jesus Monotheism"; it is at this point where the present study departs most significantly. We will not be asking "how did Jesus understand himself" or "how did those who witnessed his ministry and became part of the Church understand his identity?" Instead,

---

Testament," in *The Bible and Early Trinitarian Theology*, ed. Christopher A. Beeley, CUA studies in early Christianity (Washington, D.C: The Catholic University of America Press, 2018), 50–68; Richard B. Hays, *Reading Backwards: Figural Christology and the Fourfold Gospel Witness* (Waco, Texas: Baylor University Press, 2014). Cf. Simon J. Gathercole, *The Preexistent Son: Recovering the Christologies of Matthew, Mark, and Luke* (Grand Rapids: Eerdmans, 2006).

[20] Fletcher-Louis, *Jesus Monotheism*.

[21] Fletcher xiv. For the second thesis, cf. Sigurd Grindheim, *God's Equal: What Can We Know about Jesus' Self-Understanding?*, Library of New Testament studies 446 (London ; New York: T & T Clark, 2011).

we will ask what relationship the New and Old Testaments—treated as a singular, canonical text—portray between Jesus and Yahweh, the God of Israel.

c. Luke's Christology of Divine Identity – Nina Henrichs-Tarasenkova[22]

In her 2016 study, *Luke's Christology of Divine Identity*, Nina Henrichs-Tarasenkova developed the approach of a "divine identity" Christology in a lengthy study of Luke. Recognizing that the attribution of the predicate θεός (*Theos*; "God") would not have had a definite significance in the first century, Henrichs-Tarasenkova set out to consider how Luke's narrative portrayed Jesus as God even in the absence of the word θεός.[23] From her analysis of Gospel's narrative, she argues "that although Luke does not explicitly call Jesus θεός, he presents Jesus by means of indirect characterizations as the one God of Israel with YHWH and as such worthy of worship reserved for YHWH." [24] The significance of this study lies, perhaps, in its application of the concept of "divine identity" to the exegetical question of Luke's narrative portrayal of Christ, as opposed to the historical question of Christological origins explored by Bauckham and others. If her argument is accepted, it would suggest that, according to Luke, Jesus being God means that in some way, Jesus is Yahweh, the particular God of Israel.

B. Christ as the Idealized Human Figure[25]

In "divine identity" Christologies, a certain concept of God's unique identity is articulated and then Christ is shown to align with this conceptual paradigm. In contrast to this approach, Daniel Kirk draws together a portrait of "idealized human figures" in ancient Judaism and argues that, as far as the Synoptics are concerned, this paradigm is a better fit for their portrait of

---

[22] Nina Henrichs-Tarasenkova, *Luke's Christology of Divine Identity*, Library of New Testament Studies vol. 542 (New York: Bloomsbury, 2016).

[23] Ibid., 4–6.

[24] Ibid., 24.

[25] Kirk, *A Man Attested by God*.

Christ than that of the divine identity. Against Bauckham, Hurtado, and other proponents of an early, high Christology, Kirk argues that various statements in Jewish "biblical and post-biblical" literature are indications "that God can share such divine roles and instances in which we see human participation in the divine identity."[26] Kirk's methodology is similar to that of the "divine identity" Christologies, yet he comes to a contrary conclusion and does not attempt to draw any theory of Christological origins from his study.

C. An Old Testament Christology[27]

The contrast between Kirk and Bauckham sets the ground for a more recent Christological study, though this one from an Old Testament perspective. In *God's Messiah in the Old Testament*, Andrew Abernethy and Gregory Goswell trace the theme of the "messiah" (narrowly conceived of as a Davidic king) across the Old Testament.[28] They argue that the messiah in the Old Testament is portrayed in purely human terms and argue that many texts Christians have traditionally treated as "messianic" do not refer to a human, Davidic king (e.g. Isa 7:14, Zech 9:17).[29] Instead, many texts, like Zechariah 9:17 refer in their context to the exalted divine king, Yahweh himself. Thus, by applying such texts to Jesus in the New Testament, the biblical authors are not suggesting Jesus is the human messiah but that he is the fulfilment of the expectation for rule of Yahweh himself: "What are separate strands of hope in the Old Testament—the Messiah is coming and God is coming—are dramatically brought together in the New Testament in one person, the Lord Jesus Christ."[30]

Abernethy and Goswell, like Kirk, see the messianic figure as an exalted human; Christ is the fulfillment of this figure. However, along with Bauckham and others, they also recognize that Jesus is identified with

---

[26] Ibid., 2.

[27] Abernethy and Goswell, *God's Messiah*.

[28] Cf. James Rutherford, "Review of God's Messiah in the Old Testament," *Reformed Theological Review* 80, no. 3 (2021).

[29] On the human messiah of the Old Testament, see also Christopher Wright, *Knowing Jesus Through the Old Testament*. (Westmont: InterVarsity Press, 2014).

[30] Abernethy and Goswell, *God's Messiah*, 227.

Yahweh himself. As in our present study, *God's Messiah in the Old Testament* considers the canonical portrait of Jesus, though their emphasis is firmly on the Old Testament.

D. Summary: Historical Versus Canonical Frameworks

Adopting the theological framework we have from the start, our approach is rather different than these studies. We are presupposing the central claim of Christianity, affirmed at Nicaea and then Chalcedon, that Christ is "God," where this later term relates to the Bible's portrayal of Yahweh, the God of Israel. Furthermore, this chapter presupposes that this claim has precedence in the New Testament. However, even with these points conceded, the question is still open, what exactly does it mean for Christ to be God as the New Testament portrays this claim? Indeed, what is the concept of God that permits such a claim?

We will not try to prove that the New Testament teaches the Trinity, or whether or not it teaches that Jesus is God. Instead, reading the Bible within a Trinitarian frame of reference, we have already seen that the Old Testament at least teaches plurality and unity in God, if not Triune plurality. Coming to the New Testament, we have good reason to believe that the authors assume the Trinity; thus, we will not treat the Trinity as the product of second exegesis, later reflection and synthesis based on the biblical text. Assuming that the New Testament presupposes the Trinity (as opposed to containing the seeds of a later doctrine), we are going to ask, what is the Trinitarian teaching presupposed in the New Testament? That is, how does the New Testament understand God's plurality and unity? What are the conditions and understandings that allow the New Testament to include Jesus in the "divine identity," as Bauckham and others put it?

For many contemporary New Testament scholars, the framework brought to questions of Christ's divinity and the concept of God is that of history. Bauckham and others ask what concept of God 1st-century Jews held and how this affects our understanding of the biblical portrayal of Christ. "God" on such a view is defined within the "plausibility structures" or "social imaginary" of first-century Jews, that is, within the intuitive understanding of God and the world, with implicated expectations, that is generally shared by those in a specific culture and by which they interpret not only their experience but the plausibility and contours of the things and ideas they encounter.[31] This could be called a "descriptive" framework, for it seeks to describe how someone in the 1st century would perceive the biblical data and other such questions. However, a canonical reading is not so much concerned with the plausibility structures of the 1st-century world but with the plausibility structure of the implicit world of the Bible, with the ideological structure or social imaginary that is portrayed by the whole.

Thus, here in Part 3, we will ask what it means for Jesus, the Father, and the Spirit to be God and for God to be one in the New Testament. Because the New Testament focuses on Jesus, much of our discussion will concern the 2nd Person of the Trinity. In Chapter 11, we will look at Jesus as the fulfilment of Isaiah's divine eschatological agent, then we will turn to texts which seem to identify Jesus directly with Yahweh in Chapter 12. Next, in Chapter 13, we will consider three texts where Jesus is granted exalted, even divine status, alongside God. In Chapter 14, we will consider the Spirit in the New Testament, looking in particular at 2 Corinthians 3:17-18, where the Spirit is called Yahweh. We will conclude in Chapter 15 by considering the oneness of God in the New Testament.

---

[31] Charles Taylor, *Modern Social Imaginaries*, Public Planet Books (Durham: Duke University Press, 2004), chap. 2; Peter L Berger, *The Sacred Canopy: Elements of a Sociological Theory of Religion* (N.Y.: Doubleday, 1967), chaps. 1–2. cf. Polanyi, *The Tacit Dimension*; Carl R. Trueman, *The Rise and Triumph of the Modern Self: Cultural Amnesia, Expressive Individualism, and the Road to Sexual Revolution* (Wheaton: Crossway, 2020), chaps. 1–2; Rikk E. Watts, *Isaiah's New Exodus in Mark*, Biblical studies library (Grand Rapids: Baker Books, 2000), chap. 2.

11

JESUS, ISAIAH'S DIVINE ESCHATOLOGICAL AGENT

In Chapter 8, we argued that Isaiah presents three portraits of an eschatological agent who was identified with Yahweh. As we turn to the New Testament, each of these figures is identified with Jesus and, in several contexts, this identification depends on this eschatological figure's identity with Yahweh.

In his book *Isaiah's New Exodus in Mark*, Rikk E. Watts has argued that the narrative of Mark presents Jesus as the agent who brings about Isaiah's prophesied new exodus. In particular, Watts argues that Jesus is portrayed as the "Yahweh-Warrior" whom Isaiah prophesied would come and deliver his people (e.g. Isa 40:10-11; 51:9; 52:10). In light of imagery that intimated "a divine conflict" earlier in Mark (1:7, 10, 14ff), Watts argues that Jesus is portrayed by Mark as the prophesied divine warrior. For example, in the account of the strong man in Mark 3, Watts argues that an allusion to Yahweh's prophesied action explains many features of the passage. For example, "that Yahweh's warrior activity in Isaiah is so that Zion and 'all flesh' may know that 'I am Yahweh your Saviour' (Isa 49:23-26), is especially pertinent to the central issue here, namely coming to 'know' that Jesus' actions constitute Yahweh's salvation (Mark 1:14ff)."[1] That Jesus would be identified with Yahweh fits well with our analysis of Isaiah's eschatological

---

[1] Watts, *Isaiah's New Exodus in Mark*, 150, cf. ch. 6.

agent and finds confirmation in the other Gospels. By giving careful attention to Jesus's Nazareth sermon, where the Lord quotes Isaiah 61, and other Isaianic themes in Luke, David Seccombe has argued that the passion narrative in Luke is intended to equate Jesus with the suffering servant, whom we saw was (like the figure in Isaiah 61) identified with Yahweh. In this passion narrative, "What Luke gives his readers is not an abstract notion of the goodness of Jesus but an apologetic defence of his righteousness, designed to undergird his identity as the 'Just One.'"[2]

The Gospel of Matthew also draws on the account of the eschatological agent. Matthew notoriously declares the fulfilment of the promised Davidic descendent in Isaiah 7:14 as Jesus (Matt 1:18-25). Many of Matthews "fulfilments" are quite complicated, though others are not. The fulfilment of Isaiah 7:14 is often taken to be an example of a complicated use of the Old Testament; most New Testament commentators (following the Old Testament commentators) do not consider this prophecy to be about Jesus in the context of Isaiah. However, in Chapter 8, I argued that the context of this prophecy points to the miraculous birth of a divine king from the Davidic line, which obviously finds its fulfilment in Jesus. The following verses make this all the more clear, identifying the Immanuel as Yahweh (Isa 8:18) and the Mighty God (9:6). If the figure in Isaiah 7 is a future Davidide, then his continuity with the figure in Isaiah 8-11 is clear. Given that the latter figure is identified with Yahweh, the Immanuel sign is given greater significance; this child is literally "God with us." Matthew explicitly identifies this figure with Jesus, to which Luke also alludes (Luke 1:26-27; 34-38).

In Acts 8:35, Philip responds to the Ethiopian eunuch's question concerning Isaiah 53:7-8. He tells him "him the good news about Jesus," clearly identifying the suffering servant with Jesus. Isaiah 53 is frequently alluded to throughout the New Testament in the context of Jesus' ministry (e.g. Matt 8:14-17; Mark 9:12; John 12:38; Rom 10:16; 2 Cor 5:21; 1 Pet 2:18-25). The significance of this identification emerges when we remember that Isaiah 53:1 equates the Servant with Yahweh himself acting for the sake of his people. In each of these cases, whether an individual text or the trajectory

---

[2] David Seccombe, "Luke and Isaiah," in *The Right Doctrine from the Wrong Texts?: Essays on the Use of the Old Testament in the New*, ed. G. K. Beale (Grand Rapids: Baker Books, 1994), 256.

of an entire book, the Evangelists, Philip, and the Apostles identify Jesus as the fulfillment of Isaiah's eschatological agents as expounded in Isaiah 7, 53, and 61. This agent is identified with Yahweh, so to say that Jesus is this agent is to say that Jesus is, in some sense, Yahweh. Looking closely at Hebrews 2:13 will serve to strengthen this point.

A. Hebrews 2:13

καὶ πάλιν· ἐγὼ ἔσομαι πεποιθὼς ἐπ' αὐτῷ, καὶ πάλιν· ἰδοὺ ἐγὼ καὶ τὰ παιδία ἅ μοι ἔδωκεν ὁ θεός.

And again, "I will trust upon him"
And again, "Behold, I and the children whom God has given me." – Hebrews 2:13

Hebrews is a complex book, engaging extensively with the Old Testament to provide a compelling argument for the superiority of Christ. R.T. France describes it as "a pastoral exhortation, interspersed with earnest appeals to the recipients to stand firm in their faith."[3] "It seeks to strength [older and tired individuals] who were in danger of relinquishing their Christian commitment."[4] After describing Christ's exalted status (Heb 1:1-4), the unnamed author of Hebrews immediately begins to contrast the Son with "the angels" (1:5-14). Chapter 2, verses 1-4 are the first of a series of "warning passages" that occur throughout the book, hinting at the books purpose to warn against apostasy and exhort its hears to perseverance (the most controversial being 6:4-12).[5] After this warning, the author briefly resumes his contrast between Christ and the angels from 2:5-9 before transitioning to the recurring theme of Christ's solidarity with humanity (2:10ff). This solidarity is tied to the argument concerning angels via the quotation from Psalm 8 (Heb 2:6-8). That Christ was "made for a little while lower than the

---

[3] R. T. France, "Hebrews," in *The Expositor's Bible Commentary*, ed. Tremper Longman and David E. Garland, Rev. ed. (Grand Rapids: Zondervan, 2006), 19.France 19

[4] William L. Lane, *Hebrews 1-8*, ed. David A. Hubbard, Glenn W. Barker, and Ralph P. Martin, vol. 1, Word Biblical Commentary Vol. 47a (Nashville: Word Books, 1991), xlvii.

[5] Ibid., 1:XCVI.

angels" (Heb 2:7, ESV) forms a segue for the author to Christ's vicarious suffering; however, though the author turns to the humiliation of Christ, Christ's exaltation remains in sight (2:8-9). In verses 12-13, the author quotes from Psalm 22:22 and Isaiah 8:17-18 (LXX) to illustrate Christ's solidarity, that "he is not ashamed to call them brothers" (2:11 ESV). These two quotes are often treated as the more difficult of the set: "From our modern exegetical point of view, the argument would have been stronger if he had confined himself to the quotation from Psalm 22 alone! ... That phrase, which in Isaiah 8 denotes literally the prophet's children is picked up by our author in the next verse as a designation of humanity in general."[6] The author must, in some way, identify Jesus with the speaker of Isaiah 8:16-17, whether typologically or—as I will argue—directly.[7]

Our discussion of the Isaiah passage in Chapter 8 showed that France's claim concerning the quoted phrase, that Isaiah is the speaker, is not as evident as he makes it out be. To the contrary, there is significant textual evidence that Yahweh continues to be the speaker in this verse. The reading

---

[6] France, "Hebrews," 55.

[7] For a survey of indirect approaches, see Brian Pate, "Who Is Speaking? The Use of Isaiah 8:17-18 in Hebrews 2:13 as a Case Study for Applying the Speech of Key OT Figures to Christ," *Journal of The Evangelical Theological Society* 59, no. 4 (2016): 731–745; Rodrigo (Rodrigo Franklin) De Sousa, "The Hermeneutics of the Scriptural Citations in Hebrews 2:12-13," *Biblical Research* 64 (2019): 83–101. A recent trend in theological exegesis is to identify this as an instance of "prospological" exegesis; I am not convinced of the presence of prospology in the New Testament. Matthew Bates identifies prospological exegesis in this way, "Prosopological exegesis is a reading technique whereby an interpreter seeks to overcome a real or perceived ambiguity regarding the identity of the speakers or addressees (or both) in the divinely inspired source text by assigning nontrivial prosopa (i.e., nontrivial vis-à-vis the 'plain sense' of the text) to the speakers or addressees (or both) in order to make sense of the text." "Nontrivial" means that the one the New Testament claims to be speaking is not the speaker according to the plain sense of the Scripture in question. It is not clear to me that the Patristic examples given for this technique were convinced about the "nontriviality" of their readings; indeed, they were more ready to find Christ in the Old Testament than contemporary scholarship is. More importantly, proponents are too eager to follow the scepticism of modern scholarship; as we have seen, the Old Testament context supports the judgements of the New Testament authors more often than naught. See Gentry for a criticism of this technique. Matthew W. Bates, *The Hermeneutics of the Apostolic Proclamation: The Center of Paul's Method of Scriptural Interpretation* (Waco, Tex: Baylor University Press, 2012), 218, cf. 183, 53–54; Gentry, "A Preliminary Evaluation and Critique of Prosopological Exegesis."

proposed in Chapter 8, that these "children" are God's disciples, also suggests that France is demanding to much from this quote. That is, in the context of Hebrew 2, does it have to refer to "humanity in general"? It does not; in the immediate context, those with whom Christ shows solidarity are not humanity in general but redeemed humanity, the "sons" to which he has suffered to bring to glory (2:10).

In the greater argument of Hebrews, Jesus has already been identified with God. Not only has he received "glory and honor" (2:8-9) but he is seen to be the pre-existent Son, "through whom also he created the world" (1:2, ESV). This Son is "the radiance of the glory of God and the exact imprint of his nature, and he upholds the universe by the word of his power" (1:3, ESV). The language used by the author makes the Son the perceptible extension (ἀπαύγασμα; *apaugasma*, "radiance") of God's glory, who shares perfect equality with God (χαρακτήρ; *charakter*, "exact imprint"). This association with God is strengthened when, in contrast with the angels, the author of Hebrews quotes Psalm 45 to the effect that Jesus the Son is "God" (θεός, אֱלֹהִים; *theos, 'elohim*) (Ps 45:6-7). We will return to the language of Hebrews 1:1-4 a bit later, but for now the point I want to make is that in context, the superiority which Christ has over the angels is explicated through his identity with Yahweh, the one God of Israel. Thus, when the author returns to the theme of Christ's exaltation in 2:8-9, he speaks of Christ as exalted through identity with Yahweh, not merely as an elevated man. This observation gives us an angle from which to approach the author's use of Isaiah 8:16-17.

As we saw in Chapter 8, the speaker in these verses is Yahweh himself somehow distinguished from Yahweh. This would seem to be the picture portrayed by the author of Hebrews thus far: Jesus is God alongside God, the exact imprint (χαρακτήρ; *charaketer*) of Yahweh. Jesus as Yahweh is the one speaking in Isaiah 8:16-17, yet he speaks as Yahweh who has humbled himself in solidarity with the redeemed of Israel; he is Immanuel, truly Yahweh (Isa 7:14, 8:8, 16-18) yet also a son given to his people (Isa 9:2-7). If our argument concerning Isaiah 8:16-18 is cogent, then the clearest reading of Hebrews 2:13 is that the author applies this text to Jesus because Yahweh the Son who came as Jesus is the speaker in the context of Isaiah. So, the author of Hebrews draws forth the same resonances we identified in our exegesis: the Davidic eschatological figure is Yahweh, revealed to us as the man Jesus Christ.

Thus far, I have argued that the New Testament sees Christ as the fulfilment of Isaiah's divine eschatological agent. In particular, I have argued that Hebrews 2:13 draws on this very identification. Looking at the New Testament from another perspective, it will be argued that Jesus is identified with Yahweh in Mark 1:3, Romans 10:13, John 8:58, and John 12:37-41.

JESUS, THE OLD TESTAMENT'S "LORD"

A. Mark 1:2-3

ἰδοὺ ἀποστέλλω τὸν ἄγγελόν μου πρὸ προσώπου
σου, ὃς κατασκευάσει τὴν ὁδόν σου· φωνὴ βοῶντος
ἐν τῇ ἐρήμῳ· ἑτοιμάσατε τὴν ὁδὸν κυρίου, εὐθείας
ποιεῖτε τὰς τρίβους αὐτοῦ.

²Behold, I send my messenger before your face, who
will prepare your way. ³A voice of one shouting in the
wilderness, "Prepare the way of the Lord, make straight
his paths."

From the outset of his Gospel, Mark introduces both John the Baptist and
Jesus through a compound quote of Malachi 3:1 and Isaiah 40:3. What
interests us at this point of our investigation is the way that Mark 1:3
introduces Jesus. Before considering the text itself, we can observe how Mark
has used it to introduce John. Both Malachi 3:1 and Isaiah 40:3 are connected
through their description of an agent who would prepare the way for
Yahweh. In the first case, Malachi 3:1-5 describes two messengers, a
prophetic one and a divine one.[1] The first messenger, introduced in 3:1, is

---

[1] Beth Glazier-McDonald, "Mal'ak Habběrît: The Messenger of the Covenant

said to "prepare the way before me," with Yahweh speaking. In this passage, "Malachi announces that God himself will intervene to judge and refine."[2] It is this messenger which Mark aligns with John; Mark present John as making the way ready for Jesus, as indicated by his words in Mark 1:7-8.

In Isaiah 40:3, Isaiah looks to the day when Yahweh would come to redeem his people. After introducing God's salvation in light of the finished judgment of Israel (40:1-2), Isaiah writes of the "voice of one calling out" (קוֹל קוֹרֵא; *qol qore'*) for "the way of YHWH" (דֶּרֶךְ יהוה; *derek YHWH*) to be prepared. Mark connects this "voice of one calling out" with Malachi's messenger in the compound quotation. Both Old Testament passages also share the idea of a "way" (ὁδόν, *hodon*) being prepared, and in Isaiah's passage, the "wilderness" (ἐρήμος, *eremos*) sets the location of John the Baptist's ministry (Mark 1:4).[3] In context, John is presented as the one who makes the way for Jesus. However, through the eyes of "Isaiah" (Mark 1:2), John is presented as the messenger preparing the way for Yahweh: "vv. 2-8 appear to leave no room for a human figure in the eschatological drama other than John himself, the forerunner sent to prepare for the eschatological coming of God." [4] Consider the passages in parallel:

Malachi 3:1

הִנְנִי שֹׁלֵחַ מַלְאָכִי וּפִנָּה־דֶרֶךְ לְפָנָי

Behold, I am sending my messenger, he will prepare a way before me.

ἰδοὺ ἐγὼ ἐξαποστέλλω τὸν ἄγγελόν μου, καὶ ἐπιβλέψεται ὁδὸν πρὸ προσώπου μου (LXX)

Behold, I send my messenger, and he will look upon the way

---

in Mal 3:1," in *Hebrew Annual Review, Vol 11, 1987: Biblical and Other Studies* (Columbus, Ohio, 1987), 96–97.

2 Abernethy and Goswell, *God's Messiah*, 178.

3 France 56.

4 France 61-62.

before my face.

ἰδοὺ ἀποστέλλω τὸν ἄγγελόν μου πρὸ προσώπου σου, ὃς κατασκευάσει τὴν ὁδόν σου· (Mark 1:2 NA28)

Behold, I send my messenger before your face, who will prepare your way.

Isaiah 50:3

קוֹל קוֹרֵא בַּמִּדְבָּר פַּנּוּ דֶּרֶךְ יְהֹוָה יַשְּׁרוּ בָּעֲרָבָה מְסִלָּה לֵאלֹהֵינוּ׃

A voice of one shouting in the wilderness, "make clear the way of YHWH, make straight a highway in the desert for our God."

φωνὴ βοῶντος ἐν τῇ ἐρήμῳ Ἑτοιμάσατε τὴν ὁδὸν κυρίου, εὐθείας ποιεῖτε τὰς τρίβους τοῦ θεοῦ ἡμῶν (LXX)

A voice of one shouting in the wilderness, "prepare the way of the Lord, make straight the paths of our God."

φωνὴ βοῶντος ἐν τῇ ἐρήμῳ· ἑτοιμάσατε τὴν ὁδὸν κυρίου, εὐθείας ποιεῖτε τὰς τρίβους αὐτοῦ (Mark 1:3, NA28)

A voice of one shouting in the wilderness, "Prepare the way of the Lord, make straight his paths."

It is immediately clear that Mark is not drawing on Malachi in any straightforward manner. Commentators generally agree that the unique form of this first part comes from the combination of Malachi 3:1 with Exodus 23:20.[5] In the latter text, Yahweh declares that his "angel" (מַלְאָךְ; mal'ak) will

---

[5] Rikk E. Watts, "Mark," in *Commentary on the New Testament Use of the Old Testament*, ed. G. K. Beale and D. A. Carson (Grand Rapids: Baker Academic, 2007), 113. Cf. Glazier-McDonald, "Mal'ak Habběrît."

go before the people of Israel into the promised land prepared for them. In the first quotation, from Malachi and Exodus, it is not immediately clear for whom the messenger will prepare the way. However, in the eschatological context of Malachi, it appears to be Yahweh himself, as it is with the later reference to the coming of Elijah (Mal 4:5; cf. Matt 11:14ff, Mark 9:11ff; Luke 1:17ff). This corresponds well with Isaiah 40:3, where the Hebrew and Septuagint both have "the one calling out" preparing the way for Yahweh himself (יהוה, κυρίου; *YHWH, kuriou*), "our God" (לֵאלֹהֵינוּ, τοῦ θεοῦ ἡμῶν; *le'lohenu, tou theou hemon*). In Mark's quotation, "our God" is replaced with a pronoun (αὐτοῦ; *autou*, "his"); France claims concerning this substitution: "while this might be no more than a simplifying substitution of pronoun for noun, making no difference to the understanding of the text, it also, by avoiding the direct use of θεός (theos, "God"), allows the Christian reader to understand the κύριος (kurios, "Lord") of the previous line to refer to Jesus."[6] Similarly, Watt's writes that through this substitution, "Mark makes the forthright claim that Israel's new-exodus hopes have been inaugurated in Jesus."[7] In a sense this is true: by focusing on the κυριός as the object of the messenger's preparatory work, Mark clearly draws the connection with Jesus in such a way that the presence of "τοῦ θεοῦ ἡμῶν" might have obscured, drawing the reader as it were towards the one to whom Jesus is related as a son (Mark 1:11). However, this substitution in no way diminishes the weight of Mark's use of Isaiah and Malachi. That is, in both contexts, the one for whom the messenger prepares the way is Yahweh himself. The use of κυρίος in the LXX of Isaiah 40:3 is not rendering אָדוֹן (*adon*; "Lord") but יהוה, thus the first instance of κυρίος in Mark's Gospel does not lead the reader to associate the title in contrast with κυρίος καίσαρ (*kurios kaisar*; "Caesar is lord") or with the Hebrew אָדוֹן. Instead, Jesus is identified with יהוה himself, the one God of Israel. The same use of κυρίος with reference to Christ in the place of an Old Testament reference to Yahweh occurs in Romans 10:13.

---

[6] R. T. France, *The Gospel of Mark: A Commentary on the Greek Text* (Grand Rapids: Eerdmans, 2002), 64.

[7] Watts, "Mark," 119.

B. Romans 10:13

πᾶς γὰρ ὃς ἂν ἐπικαλέσηται τὸ ὄνομα κυρίου σωθήσεται.

For "everyone who calls upon the name of the Lord will be saved."

Romans 10:13 is located in a theologically rich chapter that poses many exegetical problems.[8] However, acknowledging that these complexities exist, we can understand the aspect of verse 13 that is important to our argument without addressing these questions. It is enough for our purposes to acknowledge that Romans 10:5-13 juxtaposes the Old Covenant with the New Covenant concerning the particular question of "righteousness," particularly contrasted as "the righteousness that is based on the law" (10:5) and "the righteousness that is based on faith" (10:6, ESV). In the later part of this passage, Paul narrows in on the connection between "belief," "confession," and "righteousness" (10:10). In verse 9 belief and confession as coordinated with being saved and receiving "righteousness" (v. 10) are explicated in this way, "if you confess with your mouth Jesus is Lord and believe in your heart that God raised him from the dead, you will be saved" (ESV). Following this statement are two quotes from the Old Testament (Isa 28:16 [LXX] in 10:11; Joel 2:32 in 10:13) used to substantiate this salvation/righteousness relating to belief and the confession concerning Christ. The second is the quotation which we are interested in.

In verse 12, Paul proclaims that there is no distinction between Jews and

---

[8] Cf. Karen Pidcock-Lester, "Romans 10:5-15," *Interpretation* 50, no. 3 (July 1996): 288; James R. Lowther, "Paul's Use of Deuteronomy 30:11-14 in Romans 10:5-8 as a Locus Primus on Paul's Understanding of the Law in Romans" (Doctoral Dissertation, Southwestern Baptist Theological Seminary, 2001); Akio Ito, "The Written Torah and the Oral Gospel: Romans 10:5-13 in the Dynamic Tension Between Orality and Literacy," *Novum testamentum* 48, no. 3 (2006): 234–260; P. J. Bekken, *The Word Is Near You: A Study of Deuteronomy 30:12-14 in Paul's Letter to the Romans in a Jewish Context*, Beihefte zur Zeitschrift für die neutestamentliche Wissenschaft und die Kunde der älteren Kirche 144 (Berlin; New York: de Gruyter, 2007); Mark Seifrid, "The Near Word of Christ and the Distant Vision of N. T. Wright," *Journal of the Evangelical Theological Society* 54, no. 2 (June 2011): 279–297; Willem Oliver, "Romans 10:5-13 Revisited," *Hervormde Teologiese Studies* 71, no. 3 (2015): 1–12.

Greeks because "the same Lord is Lord of all." Given the basic confessional claim in verse 9, that "Jesus is Lord," and the following exposition of "calling on" and "believing in" in terms of the Gospel proclamation (Romans 10:14-17), the "Lord" here is, minimally, Jesus.[9] The same logic follows for the reference to the "Lord" in verse 13, "everyone who calls on the name of the Lord will be saved." When we look at Joel 2:32, "Lord" is the LXX rendering of the Hebrew YHWH:

וְהָיָה כֹּל אֲשֶׁר־יִקְרָא בְּשֵׁם יְהוָה יִמָּלֵט
And it will happen that everyone who calls on the name of YHWH will be delivered.

καὶ ἔσται πᾶς, ὃς ἂν ἐπικαλέσηται τὸ ὄνομα κυρίου, σωθήσεται,
And it will be that everyone who calls upon the name of the Lord will be saved. – Joel 2:32

Thus, when Paul uses Joel 2:32 to refer to Jesus, he is implicitly identifying Jesus with Yahweh. Jesus is the one on whom people will call in eschatological Day of the Lord; he is Yahweh whose day of judgment is coming for unbelievers and salvation for those who call upon him.

C. John 8:58

εἶπεν αὐτοῖς Ἰησοῦς· ἀμὴν ἀμὴν λέγω ὑμῖν, πρὶν Ἀβραὰμ γενέσθαι ἐγὼ εἰμί.

Jesus said to them, "Truly, truly I say to you, before Abraham was, I am."

Commentators take various stances on the use of the phrase "I am" (ἐγὼ εἰμί; *ego eimi*) in the book of John. On the one hand, it is a regularly used formula for identification (e.g. John 9:9); on the other hand, it is part of the Greek phrase used to translate the climactic revelation of God's name in

---

[9] I say minimally because it may be an instance of either non-exhaustive reference or a inclusive usage of the term, both of which categories are discussed in Chapter 18.

Exodus 3:13-15. In a book that does not hesitate to identify Jesus with God, even from its first verses, it is hard to miss the unique connotations this common phrase takes when spoken by Jesus. There are several instances where this is more prominent (6:24; 8:24, 28), John 8:58 being the most significant.

In John 8, Jesus is engaging with the Jewish leadership. He identifies them as children of Satan, but they seek to identify themselves with Abraham. Throughout the chapter, Jesus stresses his unique relationship to the Father; if they reject Jesus, they have rejected God the Father. They cannot be Abraham's true offspring if they deny the God Abraham worshipped. In verse 51, Jesus again promises eternal life to those who believe; they "will never see death."[10] For the Jewish leadership, this is too far: Jesus makes himself to be greater than Abraham and the prophets, for they died but Jesus promises eternal life for those who trust in him (vv. 52, 53). Convinced he has a demon and fed up with him, they conclude their response, "Are you greater...? Who do you make yourself to be?" (v. 53)

Jesus' response to their questions does nothing to assuage their concerns. Jesus denies giving glory to himself; he is not claiming status that is not rightfully his. No, his father, "of whom you say, 'He is our God,'" he glorifies Jesus (v. 54). Not only do they fail to recognise God's testimony concerning his son, they do not even know him—but Jesus knows him. Indeed, not only is Jesus greater than Abraham, "Your father Abraham rejoiced that he would see my day. He saw it and was glad" (v. 56). If Jesus claims thus far are audacious; he now claims that Abraham looked with joy to Jesus' day, and indeed saw it. The Jewish leaders interpret this statement as claim to have seen Abraham, clearly false given Jesus' age (v. 57). It is in response to this, to the leaders' shock at Jesus' bold claims to have seen (or been seen by) and be greater than Abraham, that leads Jesus to make his final claim. The reason these things are true is, "before Abraham was, I AM." After all the claims Jesus has made and juxtaposed with a temporal clause framing the "I AM" as a claim to pre-exist Abraham (to not be merely "not yet fifty years old"), it is hard to miss what Jesus is saying. The Jewish leaders certainly didn't, "they picked up stones to throw at him"—perceiving his claim as

---

[10] Unless stated otherwise, the Scripture citations in this section other than John 8:58 and Exodus 3:13-15 are from the ESV.

blasphemy.

Jesus has taken a fundamental self-revelation of God in the Old Testament and applied it to himself. Here, the Jewish leaders ask who Jesus thinks he is; in Exodus 3, Moses seeks to know who the God is who speaks to him, that he might declare his "name" to Israel when they ask. I argue elsewhere that God's response, "I am who I am" is a claim to be self-interpreting or self-revealing—He is exactly, no more and no less, than who he has revealed himself to be in his relationship with Israel thus far and into the future.[11]

וַיֹּאמֶר אֱלֹהִים אֶל־מֹשֶׁה אֶהְיֶה אֲשֶׁר אֶהְיֶה וַיֹּאמֶר כֹּה תֹאמַר לִבְנֵי יִשְׂרָאֵל אֶהְיֶה שְׁלָחַנִי אֲלֵיכֶם:

And God said to Moses, "I am who I am." And he said, "Thus you shall say to the sons of Israel, 'I AM sent me to you.'"

καὶ εἶπεν ὁ θεὸς πρὸς Μωυσῆν Ἐγώ εἰμι ὁ ὤν, καὶ εἶπεν Οὕτως ἐρεῖς τοῖς υἱοῖς Ισραηλ Ὁ ὢν ἀπέσταλκέν με πρὸς ὑμᾶς. (LXX)

And God said to Moses, "I Am the One Who Is." And he said, "Thus you shall say to the sons of Israel, 'The One Who Is' sent me to you.'" – Exodus 3:14

In Hebrew, the summary of this phrase from God's perspective is אֶהְיֶה ('ehyeh), "I AM." From the perspective of God's people, the אֶהְיֶה is יהוה (yihveh)(or יְהוָה: Yahweh, as the name is probably pronounced), "He Is." The LXX captures the first אֶהְיֶה with ἐγώ εἰμι (ego eimi, "I am") but gives an interpretive gloss to the second, ὁ ὤν (ho on), "the one who is." In the philosophical context of the Hellenised world, this latter phrase may suggest a more philosophical idea such as "being" or "existence." Nevertheless, someone reading from the LXX tradition may still make the connection between Jesus words and this passage from the one use of ἐγώ εἰμι, but if they were reading the Hebrew or a more literal translation, the connection is all the more clear:

---

[11] See my forthcoming *Portraits of a Great God* and the literature cited there.

καὶ εἶπεν οἱ θεοὶ πρὸς Μωυσῆν **ἐγώ εἰμι ὅ εἰμί**, καὶ εἶπεν οὕτως ἐρεῖς τοῖς υἱοῖς Ισραηλ **ἐγώ εἰμι** ἀπέσταλκέν με πρὸς ὑμᾶς.[12]

And God said to Moses, "I am who I am," and he said, "Thus you will say to the sons of Israel, 'I AM' sent me to you."

Jesus does not just call himself "Yahweh," "He Is," as if from the creatures' perspective, but takes up God's own perspective, "I AM." He could have made no higher claim for himself than this; it is because He Is that he saw and was seen by Abraham and could promise eternal life. The Jewish leaders recognise the claim, and their response would have been appropriate if Jesus claimed this erroneously. Thus, after differentiating himself clearly from Yahweh, the God of Abraham and the one whom the Israelites claimed to serve, Jesus simultaneously identifies himself as Yahweh, united with yet in distinction from God the Father, who is himself Yahweh. Moreover, if we are right to identify Jesus with the Angel of Yahweh in the Old Testament, then it was Jesus who spoke the words of Exodus 3:13-15, expressed here as it was there in answer to the question, who are you? Once again, we have seen an instance where Jesus or his apostles identify him with Yahweh.

D. John 12:37-41 and Isaiah 6

ταῦτα εἶπεν Ἠσαΐας ὅτι εἶδεν τὴν δόξαν αὐτοῦ, καὶ ἐλάλησεν περὶ αὐτοῦ.

Isaiah said these things because he saw his glory and spoke concerning him. – John 12:41

Though Jesus had done many mighty things, boldly proclaiming himself to be Yahweh and attesting to this with signs, his own people continued to reject him. According to John, this was not unanticipated; instead, this was spoken

---

[12] My translation, adapted from the LXX. Alternatively, ἐγώ εἰμι ὅ ἐγώ εἰμι or εἰμί ὅ εἰμί (cf. 1 Cor 15:10). The verb is sufficient to translate the same clause in Hebrew; however, Koine style would seem to prefer an explicit subject in this case. The meaning is the same in any of the three constructions offered.

of beforehand by the prophet Isaiah. John first cites Isaiah 53:1, where Isaiah points to the incarnate Yahweh suffering for his people; the prophet laments the lack of response to the good news, point to the fact that the "Arm of the Lord" has not been revealed. I argued above, following Motyer, that "the Arm of the Lord" is the suffering servant presented as Yahweh acting in his strength; that the arm has not been revealed points to a greater theme in Deuteronomy and the prophets, that regeneration or the new, circumcised heart is need to receive God.[13] John then cites Isaiah 6:10, which gives the other side of the picture: they have not believed because they have not received the power to do so from God (Isa 53:1) and because they have been blinded by God, their hearts are hard and hardened by the continued prophetic word (Isa 6:10).[14]

Isaiah 6:10 is part of Isaiah's commission: in chapter 6, Isaiah experiences a vision of Yahweh "upon a throne, high and lifted up" (v. 1, ESV). Isaiah is in the heavenly temple and witnessing the worship of seraphim and the holiness of God, he is convinced that he will die (v. 5). However, being cleansed through the action of a Seraph, he then receives a commission from Yahweh. Isaiah ministry will be to preach in order to harden the people in their sin until judgment comes, but a remnant will remain (vv. 9-13).

What draws our attention to this passage is the verse that follows this quote. John tells us in verse 41 that the prophet Isaiah said these words "because he saw his glory and spoke concerning him." The obvious antecedent—and the only one available—for "he/his" is Jesus, who is the immediate object of interest. John quotes these passages from Isaiah to explain unbelief in the presence of Jesus' signs. "These things," which Isaiah said, probably refers to both quotes. Isaiah 53:1 speaks of the Arm, speaking of Jesus (see Chapter 8), and so "spoke concerning him" makes sense. What draws our attention is the phrase "he saw his glory." After a quote from Isaiah 6:10, no one familiar with that chapter can miss the reference: in chapter 6 Isaiah witnesses the glory of God enthroned in the heavens, as the Seraphim

---

[13] Chapter 8 above and Rutherford, *Prevenient Grace*.

[14] John changes the imperatives in the Hebrew and Greek text to perfect verbs, reflecting on the results of Isaiah and the prophets' ministry as opposed to the commission for ministry.

put it, "Holy, holy, holy is the Lord of hosts; the whole earth is full of his glory" (Isa 6:3). If the one whom Isaiah saw is Jesus, then John is identifying the one seated on the throne with Jesus. Jesus is thus identified with Yahweh the king.

That John would make this identification is no surprise. We already saw that Jesus identifies himself as Yahweh in John 8:58. John identifies Jesus with the creator God, while also differentiating him, in John 1:1-5. Throughout the Gospel, Jesus is identified as God in various ways. Even here, John identifies Jesus with the Arm of YHWH in 53:1, who is Yahweh. Earlier, following Augustine and Calvin—among others—I suggested that references to God in the Old and New Testament cannot always be parsed down to one or another of the persons.[15] That is, "Yahweh" (יהוה, κυριός; YHWH, Kurios) or "God" (אֱלֹהִים, θεός; 'elohim, theos) may refer to the Father, the Son, the Spirit, or God as one. In the case of Isaiah 6, the figure on the throne is not differentiated, so we cannot clearly identify him as Father, Son, or Holy Spirit. This is the case in most of these theophanies. John's statement does not necessarily lead us to conclude that it is the 2nd Person whom Isaiah sees. Instead, if Isaiah saw the glory of the undifferentiated Godhead, then he saw the glory of the Father, Son, and Spirit. John can say that Isaiah saw Jesus only because for John, Jesus is Yahweh.

---

[15] For Augustine, see *De Trinitate* II.10.18-19. For Calvin, see John T. Slotemaker, "'"Fuisse in Forma Hominis" Belongs to Christ Alone': John Calvin's Trinitarian Hermeneutics in His *Lectures on Ezekiel*," *Scottish Journal of Theology* 68, no. 4 (November 2015): 421–436.

13

JESUS BESIDE YAHWEH

And the Word was with God – John 1:1b

In the previous chapter, we looked at various instances where Jesus is identified with Yahweh. In this chapter, we will now consider several passages where Jesus is said to be God while simultaneously being differentiated from him. Jesus is Yahweh while being beside Yahweh. Many passages could be added to these ones, but I believe these will sufficiently represent conclusions we could draw from a broader engagement with the New Testament testimony.

A. The Divine Son in John 1:1

Ἐν ἀρχῇ ἦν ὁ λόγος, καὶ ὁ λόγος ἦν πρὸς τὸν θεόν, καὶ θεὸς ἦν ὁ λόγος. οὗτος ἦν ἐν ἀρχῇ πρὸς τὸν θεόν.

In the beginning was the Word, and the Word was with God, and the Word was God. He was in the beginning with God.

When we think of Jesus' deity, John 1:1 is the passage that often comes to mind. Thousands of pages have been written since the early days of the church on the prologue of John and it's Christology. Of particular interest has been the word ὁ λόγος (*ho logos*), the Word, and its parallels in Semitic, Hellenistic, and Second Temple literature. Depending on what one makes of the purpose and audience of John's Gospel, these different theories present themselves with varying degrees of usefulness. However, read in its current context, as part of the canonical Scriptures, a clearer explanation of the use of the term emerges. John uses language from the Genesis creation account, indicating that this is the primary background he has in mind. Read against this background, the implications of this passage for our thesis are strengthened. In what follows, I will primarily interact with the LXX of Genesis. It represents a literal translation of the Hebrew in the early verses (even down to the word order) and the differences in the later verses will not affect our interpretation, so nothing is lost in working from this text.

a. John 1:1-5 and Genesis 1:1 – 2:7

Ἐν ἀρχῇ ἦν ὁ λόγος, καὶ ὁ λόγος ἦν πρὸς τὸν θεόν, καὶ θεὸς ἦν ὁ λόγος. οὗτος ἦν ἐν ἀρχῇ πρὸς τὸν θεόν. πάντα δι' αὐτοῦ **ἐγένετο,** καὶ χωρὶς αὐτοῦ **ἐγένετο** οὐδὲ ἕν. ὃ γέγονεν ἐν αὐτῷ **ζωὴ** ἦν, καὶ **ἡ ζωὴ** ἦν **τὸ φῶς τῶν ἀνθρώπων·** καὶ **τὸ φῶς ἐν τῇ σκοτίᾳ** φαίνει, καὶ ἡ σκοτία αὐτὸ οὐ κατέλαβεν. (John 1:1-5)

In the beginning, the Word was, and the Word was with God, and the Word was God. This one was in the beginning with God. All thing **came to be** through him, and not even one thing **came to be** apart from Him. What **came to be** was **alive** in him, and **the life** was **the light of humans,** and **the light** shone in **the darkness,** and the darkness did not overcome it.

Ἐν ἀρχῇ ἐποίησεν ὁ θεὸς τὸν οὐρανὸν καὶ τὴν γῆν. ... καὶ **εἶπεν** ὁ θεός **Γενηθήτω φῶς.** καὶ **ἐγένετο φῶς.** καὶ εἶδεν ὁ θεὸς **τὸ φῶς** ὅτι καλόν. καὶ διεχώρισεν ὁ θεὸς ἀνὰ μέσον **τοῦ φωτὸς** καὶ ἀνὰ μέσον **τοῦ σκότους.** ... Ἐξαγαγέτω τὰ ὕδατα ἑρπετὰ ψυχῶν **ζωσῶν** καὶ πετεινὰ πετόμενα ἐπὶ τῆς γῆς κατὰ τὸ στερέωμα τοῦ οὐρανοῦ. καὶ **ἐγένετο** οὕτως. ... ὃ ἔχει ἐν ἑαυτῷ **ψυχὴν ζωῆς** ... καὶ ἔπλασεν ὁ θεὸς **τὸν ἄνθρωπον** χοῦν ἀπὸ τῆς γῆς καὶ ἐνεφύσησεν εἰς τὸ πρόσωπον αὐτοῦ πνοὴν **ζωῆς** (Genesis 1:1, 3-4, 20, 30; 2:7)

> **In the beginning, God made** the heavens and the earth.
> ... and God **said**, "**let light be**." And **light came to be**.
> And God saw that **the light** was good. And God divided
> between **the light** and between **the darkness**. ... "Let the
> waters bring forth creeping creatures with the spirit of **life**
> and let birds fly above the earth across the firmament of
> heaven. And **it was** so. ... **which has in itself a spirit of**
> **life** ... and God formed **the man** out of the dust of the
> earth and he breathed into his face a breath of **life**.

Above I have juxtaposed the first verses of John's prologue with selection of verses from the creation account in Genesis 1-2, along with an intentionally wooden translation of both texts. These parallels have been observed before, but the significance of this sustained allusion to Genesis 1-2 is crucial to our purpose.[1] In John 1:1-5 we find one phrase adapted from Genesis and four semantic links to the Genesis creation account: ἐν ἀρχῇ ἦν ὁ λόγος (*en arche en ho logos*; "in the beginning the word was") and ἐν ἀρχῇ ἐποίησεν ὁ θεος (*en arche epoiesen ho theos*; "in the beginning God made"), speech (ὁ λόγος / εἶπεν; *ho logos / eipen*),[2] coming into existence (γίνομαι; *ginomai*), light and darkness (φῶς, σκοτία; *phos, skotia*), and life (ζωή, ζάω; *zoe, zao*). Below, I will argue that these connections establish the agency of the Word in the entire act of creation and serve to identify him with God.

The first observation we may make is that John puts the Word *before* creation; even before the Word is stated to be God, he is shown to be him. Even before we read that the Word is beside God, John has placed the Word within the plurality of God we saw in the Old Testament, אֱלֹהִים (*'elohim*). The Word is not simply אֱלֹהִים (*'elohim*) but is also there with him. The following parallels between John and Genesis suggest the reason for calling Jesus "the Word"; ὁ λόγος (*ho logos*) is the nominal form of the aorist verb "he said" in the LXX of Genesis 1. In the Genesis account, speech is the instrument God

---

[1] E.g. Craig A. Evans, *Word and Glory: On the Exegetical and Theological Background of John's Prologue* (A&C Black, 1993).

[2] For the reader unfamiliar with Greek, εἶπεν (*eipen*) is the aorist 3ms form of the Greek verb λέγω (*lego*) to which the noun λόγος (*logos*) is related, meaning "to speak" and "word" respectively.

uses to create all things; by calling Jesus "the Word," John identifies *Jesus* as that instrument. It was not impersonal speech or thought but the 2nd-person of the Trinity that achieved God's creative purpose. Having identified Jesus with God's creative speech, the claims that all things came to be through the Word follow; everything that created was created when God said "let it be." John then uses the creation language to portray the incarnation: this same Word who created has entered the creation and defeated the darkness, as he had pushed back the darkness in the beginning.

John thus identifies Jesus as the personal agent of God's creative work, himself God—part of the plurality indicated by אֱלֹהִים (*'elohim*). His three-part description of the Word indicates as much, showing both that Jesus is אֱלֹהִים but not alone as such. "In the beginning was the Word" implicates Jesus in the being of God, "In the beginning he, the God(s), created." Then, "the Word was with God" differentiates Jesus from God so that the plurality is not collapsed. Finally, "and the Word was God" secures this divine identification in differentiation. Much ink has been spilled on the use of the anarthrous θεός (*theos*, "God") here (that is, without the article). Carson and others argue that the construction as it is found, with an anarthrous predicate θεός and the articular subject ὁ λόγος (*ho logos*), would more properly indicate a qualitive relationship, "what God was the Word was."[3]

This is, of course, true enough, but it is not the only possibility. That is, vary rarely are the biblical writers interested in the qualitative relationship between Jesus and the Father; that is, they incorporate Jesus into the divine identity, or identify him as Yahweh, the one True God, assuming that whatever God is, Jesus is (as God). The focus, as we have seen, is on the former equation (Jesus is Yahweh) rather than the latter (Jesus is what Yahweh is). Nevertheless, this reading is grammatically possible and makes good sense of John's prologue: Jesus is God and is differentiated from God, yet this differentiation does make Jesus ontologically different or less than God. However, another reading presents itself that maintains John's purpose

---

[3] Carson offers this rendering. Or "the Word was divine," but given its contemporary ambiguity, "divine" is hardly fitting. D. A. Carson, *The Gospel According to John*, The Pillar New Testament Commentary (Leicester; Grand Rapids: IVP; Eerdmans, 1991).

perhaps better than this.

If John's purpose is to identify Jesus with God while nevertheless differentiating him from God—which is the pattern of Trinitarian identification in the Old Testament—then the anarthrous construction is entirely appropriate. On the one hand, it serves the grammatical purpose of clarifying the predicate: the articular noun is the subject, the anarthrous the predicate. The present constructions ensures that we read it: The Word was God, not God was the Word. These are not interchangeable propositions: the Word is God, but not exclusively (God is the unity among plurality); the opposite is not true, the Word is not the unity of divine plurality.

On the other hand, though Jesus does not exhaust all that can be said about אֱלֹהִים (*'elohim*, "God(s)"), he is nevertheless God, identified with אֱלֹהִים. John has thus far put Jesus on the creator side of the creator-creature distinction, with אֱלֹהִים in 1a, then differentiated him from God in 1b. What remains is to assert that differentiation does not negate identity, namely, that Jesus does not exhaust אֱלֹהִים (a statement of pure identity), and that he is not a creature alongside אֱלֹהִים. Instead, Jesus is one of the divine persons, part of the plurality of the one God, what we call one of the persons of the Trinity. The phrase θεός ἦν ὁ λόγος (*theos en ho logos*, "the Word was God") seems to achieve this well: not quite "a god"—plurality without unity—nor what God was—qualitative identity—but a clear identification with God without making the predicate/subject interchangeable, as ὁ θεός ἦν ὁ λόγος (*ho theos en ho logos*, either "God was the Word" or "the Word was God") would suggest.

In John 1, the evangelist looks at the Creation narrative and finds Jesus there. Jesus is not "God," full stop. He is the instrument of God's creation, there with God—differentiated from him—yet nevertheless united with him. The LXX text does not open the possibility of God's plurality in unity, but the Hebrew text does, as we considered earlier. Reading John with the Hebrew text in mind, it is clear that John has not missed God's plurality and has carefully situated Jesus the Word as one of the many and one with the many, united as the one true God while differentiated as one of the Divine persons.

B. Philippians 2:1-5

Τοῦτο φρονεῖτε ἐν ὑμῖν ὃ καὶ ἐν Χριστῷ ᾽Ιησοῦ, ὃς ἐν μορφῇ θεοῦ ὑπάρχων οὐχ ἁρπαγμὸν ἡγήσατο τὸ εἶναι ἴσα θεῷ, ἀλλ᾽ ἑαυτὸν ἐκένωσεν μορφὴν δούλου λαβών, ἐν ὁμοιώματι ἀνθρώπων γενόμενος· καὶ σχήματι εὑρεθεὶς ὡς ἄνθρωπος ἐταπείνωσεν ἑαυτὸν γενόμενος ὑπήκοος μέχρι θανάτου, θανάτου δὲ σταυροῦ. διὸ καὶ ὁ θεὸς αὐτὸν ὑπερύψωσεν καὶ ἐχαρίσατο αὐτῷ τὸ ὄνομα τὸ ὑπὲρ πᾶν ὄνομα, ἵνα ἐν τῷ ὀνόματι ᾽Ιησοῦ πᾶν γόνυ κάμψῃ ἐπουρανίων καὶ ἐπιγείων καὶ καταχθονίων καὶ πᾶσα γλῶσσα ἐξομολογήσηται ὅτι κύριος ᾽Ιησοῦς Χριστὸς εἰς δόξαν θεοῦ πατρός.

Have the same mindset, all of you, that Christ Jesus had, who being in the form of God did not regard being equal with God as something to seize.[4] Rather, he made himself nothing, taking the form of a servant and becoming like humans. Being found in shape as a human, he humbled himself by being obedient unto death, even the death of a cross. Therefore, God has also exalted him and gifted him the name above all names, in order that at the name of Jesus every knee should bow, in heaven, on earth, and under the earth, and every tongue confess that Jesus Christ is lord to the glory of God the Father.

There is a beautiful symmetry in the descent and ascension of Christ in the second chapter of Philippians. That Christ did not need to "seize" equality with God simultaneously reflects Christ's pre-incarnate status while anticipating his self-emptying condescension. Christ, we are told, did not count equality as something to be seized because he already had it, "being in

---

[4] ἁρπαγμὸν (*harpagmon*): the Biblical usage of is almost always in the context of theft or plundering.

the form of God." Yet "seize" or "steal" (ἁρπαγμὸν; *harpagmon*) also echoes the final verses in antithesis, where God "gifts" (ἐχαρίσατο; *echarisato*) the exalted name to Jesus. At first glance, μορφῇ (*morphē*), "form," might communicate less than identity, for in English, "form" often refers to external appearance. The word μορφῇ often does connotes external appearance (e.g. Judges 8:13, Job 4:16, LXX), but it is also used for true identity.[5] In the immediate context, Jesus being in the form of God meant equality with God need not have been seized: being in the form of God meant being equal with him. In addition, taking on the form of the servant is glossed as "becoming like humans." "Shape" (σχήματι, *schemati*) in the following verse more clearly refers to external appearance. In ancient Greek philosophy and post-New Testament theology, μορφῇ is used alongside εἶδος (*eidos*; "form," "idea") and οὐσία (*ousia*) for the "essence" or definition of something: they refer to what something truly is, not merely its appearance. We see this sense of μορφῇ as what-it-is (without the philosophical baggage of the extra-biblical usage) in the use of cognates from the same root in Philippians and elsewhere (3:10, 21; Rom 8:29, 12:2; 2 Cor 3:18; Gal 4:19). Jesus is thus what God the Father is, yet he is not God the Father: Jesus is acted on by God and relates to God.

C. Hebrews 1:1-4

Πολυμερῶς καὶ πολυτρόπως πάλαι ὁ θεὸς λαλήσας τοῖς πατράσιν ἐν τοῖς προφήταις ἐπ᾽ ἐσχάτου τῶν ἡμερῶν τούτων ἐλάλησεν ἡμῖν ἐν υἱῷ, ὃν ἔθηκεν κληρονόμον πάντων, δι᾽ οὗ καὶ ἐποίησεν τοὺς αἰῶνας·
ὃς ὢν ἀπαύγασμα τῆς δόξης καὶ χαρακτὴρ τῆς ὑποστάσεως αὐτοῦ, φέρων τε τὰ πάντα τῷ ῥήματι τῆς δυνάμεως αὐτοῦ, καθαρισμὸν τῶν ἁμαρτιῶν ποιησάμενος ἐκάθισεν ἐν δεξιᾷ τῆς μεγαλωσύνης ἐν ὑψηλοῖς, τοσούτῳ κρείττων γενόμενος τῶν ἀγγέλων ὅσῳ διαφορώτερον παρ᾽ αὐτοὺς

---

[5] The one other use of this word in the NT is in the so-called longer ending of Mark, which is probably not original, Mark 16:12.

κεκληρονόμηκεν ὄνομα.

God, having formerly spoken in various and many ways to the fathers by the prophets, in these last days spoke to us by a Son, whom he made the inheritor of all things, through whom he also made the ages:

Who, being the effulgence of his glory and the exact imprint of his reality, and upholding all things by the word of his power, having made purification for sins, he sat down at the right hand of the majesty on high, becoming so much greater than the angels in as much as the name he has inherited is more excellent than them.

The main line of argument in the book of Hebrews is the pre-eminence of the New Covenant instituted in Christ over the Old Covenant instituted under Moses at Sinai. A significant portion of this argument is dedicated to the superiority of Jesus as a better mediator and priest than those of the Old Covenant. From the opening lines, the superiority of Christ is in view. As it concerns our argument, it is important to first observe that God has acted towards his Son, differentiating them, and that the Son is simultaneously stated to be equal to God. Four statements about the Son stand out for our purposes.

First, we are told that God "made the ages" through Jesus; as in John 1, the author of Hebrews makes Jesus the agent of God's creative activity. Second, Jesus is identified as the "effulgence of his glory." "Effulgence" and the following terms I translate "imprint of his reality" are used as technical terms in ancient literature, leading to all sorts of speculation about the platonic leanings of the author of Hebrews, yet they also have a relatively generic meaning which helps us make sense of them here. Ἀπαύγασμα (*apaugasma*; "effulgence") is the extension of something outwards, leading to the translation "radiance," for it is sometimes used of the rays of the Sun. Here, Jesus is the pouring forth or shining forth of God's glory, the extension of God's glory into the created world, so the revelation of God, as verses 1-2 have indicated. The close connection between the source and that which comes forth from it identifies Jesus closely with God's glory, one who makes it known as very much a part of it.

Third, the sense of this phrase is reinforced by the next one, "the exact imprint of his reality." "Exact imprint" or χαρακτήρ (*charakter*) often carries the sense of a representation or reproduction of something, intimating a close relationship, a likeness, between two different things. Jesus is the "exact imprint" of God's "reality," his ὑπόστασις (*hupostasis*). In later theological discourse, ὑπόστασις was used for the "person," for the individual rather than the universal (for "*a human*" in contrast with "humanity"). Prior to this, the term closely mirrored οὐσία (*ousia*) as the fundamental existent or "substance," though it was not so much used for the definition or "essence"—as οὐσία often was. Less technically, ὑπόστασις was used for something's reality, that which something is (though not conceived of in the philosophical sense of *quiddity*) (in the Bible, Heb 11:1). In this context, it indicates the closeness of the identity described by χαρακτήρ: Jesus is the exact imprint of what God really, truly is. This is why Jesus may reveal God's glory, for has the same glory, yet he is distinct as the messenger, sent by God to make known his glory.

Fourth, Jesus upholds all things by the "word of his power." Not only is Jesus God's agent of creation; he is also the agent who sustains all creation in existence, moment by moment. The use of "word" connects this act of sustenance to the Genesis creation account; as in the prior cases, Jesus is differentiated from yet identified with God in creation. In all these ways, the author of Hebrews puts Jesus on the creator side of the creator-creature distinction, alongside of God the Father.

14

THE LORD IS THE SPIRIT

¹⁷ Now, the Lord is the Spirit; and where the Spirit (that is, the Lord) is, there is freedom. ¹⁸And all of us, beholding the glory of the Lord with unveiled faces, are being transformed into the same image, from glory into glory, as from the Lord, namely, the Spirit. – 2 Cor 3:17-18

In Part 2, we saw that the persons of the Trinity—God's plurality—were united as one person, Yahweh. In texts where God was shown to be plural, both persons are called Yahweh. Thus far, we have seen that Jesus identifies himself and is identified as Yahweh. Turning to the Holy Spirit, we will see from two key texts that he is likewise called Yahweh. This is the highest possible statement of the Spirit's divinity: there are many beings called God, but only the three Trinitarian persons are called Yahweh. If the Spirit is Yahweh, then he is God in the most significant sense.

A. Matthew 28:19-20

¹⁹πορευθέντες οὖν μαθητεύσατε πάντα τὰ ἔθνη, βαπτίζοντες αὐτοὺς εἰς τὸ ὄνομα τοῦ πατρὸς καὶ τοῦ υἱοῦ καὶ τοῦ ἁγίου πνεύματος, ²⁰διδάσκοντες αὐτοὺς τηρεῖν πάντα ὅσα ἐνετειλάμην ὑμῖν· καὶ ἰδοὺ ἐγὼ μεθ' ὑμῶν εἰμι πάσας τὰς ἡμέρας ἕως τῆς συντελείας τοῦ αἰῶνος.

> ¹⁹Therefore, going forth, make disciples of all peoples, baptising them into the name of the Father, of the Son, and of the Holy Spirit, ²⁰teaching them to keep all of which I have commanded you. Behold, I am with you always, until the end of the age.

The words of the "great commission" are rightly well known and significant for Christians throughout the ages. What draws our attention in this book is the verse 19. The disciples are charged with the task of "making disciples," part of this task is "baptising them into the name of the Father, of the Son, and of the Holy Spirit." Commentators are probably right to identify "into the name" as indicating ownership in some sense—we become God's—but the point that draws our attention is that this baptism is into *the name* of the three Trinitarian persons.[1] Each person shares the same name, identifying the baptised Christian with each of them equally and identifying them with each other. Against taking name as a bare marker of unity, the parallel texts from the Old Testament are pertinent; Craig Evans summarises the data in this way,

> To act or speak "in the name of" God (or the Lord) is commonplace in the Old Testament (e.g., Deut 18:5, "to stand and minister in the name of the Lord"; Deut 18:22, "If a prophet speaks in the name of the Lord"; Deut 21:5, "The Lord your God has chosen them to minister to him and to pronounce blessings in the name of the Lord"; 1 Sam 17:45, "I Come to you in the name of the Lord of hosts"; 2 Sam 16:18, "David ... blessed the people in the name of the Lord of hosts"; Ezra 5:1; Pss 20:5; 118:10, 11-12, 26; Isa 50:10, Mic 4:5; Zeph 3:12). The most interesting parallel is found in Ps 118:10-12, where three times the Psalmist complains of being surrounded by the "nations" but predicts that "in the name of the Lord" he will be able to "cut them off" (i.e., destroy them). In contrast to this imprecation stands Jesus' charge to his disciples: "Go and

---

[1] Ben Witherington, *Matthew*, Smyth & Helwys Bible Commentary (Macon, Ga: Smyth & Helwys Publishing, 2006), 535; D. A. Carson, "Matthew," in *The Expositor's Bible Commentary: Matthew–Mark (Revised Edition)*, ed. Tremper Longman III and David E. Garland, vol. 9 (Grand Rapids: Zondervan, 2010), 668.

make disciples of the nations."[2]

In these quotes, "the name" refers specifically to "Yahweh," the name by which God is known to his people. The correlation between "Yahweh" and the "name" in reference to God is so common that on occasion "the name" used absolutely refers to "Yahweh" or God via the name "Yahweh" (Lev 24:11, Deut 28:58, Ezek 22:5). The three persons are said to share the same singular name, Yahweh: thus, as in Deuteronomy 6 and throughout the Old Testament, the unity of God is declared via the singular name Yahweh, as each person is called Yahweh. The declaration that the Spirit is Yahweh is also made in 2 Corinthians 3:17-18.

B. 2 Corinthians 3:17-18

[17]ὁ δὲ κύριος τὸ πνεῦμά ἐστιν· οὗ δὲ τὸ πνεῦμα κυρίου, ἐλευθερία. [18]ἡμεῖς δὲ πάντες ἀνακεκαλυμμένῳ προσώπῳ τὴν δόξαν κυρίου κατοπτριζόμενοι τὴν αὐτὴν εἰκόνα μεταμορφούμεθα ἀπὸ δόξης εἰς δόξαν καθάπερ ἀπὸ κυρίου πνεύματος.

[17]Now, the Lord is the Spirit; and where the Spirit (that is, the Lord) is, there is freedom. [18]And all of us, beholding the glory of the Lord with unveiled faces, are being transformed into the same image, from glory into glory, as from the Lord, namely, the Spirit.[3]

In 2 Corinthians 3:17-18, Paul invokes many of the connotations surrounding the Spirit of Yahweh in the Old Testament. In the context of the New Covenant and Old Covenant distinction and the phrase "veil lies over their hearts" (κάλυμμα ἐπὶ τὴν καρδίαν; *kalumma epi ten kardian*), along with "hardened" (ἐπωρώθη; *eporothe*), the New Covenant promise of the Spirit poured out on the hearts of God's people is invoked by Paul (cf. Deut 30:1-

---

[2] Craig A. Evans, *Matthew*, New Cambridge Bible Commentary (New York: Cambridge University Press, 2012), 485.

[3] All Scripture quotations in this chapter are my own unless stead otherwise.

14; Isa 54:13; Jer 31:31-34; Ezekiel 36-37).[4] The Spirit also represents the presence of God among his people. Not unexpectedly, given what we saw in the Old Testament, Paul goes on to identify the Spirit as κυρίος (*kurios*), intending the divine name (v. 17b): "the Lord is the Spirit" (v. 17a), "the Lord, namely, the Spirit" (v. 18).

This passage is difficult, with an extended meditation on Exodus 34 that is not clear in all its details, though certainly in its intent (see the first part of 2 Corinthians 3).[5] However, despite the difficulties, I think we can see that Paul is identifying the Spirit with Yahweh in Exodus 34.[6] First, though Paul has changed the tenses, 2 Corinthians 3:16 is a quotation from Exodus 34:34, "Now, whenever Moses went in before Yahweh to speak with him, he would remove the veil, until he went out." In 2 Corinthians 3:16, Paul paraphrases this in the following way, "Now, whenever he would return to the Lord, he took off the veil." "The Lord" in 2 Corinthians 3:16 thus refers to Yahweh; this is supported by the absence of the article ("the") before "Lord" (κύριος) in this verse (suggesting it is functioning a proper noun). So, when we come to 2 Corinthians 3:17, ὁ κύριος (*ho kurios*, "the Lord") does not mean "the Lord," i.e. Jesus, but *"this* Lord," meaning Yahweh in Exodus 34.[7] This Yahweh whom we meet in Exodus 34 is the Spirit, and wherever the Spirit is present, the veil is removed: there is freedom. The presence of the Spirit in the tabernacle or on the Mountain and his effects were separated from the people, as symbolised by the veil; under the Old Covenant, only few had the privilege of the Spirit. But now, under the New Covenant, that same Spirit has been poured out on all, so that there is true freedom to behold and be transformed by Yahweh whom Moses beheld.

---

[4] Cf. C. F. D. Moule, "2 Cor 3,18b," in *Neues Testament Und Geschichte: Historisches Geschehen Und Deutung Im Neuen Testament: Oscar Cullmann Zum 70. Geburtstag*, ed. B. Reicke and H. Baltensweiler (Tübingen: Mohr Siebeck, 1972), 232–233.

[5] Cf. James D G Dunn, "2 Corinthians 3:17: The Lord Is the Spirit," *The Journal of Theological Studies* 21, no. 2 (October 1970): 309–320; Moule, "2 Cor 3,18b"; George H Guthrie, *2 Corinthians*, ed. Robert W. Yarbrough and Robert Stein (Grand Rapids: Baker Academic, 2015), 222–232.

[6] See the three works cited above.

[7] Dunn, "2 Corinthians 3," 317.

Notice how in 17b, the phrase "the Spirit of the Lord" (τὸ πνεῦμα κυρίου; *to pneuma kuriou*) appears to be in apposition (a genitive of apposition), "and where the Spirit (that is, the Lord) is, there is freedom." This was how we suggested that the phrase "the Spirit of YHWH" should be read in the Old Testament (cf. Chapter 9). At the end of verse 18, the apposition is clearer; here we read "from the Lord, namely, the Spirit" (κυρίου πνεύματος; *kuriou pneumatos*). Therefore, as in Matthew 28:19, we find that the Spirit is called Yahweh; he is the one God of Israel, as is the Son and the Father.

J. Alexander Rutherford

ONE LORD AND ONE GOD

All that remains is to consider the role of the Father as Yahweh. There is great complexity to the naming of God in the Bible, which we have already explored at points and will discuss further in Chapter 18. For the purpose of our argument thus far, we will only seek to establish that God the Father is called Yahweh, the Lord. In addition to examining the role of the Father, we will also ask if Yahweh is presented as a personal unity or if, as many 4th-century theologians contended, God as one—his unity—resolves into the Father as distinct from Son and Spirit. We will touch upon this important question here and will revisit it again in Chapter 18.

A. The Father is Yahweh

God the Father is referred to as Lord numerous times in the New Testament; exploring two examples should suffice to show that "Lord" (κύριος; *kurios*) in these instance means Yahweh (cf. Matt 4:7, 4:10, 11:25; Luke 10:21; Acts 17:24; Rom 4:8; Rom 12:19; 2 Cor 6:18). In Mark 12:35-37, Jesus interprets Psalm 110:1 with reference to himself; Jesus thus places himself in the position of the אֲדֹנִי (*'adoni*; "my lord") addressed by יהוה (YHWH) (cf. Acts 2:34). Though "Father" can on occasion be a title for Yahweh, and thus for the Father, Son, and Spirit (see below), when used relationally (our Father, the Father of Jesus), it refers to God the Father. In Hebrews 10:3-6, the author of Hebrews speaks of God's discipline of his children, quoting Proverbs 3:11-12 where twice YHWH is said to discipline his beloved children. Given that YHWH here is God the father of his children, disciplining them as does an earthly father, the term is being used for God the Father. These to passages suffice to Show that κυρίος (*kurios*, lord) as the equivalent of יהוה (YHWH) may refer to either the Father, the Son, or the Spirit. Therefore, as we saw in instances such as Isaiah 7:17-18, יהוה could speak to himself, for Yahweh may refer to the Father or the Son. That the Father may be called Yahweh should not be contentious; indeed, the tendency throughout church history has been to interpret ambiguous passages concerning Yahweh or God to the Father, even identifying the Father as the one true God (see Chapter 16).

B. God with Reference to the Undifferentiated Godhead

When θεός (*theos*; "God") is used in the New Testament, it refers to the Father many times, as when Jesus says, "my Father and your Father, my God and your God" (John 20:17, ESV). κυρίος (*kurios*; "the Lord") often refers to the Son (though not exclusively). The most regular term applied to each Trinitarian person across the Canon is not θεός, though their shared identity as the One God of is Israel is clear enough. Instead, they are designated "the Lord," Yahweh. Thus, in the Old and New Testaments, God as one and the unity of the three persons is designated not by what is ostensibly a class or universal term, אֱלוֹהַּ or θεός (*'eloah, theos*; "God," though we have argued that it is not a class term in the ontological sense), but with a concrete term, a personal name, Yahweh. Thus, when we speak of God as one within a biblical framework, interpreting that unity in terms of the universal or a oneness of essence is not possible. Speaking of God's oneness in concrete terms heightens the tension of our Trinitarian beliefs, but it does not create a contradiction, as we have already observed (see further Ch. 18). God is one and three in a similar, perhaps the same, sense: he is one person, Yahweh, in three persons, the Father, the Son, and the Holy Spirit. This point has been made occasionally throughout the history of the church, as we will address below (Chs 16-17).

On this basis, we would expect occasions where references to Yahweh our God do not resolve easily into one or another of the Trinitarian persons.

Several instances of this have already been observed: in Isaiah 6, it is not contextually clear that Yahweh enthroned in his glory is Father, Son, or Spirit. Exodus 34 does not identify Yahweh on the Mountain or in the Tabernacle as Father, Son, or Spirit; Paul identifies Yahweh as the Spirit in Exodus 34, but that does not necessarily mean Yahweh as the Spirit over against Yahweh as the Father or Son. Though there are specific moments where each person is manifest (as at Jesus baptism), the concrete reality of their unity suggests that they could manifest together, such that because Isaiah beheld the glory of Yahweh enthroned, he beheld Jesus' glory, but not necessarily the glory of Jesus alone (cf. Rev 4:1-11); as Moses beheld the glory of Yahweh, he beheld the Spirit's glory, but not necessarily the glory of the Spirit alone. More often than not, the name Yahweh and the terms we translate God and Lord are used without discrimination in the Old Testament; in the New Testament, we find more evidence of discrimination, with "God" often referring to the Father and "Lord" to the Son, yet even this is not consistent. Throughout the Gospels and the Epistles the same pattern is followed that is found in the Old Testament, where God and Lord are used for the Trinity without discrimination. For example, in Psalm 5, is the God to whom David cries the Father, or the Son, or the Spirit? We are given no contextual clues to allow us to decide the case. In the New Testament, we are given frequent contextual clues when the authors specify a person, such as "God the Father" or "the God and Father of our Lord Jesus Christ," and "our Father," or "the Lord Jesus Christ" (e.g. 1 Cor 1:3; 2 Cor 1:3; Gal 1:1; Acts 11:17). However, given the use of God and Lord without discrimination throughout the Old Testament and the continued use of these terms for all the Trinitarian persons in the New Testament (e.g. Matt 11:25; Luke 10:21; Acts 17:24), we have no biblical precedence to assume that the unqualified use of "God" or "Lord" intends one person over the other. That is, given the indiscriminate use of words referring to God in the Old Testament, which so shaped the imagination of the New Testament authors, and no indication of a radical shift in this regard, we should assume that "God" and "Lord" refer to the Trinity, not any one of the persons, when there is no clear contextual qualification otherwise. In other terms, the New Testament displays an progression in revelation as compared to the Old Testament, with greater attention paid to and insight into the intra-Trinitarian economy (the relationship between the persons of the Trinity) and the diverse economy of the persons towards the creation (see Chapter 18), but it nevertheless maintains the Old Testament position that God is one as much as he is three and can be referred to without reference to a specific Trinitarian person. We know from the New Testament that we pray to the Father by the Spirit in the name of the Son, yet often in our own prayers we pray to "God," without explicitly intending the Father alone (which is, perhaps, why we so frequently flow between the persons in our prayers). Our line of argument suggests that this ought to be the case, that our use of "God" and "Yahweh" will not directly refer to one of the persons in distinction from the others. We will explore this further in Chapter 18 .

The use of "God" primarily for the Father, often indicated by the phrase "God the Father," led 4th-century Christians to articulate the Trinitarian doctrine in terms of the monarchy of the Father, where the Father is the One God yet because of their organic union with the Father, the Spirit and the Son are also "god" (we will consider this further in the Chapter 16). However, we have seen that the use of the name "Yahweh," which is regularly used for God's unity, does not yield this same conclusion. The term God maybe be used of any of the persons, most often for the Father, and of God as one.

In addition to the many cases we have already considered where the name of our God refers to the Spirit, the Son, or the Father, there are additional cases where no one referent is clear (in the NT, e.g. Matt 1:20, 22, 24; 2:15; 4:7; 4:10; Luke 1:17, 25, 28; Acts 12:23; Rom 4:8, 11:34, 12:19, 14:6; 2 Cor 5:11, 6:17-18; James 3:9, 4:10, 4:15; Rev 22:6). Two cases worth exploring a little bit more are Ephesians 4:4-8, where each person appears to be alluded to but in a way that does not allow us to distinguish them clearly, and James 3:9. In both cases, the collocation "God and Father" does not necessarily refer to God the Father. 1 Corinthians 8:6 is the text that is most favourable to the position of the Father's Monarchy, so we will end our discussion of the Trinity in the Bible there.

C. Ephesians 4:1-6

¹Παρακαλῶ οὖν ὑμᾶς ἐγὼ ὁ δέσμιος ἐν κυρίῳ ἀξίως περιπατῆσαι τῆς κλήσεως ἧς ἐκλήθητε, ²μετὰ πάσης ταπεινοφροσύνης καὶ πραΰτητος, μετὰ μακροθυμίας, ἀνεχόμενοι ἀλλήλων ἐν ἀγάπῃ, ³σπουδάζοντες τηρεῖν τὴν

ἑνότητα τοῦ πνεύματος ἐν τῷ συνδέσμῳ τῆς εἰρήνης· ⁴"Εν σῶμα καὶ ἓν πνεῦμα, καθὼς καὶ ἐκλήθητε ἐν μιᾷ ἐλπίδι τῆς κλήσεως ὑμῶν· ⁵εἷς κύριος, μία πίστις, ἓν βάπτισμα, ⁶εἷς θεὸς καὶ πατὴρ πάντων, ὁ ἐπὶ πάντων καὶ διὰ πάντων καὶ ἐν πᾶσιν.

¹Therefore, I, the prisoner in the Lord, exhort you to walk in a manner worthy of the calling to which you were called, ²with all humility and gentleness, with patience, bearing with one another in love, ³being eager to keep the unity of the Spirit in the bond of peace. ⁴There is one body and one Spirit, as you also were called in one hope of your calling; ⁵there is one Lord, one faith, one baptism, ⁶one God and Father of all things, who is over all things, through all things, and in all things.

To be honest, I am torn on this one. On the one hand, triadic statements are replete throughout the New Testament, where the Father, Son, and Spirit are mentioned in parallel. The simplest explanation of the triadic mention of God here, "one Spirit," "one Lord," and "one God and Father" would be that it is another one of these formulas (cf. 3:14-19). However, certain aspects of this verse cause me to pause and read it more closely. The language of "oneness" is highly reminiscent of Deuteronomy 6:4-5, which we have seen to be key text portraying God as one and many. Because of the emphasis on oneness, we would expect a statement of God's unity to be found in this context, yet the only candidate would be the apparent reference to God the Father in verse 5 (perhaps "Lord" as well, cf. Ch. 18). For this reason, I am led to offer a reading of this passage where it is not a triadic statement of God's multiplicity but three steps ending in God's unity.

First, the triadic formula that precedes this one seems to have this same end, from three to one. In Ephesians 3:14-19, Paul speaks of Father, the Spirit, and Christ, highlighting different aspects of their work, ending in the shared goal of all of this, "that you may be filled up to all of God's fullness" (v. 19). After considering the distinct works of the Trinity, Paul ends with a goal that is not identifiable with any one of them: God's fullness is a

Trinitarian fullness, bringing all their apparently distinct actions into one. Thus, we are prepared to expect multiplicity in God's works to end in unity when we find a similar formula in Chapter 4.

Second, God's unity would be the appropriate note to strike in 4:1-5 as Paul is arguing for the unity of all of God's people through their shared participation in faith, in Christ's body, and their attendant realities.

Third, the references to each person get more ambiguous as the formula proceeds. There is "one body" and "one Spirit," the Spirit is of course God's gift poured out on His people effecting their unity and empowering them to live for him (e.g. 1:13, 17; 2:18, 21; 3:16; 4:3). The one Spirit is the Holy Spirit whom God has granted his people. "One Lord" is more ambiguous: Jesus is regularly called "Lord" in the New Testament, but this is not exclusively the case (as we saw in the previous chapter, cf. Ch. 18). The following two statements do not clearly specify this as a reference to Jesus, indeed, "baptism" reminds us of the formula in Matthew 28 where "name" points us to the Name, Yahweh, the Lord. The phrase "one Lord" also reminds us of Zechariah 14:9, which we discussed earlier; Zechariah 14:9 is itself an allusion to Deuteronomy 6:4, a clear statement of God's unity. Ephesian 4:5 more clearly echoes 1 Corinthians 8:6, which proves to be difficult passage. There, "One Lord" is a reference to Jesus, but perhaps not Jesus alone (see the discussion below, cf. Ch. 18). Our conclusion on the latter passage is perhaps decisive for our conclusion here. If we permit that "One Lord" there is an inclusive term, for the one Yahweh over against all so-called Lords, then we have an allusion to Jesus here but with an inclusive tone, "One Lord, who is Jesus but not Jesus alone"; in line with my conclusions in Chapter 18, where "Lord" and "God" without further delineation refer to the undifferentiated Godhead (Yahweh who is Father, Son, and Spirit), we could go one step further and say that it is fully inclusive (Father, Son, and Spirit).[1] In either case, there is a movement from the specific person, the Spirit, towards ambiguity in this epithet.

Finally, we have the reference to "one God and Father of all things"

---

[1] In the parsing provided in Chapter 18, the first would be a case of non-exhaustive reference, "Yahweh, Son (Father, Spirit)" and the second an inclusive not exclusive term, "Yahweh (Father, Son, Spirit)."

(Eph. 4:6). It may be ridiculous that I question the reference of this to the Father alone, but I persist. First, God the Father is not the only person of the Godhead called "Father"; in refence to God the Father, he is the Father of God the Son and our Father via adoption. However, even God the Son is "Father" with reference to the whole creation (Isaiah 9:6); I think this inclusive use of "Father," as a more familial equivalent of "Creator," is used in James 3:9-10 (see below) and 1 Corinthians 8:6 (below). We also find Paul using Aratus' line "For we are indeed his offspring" with reference to God in Acts 17:28-31; the "offspring" here is a creational image, thus the implied fatherhood of God is that of creation not of adoption as sons. Here in Ephesians 3"Of all things" qualifies the fatherhood of God in question not as the Father to the Son or the Father to his people, but the Father to creation. Indeed, the final phrase in Ephesians 4:6, he is "over all things, through all things, and in all things" has as its most clear parallels in several texts that refer to both the Spirit and the Son. "Over all things" is paralleled by Romans 9:5, which concerns the Son; "through all things" and "in all things" have their most clear parallels in the Spirit's presence amid the people of God as his temple (Eph 2:22, 3:17, 5:18; 1 Cor 3:16, 7:19; 2 Cor 6:16) and the earlier statement about God in Christ filling all things (Eph 1:23, cf. Jer 23:34; Col 3:11).[2] Thus, the three-fold description of "the God and Father of all things" implicates the Spirit and Son (along with, presumably, the Father) in the phrase, "the God and Father of all things."

Thus, there is reason to take the final phrase not as a reference to God the Father inclusively but to the one God as Father, Son, and Spirit. There is indeed one God in whom and for whom and through whom Christians exist and are united together. That there is "one God" is a clear allusion to Deuteronomy 6:4 as we have interpreted it. We find the very themes we identified there on display here; God's concrete unity, one God and Father, is juxtaposed with his multiplicity, one Spirit, one Lord, who is in all through and over all.

---

[2] S. M. Baugh, *Ephesians: Evangelical Exegetical Commentary*, ed. Wayne H. House, Hall W. Harris III, and Andrew W. Pitts (Bellingham, WA: Lexham Press, 2015), 307.

D. James 3:9-10

⁹ἐν αὐτῇ εὐλογοῦμεν τὸν κύριον καὶ πατέρα καὶ ἐν αὐτῇ καταρώμεθα τοὺς ἀνθρώπους τοὺς καθ᾽ ὁμοίωσιν θεοῦ γεγονότας· ¹⁰ἐκ τοῦ αὐτοῦ στόματος ἐξέρχεται εὐλογία καὶ κατάρα. οὐ χρή, ἀδελφοί μου, ταῦτα οὕτως γίνεσθαι.

⁹With [our tongue] we bless the Lord and Father, and with it we curse humans who have been made according to the likeness of God; ¹⁰from the same mouth comes forth blessing and curse. Things ought not be this way, my brothers and sisters.

Perhaps more than any other epistle, James appears to use "Lord" and "God" without reference to a particular Trinitarian person (cf. 2:1-13, 14-26). In the opening words of the epistle, he seems to describe himself as a slave of "the God and Lord Jesus Christ." That is, the construction of two anarthrous nouns (nouns without an article) followed by the "Jesus Christ" modifying the single noun "slave" suggests that that they are not two distinct things but one thing described in two ways (as would be the case if they were both determined by one article).[3]

Thus, his use of "God" is not restricted to the Father. In 1:27, he explicitly refers to God the Father, yet the previous use of "Father" with reference to God appears to be the more general sense of "Creator," without referring to any one person of the Trinity (1:17). So, when we reach 3:9-10, James has already demonstrated flexibility in his use of "Father" and "God." In these verses, the construction τὸν κύριον καὶ πατέρα (*ton kurion kai patera*), with two nouns governed by the single article, does not readily lend itself to a rendering such as, "the Lord and the Father," with two distinct objects, but as one object who is both Lord and Father. The allusion to Genesis 1-2 in the second half of verse 9 also moves away from a direct identification of "Father" with "God the Father," for humanity is made in

---

[3] Craig L. Blomberg and Mariam J. Kamell, *James: Zondervan Exegetical Commentary on the New Testament*, Zondervan Exegetical Commentary Series on the New Testament v. 16 (Grand Rapids: Zondervan, 2008), 47.

the Triune image not specifically the Father's (see our discussion in earlier chapters). Given that "Father" can be used inclusively for the Trinity as can "the Lord," the pair together in parallel with "the image of God" leads us to read this as a reference to the one God, not any one of his persons (if it is proper to speak in that way, cf. Ch. 18).

E. 1 Corinthians 8:5-6

⁵καὶ γὰρ εἴπερ εἰσὶν λεγόμενοι θεοὶ εἴτε ἐν οὐρανῷ εἴτε ἐπὶ γῆς, ὥσπερ εἰσὶν θεοὶ πολλοὶ καὶ κύριοι πολλοί, ⁶ἀλλ' ἡμῖν εἷς θεὸς ὁ πατὴρ ἐξ οὗ τὰ πάντα καὶ ἡμεῖς εἰς αὐτόν, καὶ εἷς κύριος Ἰησοῦς Χριστὸς δι' οὗ τὰ πάντα καὶ ἡμεῖς δι' αὐτοῦ.

⁵For although there may be so-called gods in heaven or on earth—as there are many gods and many lords—
⁶but for us,

> there is one God, the Father,
>> from whom are all things
>> and who is our end,
> and one Lord, Jesus Christ,
>> through whom are all things
>> and through whom are we.

This brings us to the final text we will consider, certainly a difficult one on any reading. 1 Corinthians 6:8 is a crucial text in the case for the Monarchy of the Father (which we will discuss in the next chapter). This is the view that the one God is not the unity of Father, Son, and Spirit nor an abstraction that stands behind them, but it is God the Father, or at least that is what the classical reading suggests. On the one hand, this text is rich in its Christology, for in the same breath as Paul speaks of "one God," he speaks of "one Lord, Jesus Christ."[4] On the other hand, at first glance, Jesus seems to be set apart from the "one God" of the Christian faith. However, this is only the case if we give cursory notice to the passage; a closer reading shows us that more is

---

[4] Gordon D. Fee, *The First Epistle to the Corinthians*, NICNT (Grand Rapids: Eerdmans, 1987), 415.

going on.

The first thing we should notice is that we once again have an allusion to the Great Shema; the language of "one God" echoes our interpretation of the Shema's "one," and "one Lord" alludes to Zechariah 14:9, which itself relies on Deuteronomy 6:4. The language of "one," "God," and "Lord" clearly brings us back to the Shema (the use of κυρίος [*kurios*, Lord] for יהוה [YHWH] bridging these texts).[5] Roy Ciampa and Brian Rosner sees an echo here also of Deuteronomy 10:17, "the only text in the Hebrew Bible where 'gods' and 'lords' appear in the same sentence as in 1 Corinthians 8:5."[6] As in Deuteronomy 6:4, God is both "God" and "Lord." The significance of all these passages is that in each one, "God" and "Lord" refer to God as one, his unity, not the Father over against the Son or Spirit but the God who is Father, Son, and Spirit. The "one God" is interchangeable with "the Lord," so our first reading seems to face an immediate challenge: would Paul really juxtapose "One God" with "Lord" as if these referred to two different persons?

Against the Corinthians' claim that idols are non-existent, Paul counters that there are indeed many "gods and lords"—at least of a sort—but these are not such that they challenge the unique divinity of the one God. For us, for Christians, God is one. In contrast with the "many gods," it would be an odd note for Paul to strike if he wanted to draw a distinction between God the Father and God the Son. Instead, the emphasis in context is on *one*, not "one God *and* one Lord." Indeed, given what we have seen so far, this text is even more reminiscent of the Shema than we first perceived, for here we have a parallel statement of God's unity—"one God and one Lord"—with apparent plurality, the Father and Jesus Christ. The whole reason for stating "one God" and "one Lord" separately is to contrast with the "many gods" and "many lords" that otherwise exist. Thus, Paul does not appear to be making a firm distinction here: the emphasis is not on the "and." If Paul's emphasis is on the "one," as it appears to be, then there are two ways to read this set of phrases. In both cases, they strongly resemble Hebrew parallelism

---

[5] Ibid., 411–415; Roy E. Ciampa and Brian S. Rosner, *The First Letter to the Corinthians* (Eerdmans, 2010), 381–385.

[6] Ciampa and Rosner, *The First Letter to the Corinthians*, 382.

in their form.

In the first case, the use of "Father" with reference explicitly to creation fits in with the pattern we have observed of "Father" as a title for the one God, not the person of God the Father, for whom "Father" refers rather to his relationship to the Son or to believers.[7] If we follow the usage of "Father" as we have seen elsewhere, then the phrase "there is one God, the Father" echoes James 3:9 and Ephesians 4:6, referring to God's unity. Someone may respond to this by introducing Paul's regular phrase, "God our Father and the Lord Jesus Christ," which seems parallel to this passage (Rom 1:7; 1 Cor 1:3; 2 Cor 1:2; Gal 1:3; Eph 1:2; Phil 1:2; 2 Thess 1:1-2; Phlm 3). In response to this, we may observe that Paul qualifies both "Father" and "Lord" in this phrase, it is "our Father" and the "Lord Jesus Christ." As will be argued in Chapter 18, without such qualification "Lord" is an ambiguous title (an inclusive term). "Father" is nearly always qualified in this way when referring to God the Father; in the case of exceptions, the context strongly indicates when God the Father is in view. We have explored several texts where "Father" is not qualified though it refers to God; in these cases, the term appears to refer to the undifferentiated Godhead, not God the Father. John 4 appears to be an exception, yet father language is used for God the Father so profusely throughout this book—and given that the Old Testament uses this language for the Father's relation to his people—that God the Father is undoubtedly in view here (i.e. this is not an instance of creational fatherhood). The only other exception is Acts 1:4, yet this alludes to Luke 24:49, where "Father" is qualified. Thus, it stands that where "Father" is neither immediately qualified by a relation to his people or Jesus nor such is indicated by the context, that the term is being used in the creational sense. In 1 Corinthians 8, the only qualification is creational, "from who are *all things*" (v. 6). Thus, "Father" here is not as similar to Paul's regular phrase as it first appears. The identification of "God, the Father" here as the one God, not the Father, is strengthened by the phrase "one God," which is the key statement of God's unity in the Shema.

On this reading the next lines are then a movement from general to specific: "for us, there is one God who created all things (the Father), from

---

[7] Cardozo Mindiola makes a similar observation. Cristian Cardozo Mindiola, "God the Father, Lord Jesus Christ and Their Interrelationship: 1 Corinthians 8:6 as a Test Case," *Theologica Xaveriana* 69, no. 188 (July 2019): 5.

whom and for whom are all things; yes, he is the one Lord, namely, Jesus Christ, through whom all things and through whom we exist." One God, Father, and one Lord are all statements of God's oneness—the general—and Jesus Christ is the specific, one of the persons. The parallel use of "God" and "Lord" simultaneously draws on the Shema and its echoes across Scripture (Deut 6:4, 10:17; Zech 14:9) and is motivated immediately by the "many gods" and "many lords" that are not God. Indeed, the use of "God" and "Lord" as parallel descriptors for the one God undercuts the "many gods and lords" even further: there are many gods *and* many lords, not only are they many, but they are many in their distinction. For God, he is truly one, both God and Lord in unity over against the plurality of the others. However, as in the Shema, it is not simply plurality that is being contrasted but the wrong sort of plurality, a plurality without true unity. On this reading, a movement from general to specific, which does not collapse the "one God" into Jesus Christ, asserts true plurality while it emphasises true unity.

In the second potential reading, the first colon (or set of lines) may indeed refer to God the Father. Here, "one God" and "one Lord" remain in parallel, designating God as one, but each colon moves from general to specific, One God, the Father and One Lord, the Son, both "Father" and "Son" being included in the "One God/One Lord." In favour of this is perhaps the reference to the Father as the source of creation and Jesus as its means, echoing as it does the creation narrative. However, it would also be proper to read this as general-specific language in light of our first proposal, where God as one is the creator, source of all things (cf. Isa 9:6, with reference to the Son), but God the Son is specifically the means by which we are created. This is strengthened by the fact that (to the best of my knowledge), God the Father is never stated to be our telos or end alone (perhaps Rom 11:36, but in line with the argument of this chapter, it is not clearly the Father there).

In the case of either reading, the text does not assert the monarchy of the Father (though this is true in a non-metaphysical sense, on which see Chapter 18) but the unity of God who is one in differentiation. Either reading accounts for the allusions to the Shema tradition and to the immediate demands of context, syntax, and style. However, I am inclined to believe the first reading is more probable, primarily because "Father" as used here is more consistent with statements of God's unity than the person of the

Father. So, once again, we encounter a text where God, Father, or Lord is used without referring to one person in exclusion to the others.

Here, at the end of Part 3, we have seen that the picture painted in the New Testament is that of the Old Testament. God is true unity in distinction, one person, Yahweh, in three, the Father, Son, and Holy Spirit. We are now in a place to look forward from the Bible to the history of Christian reflection on the Trinity and consider the implications of the biblical testimony to our doctrine of God as one and three.

J. Alexander Rutherford

—PART 4—
THEOLOGICAL CONCLUSIONS

16

4TH CENTURY TRINITARIANISM – PART 1

As we have seen, the Trinity was not invented in the 4th century, though this is identifiable in the Church tradition as the century when an interpretation of the Trinitarian tension achieved wide acceptance. The 4th-century debates we call "Trinitarian" were not even explicitly about the Trinity. Instead, they began with debate over the proper relationship between the Father and the Son and moved to encompass the relationship between these persons and the Spirit. We have seen that the fundamental Trinitarian tension that Nicaea tried to guard, that God is one and many, was articulated throughout the biblical eras. In post-Apostolic Christian writings, we find the Trinity presupposed in a similar way: worship is given to the Son alongside the Father, and the Spirit is intimately associated with both. As Christianity faced different challenges, especially false teaching, different aspects of the tensions between God's oneness and his many-ness where addressed.

In the 2nd and 3rd centuries, patristic scholar John Behr identifies two alternate attempts to develop an understanding of who Jesus is, especially in relation to God the Father, and the incarnation. As we considered the biblical data, we saw that the incarnation was a particular problem for the Jewish audience, that God would become a man. In this, they were not too different from the Gentiles. In the philosophical traditions leading to and through the 1st century, the idea of deity incarnate was abhorrent. Certainly, Greek mythology had gods walking among humanity, but the philosophers had long discarded these myths. Furthermore, the deities of the philosophers were, like the Christian God (though do not draw too close a connection here), far removed from the anthropomorphic gods of Greek mythology. The "gods" of mythology were just bigger and more powerful humans, with the same vices and mortality. Anyways, the incarnation was an offense to everyone, so it received significant attention in Christian theological discourse as theologians sought to present biblical beliefs in a rationally compelling way over against competing worldviews. In the thought of Ignatius, Justin Martyr, and Irenaeus, Behr identifies an emphasis on Christ's identity as a that of a continuing personal subject: the same person is both the pre-existent Word, or God the Son, and the human Jesus. For Justin in particular, the incarnation is "one phase in the biography of the Word."[1] For Hippolytus, Origen, and Paul of Samosata, identity was an issue of predication, such that "the identity of Jesus Christ is revealed in those properties that mark him out."[2] Origen and Paul would have a significant influence in the 4th century. On the one hand, almost everyone—on each side of the debates—were Origenists, thinking within the framework he developed, especially in his serious engagement with Gentile philosophy. Paul, on the other hand, was the archetypical heretic, referred to offhand throughout the 4th century to tar this or that opponent.

An important tension emerges at this time, in the 3rd to 4th centuries. Jerome tells us that the role of bishop distinct from the presbyter (or "elder") was introduced in Rome at some point after the closing of the Bible, probably the 2nd century, "to remedy schism and to prevent each individual from rending the church of Christ by drawing it to himself."[3] In the following centuries there emerged a tension between the charismatic teachers who amassed followers and developed theological schools like the philosophers and the bishops, who represented the traditional church structures.[4] Origen

---

[1] Behr, *The Way to Nicaea*, 238.

[2] Ibid., 239.

[3] Letter 146, *To Evangelus*, translated in NPNF 2.6. Cf. Peter Lampe, *From Paul to Valentinus: Christians at Rome in the First Two Centuries* (Fortress Press, 2003).

[4] See Behr, *The Way to Nicaea*; Rowan Williams, *Arius: Heresy and Tradition*, 2. ed. (London: SCM, 2001).

was a charismatic teacher who came into conflict with the bishops of his home, Alexandria. Following in the tradition of these charismatic leaders was Arius.

In his careful treatment of Arius, Rowan Williams identifies him as a "conservative," not as someone who holds conservative moral beliefs or orthodox Christian doctrine but as a traditionalist, who held to the teachings he received and continued to develop it with the tools he had at hand, which Williams suggests was neo-platonic philosophy.[5] Like Origen before him, Arius' efforts in this manner led him into conflict with the bishop of Alexandria, Alexander, and soon the whole Christian world. We are told by Athanasius and others that Arius was something of a populist, spreading his teaching among the masses. His text, the *Thalia*, appears to have been composed in meter associated with "vulgar entertainment" (sotadeans); "it is clear that Arius was deliberately choosing a popular medium and endeavouring to present his teaching in a widely attractive form."[6] What remains of his writings demonstrates an effort to engage with Scripture and tradition from a framework heavily accommodated to Neo-Platonism. As in the Neo-Platonic tradition, God for Arius was entirely incomprehensible, yet as a Christian, Arius did not want to dispense with the knowledge of God entirely; our knowledge of God is grounded solely in God's grace and freedom,

> Therefore, God himself, as he is, is inexpressible to all; neither an equal nor someone alike, this one alone has none co-glorious. We say he is ingenerate on account of the generate according to nature.[7]

---

[5] Williams, *Arius*. Cf. Rowan Williams, "The Nicene Heritage," in *The Christian Understanding of God Today: Theological Colloquium on the Occasion of the 400th Anniversary of the Foundation of Trinity College, Dublin*, ed. James M. Byrne (Dublin: Columba Press, 1993), 45–48..

[6] M. L. West, "The Metre of Arius' 'Thalia,'" *The Journal of Theological Studies* 33, no. 1 (1982): 105. Cf. Philostorgius, *Church History*, II.2.

[7] Αὐτὸς γοῦν ὁ θεὸς καθό ἐστιν ἄρρητος ἅπασιν ὑπάρχει. ἴσον οὐδὲ ὅμοιον, οὐχ ὁμόδοξον ἔχει μόνος οὗτος. ἀγέννητον δὲ αὐτόν φαμεν διὰ τὸν τὴν φύσιν γεννητόν. Arius, *Thalia* quoted by Athanasius in his *De Synodis*, in Hans-Georg

Jesus is the means by which God has made himself known, but we only know, as it were, the effects of God; who he is in himself (καθό ἐστιν; *katho estin*) is hidden to us—as it is to Jesus. The Son, according to Arius, "has nothing that is God's own according to subsistent propriety, for he is not equal, nor moreover is he consubstantial with him."[8] Jesus is the one and only mediator of our knowledge of God but is separated by the infinite chasm between the Creator and his creature. As Arius teachings drew more attention, the conflict between him and Alexander grew and began to threaten the unity of Christians across the Empire. So, the newly converted Constantine convened a council in the city of Nicaea (325 AD) to resolve the matter.

However, it did not end here: for the rest of the 4th century, the empire swayed back and forth between the so-called Arians (as Athanasius would call them) and those who came to identify themselves with Nicaea. We are not to imagine that Arius was able to amass a huge following nor that he swayed many presbyters and bishops with his teaching; instead, the emphasis of his theology resonated with many other 4th-century Origenians, who defended him at first or merely opposed the doctrine espoused at Nicaea. The loose alliance of figures among whom Arius would find a home may perhaps be called "Eusebians" because of the prominence of the bishops named Eusebius, of Nicomedia and of Caesarea. Athanasius will identify Arius with others, οἱ περὶ εὐσέβιον (*hoi peri eusebion*), "those around Eusebius."[9] These bishops disavowed the title "Arian," for Arius was a mere presbyter and they were bishops.[10] Among those who would eventually emerge as the "orthodox," varying emphases and terminologies emerged. Contemporary treatments of this period discuss multiple competing positions, some closer to Arius and others to what would become known as

---

Opitz, *Athanasius Werke - Bd. 2 Die apologien: Leiferung 6-7* (Berlin; Leipzig: Walter de Gruyter & Co., 1940), 242, ln. 11. Cf. the translation in, Williams, *Arius*, 106–107.

[8] ἴδιον οὐδὲν ἔχει τοῦ θεοῦ καθ᾿ ὑπόστασιν ἰδιότητος, οὐδὲ γάρ ἐστιν ἴσος, ἀλλ᾿ οὐδὲ ὁμοούσιος αὐτῷ. Opitz, lns. 16-17.

[9] E.g. *De Decretis* 20.1; De Synodis 15.2, 18.

[10] At the council of Antioch, AD 341: "for how could we as bishops be followers of a presbyter?" Quoted in Williams, *Arius*, 82.

Nicene or Orthodox.[11] Basil of Caesarea, for example, was hesitant about ὁμοούσιος (*homoousios;* "consubstantial"), the most controversial term at Nicaea (see his correspondence with Apollinaris of Laodicea).[12]

The development of theology in this century is complex, and the emergence of the Nicaean doctrine as the accepted orthodoxy was not *fait accompli*. When a unified sense of being "conciliar" emerged at the end of the century—that is, an understanding among bishops, clergy, and theologically involved lay orders (such as the monks) of continuity with the Nicaean-Constantinopolitan tradition—various emphases and tendencies existed among the conciliar church. Various theological trajectories came into conflict and found various levels of synthesis in late 4th century theology.[13] It is surprising at first to realise that the view of Nicaea as the significant statement of orthodox theology and a measure of catholicity did not emerge immediately in AD 325 but was a product of reflection on Nicaea itself and the recognition of its value for demarcating right belief from false teaching. The first mentions of what would be recognised as the key terminology of Nicaea, ὁμοούσιος (consubstantial), come decades after the council.[14] The recognition of Nicaea's significance, as the fundamental statement of traditional Christian orthodoxy, did not reach its zenith until Ephesus I (AD 431), where the production of further creeds was prohibited, and Chalcedon (AD 451), where the Constantinopolitan Creed was recognised as part and

---

[11] For a detailed treatment, see Behr and Ayres. For an insightful and more textbook approach, see Young. Behr, *The Nicene Faith: Vol 2 of Formation of Christian Theology*; Ayres, *Nicaea and Its Legacy*; Frances M. Young, *From Nicaea to Chalcedon: A Guide to the Literature and Its Background*, 2nd ed. (London: SCM Press, 2010); Behr, "Response to Ayres: The Legacies of Nicaea, East and West."

[12] On Basil, see G. L. Prestige, *St Basil the Great and Apollinaris of Laodicea* (London: SPCK, 1956).

[13] Cf. Ayres, *Nicaea and Its Legacy*, 43–84. Cf. Behr, "Response to Ayres: The Legacies of Nicaea, East and West"; Behr, "Calling upon God as Father: Augustine and the Legacy of Nicaea."

[14] On the gradual acceptance of the term, see J. N. D. Kelly, *Early Christian Doctrines* (London: Adam & Charles Black, 1958), 245–247; George Christopher Stead, *Divine Substance* (Oxford: Clarendon Press, 1977), 260; Hanson, *The Search*, 36–437; Johannes Zachhuber, *The Rise of Christian Theology and the End of Ancient Metaphysics: Patristic Philosophy from the Cappadocian Fathers to John of Damascus* (Oxford University Press, 2020), 77.

parcel of the Nicaean tradition and where the role of the council was identified as applying the sufficient Nicaean Creed, not drafting another creed or adding to it.[15]

Thus, to consider 4th-century Trinitarian theology or conciliar Trinitarianism is not to consider a single theology but a loose alliance of theologians and their distinctive thought, out of which emerges cohesion and agreement on this or that point. The significance of the Nicaean Creed by the end of the 4th century and the 5th century can hardly be overstated, but granted its significance, the Creed itself left much unsaid. It was left to those who held forth the Creed to offer an interpretation of its language, to answer the challenges raised against it, and to offer an account of the relations between the Father, Son, and Spirit that would answer the charges of Arius and those who were likeminded. The key challenge was to uphold the essential unity of the Father and Son, and later the Spirit. They were all on the same side of the Creator-Creature distinction, though how to articulate that claim was not simple. In this chapter, we will briefly consider the Creed itself, then we will turn to the influential interpretation of it offered by Athanasius, Basil, and Gregory of Nazianzus. The careers of the latter two coincide with the Council of Constantinople (AD 381), which plays an important role in extending the same logic used to defend the deity of the Son to the Spirit.[16]

A. The Nicaean Creed

We believe in one God, the Father almighty, maker of heaven and earth, of things both visible and invisible; in one Lord, Jesus Christ, the Son of God, the only-

---

[15] On the reception of Nicaea in the 4th century, see Behr, *The Nicene Faith: Vol 2 of Formation of Christian Theology*. On the reception of Nicaea in the 5th century, see Mark S. Smith, *The Idea of Nicaea in the Early Church Councils, AD 431-451* (Oxford: Oxford University Press, 2018). On Chalcedon, see the translation of Price and Gaddis and the Definition in Session V. Michael Gaddis and Richard Price, *The Acts of the Council of Chalcedon*, 3 vols., Translated Texts for Historians (Liverpool: Liverpool University Press, 2005).

[16] This is not to say the Spirit was neglected in the earlier debates; Athanasius will once use the term ὁμοούσιος for the Spirit, in *Ad Serapion* 1.27.

begotten, begotten from the Father before all ages, true God from true God, begotten not made, consubstantial [ὁμοούσιον; *homoousion*] with the Father, through whom all things came to be, who on account of us humans and on account of our salvation came down, was incarnated [σαρκωθέντα; *sarkothenta*], became human [ἐνανθρωπήσαντα; *enanthropesanta*], suffered, rose again on the third day, ascended into heaven, and is coming to judge the living and the dead; and in the Holy Spirit.

But those who say there was a time when he was not, before he was begotten he was not, that he came to be from things that were not, or from a different reality [ὑποστάσεως; *hupostaseos*] or substance [οὐσίας; *ousias*], who assert that the Son of God is subject to turning [τρεπτὸν; *trepton*] or subject to change [ἀλλοιωτὸν; *alloioton*], persons such as this the Catholic and Apostolic church anathamatises.[17]

The Nicaean Creed echoes various personal creeds that existed around this time, bearing evidence that it was drafted out of materials at hand, not *de novo* for the present situation. There are also clear echoes of Scripture, including many passages we have examined (for "one God" and "one Lord," see 1 Cor 8:5-6, cf. Eph 4:4-6). The positive statements of the Creed are such that most Christians could not disagree, much of it being the language of Scripture. As shown by the anathemas, the contrast between "begotten" versus "made" and the atemporality of this begetting ("before all ages") addressed the very error perceived to be Arius', that the Son was created. They place the Son on the Creator side of things, not the created. However, more than placing the Son with God, the statement asserts their substantial identity with the term ὁμοούσιος. It is thought that this term was used solely to preclude Arius and his sympathizers from ascribing to the Creed. Before this, the term was used

---

[17] My translation of the text according to the Definition of Chalcedon. There was flexibility in the text of Nicaea in the 4th and 5th century. Printed in ACO 2.2, Session V, sec. 32.

in various ways that were contrary to Christian theology (such as partaking of a shared material reality); indeed, it was associated with the heresy of Paul of Samosata.[18] The term succeeded in excluding Arius and his sympathisers, but proved to be a hard sell for those who otherwise agreed with the theology of Nicaea and the bishops who aligned themselves with it.[19] Negatively, the term served to exclude Arius and others; positively, it would be later theologians who unpacked a sense appropriate to the Creed. Before turning to Athanasius and his interpretation of ὁμοούσιος (*homoousios;* "consubstantial"), it is important to observe that isolated from the biblical context, the statement "one God, the Father" asserts the monarchy of God the Father. The one God of Christianity, according to Eastern Trinitarian thought in the 4th century, is actually God the Father.[20] How much the bishops present at Nicaea had thought through the implications of this claim and how the Son and Spirit were likewise placed with the Father on the Creator side of things is unclear, but this belief in the Monarchy of the Father become a key tenant in the thought of Athanasius, Apollinaris, Basil of Caesarea, and Gregory of Nazianzus (among others). In the writings of these theologians, it is developed as perhaps the most significant sense of the term ὁμοούσιος. However, Gregory of Nyssa will on occasion strike a different note with his use of the term (see Ch. 17).

B. Athanasius

Though they were seeking to resolve what we have been calling the Trinitarian tension, it is important to observe that the impetus behind 4th-century theology was not synthesising the whole testimony of Scripture but to answer the particular challenges of Arius and others. Though everyone

---

[18] On the use of the term at Nicaea, Hanson, *The Search*, 202; Williams, *Arius*, 68–70; Behr, *The Nicene Faith: Vol 2 of Formation of Christian Theology*, 157.. For the later objections to the term, see G. L. Prestige, *God in Patristic Thought*, 2nd ed. (London: SPCK, 1952), 209; Stead, *Divine Substance*, 242–244; Hanson, *The Search*, 190–197; Williams, *Arius*, 134–135; Behr, *The Way to Nicaea*, 187–188, 218–220; Behr, *The Nicene Faith: Vol 2 of Formation of Christian Theology*, 137.

[19] Cf. Prestige, *St Basil the Great and Apollinaris of Laodicea.*

[20] See, for example, Behr, "Calling upon God as Father: Augustine and the Legacy of Nicaea."

was wrestling with the Trinitarian tension, the parameters of the 4th-century discussion were set by the controversies that arose. Arius and the Eusebii placed Jesus on the creature side of the Creator-creature distinction, so Athanasius and others needed to show that Jesus was not a creature but the Creator himself. This meant showing how Jesus was not *made*, though they need to account for the language of Father and Son and "begotten," and showing how Jesus was identical in definition or essence with the Father. They needed to show that Jesus was identical to God and himself God and that there was no substance behind Jesus and the Father that made them both God. They need to uphold the fact that though Christ came from God, he was simultaneously, as God, uncreated and eternal. Finally, they needed to uphold the claim that there were not several gods but one God, the Father almighty. It is evident how these problems are closely related to the Trinitarian tension, yet they are not identical with it. In the works of Athanasius, his associate Apollinaris (this was before Apollinaris was declared heterodox from the First Council of Constantinople (AD 381) onward), Basil of Caesarea, and Gregory of Nazianzus, a similar solution to all these problems was attained

Against the charge that Jesus was a creature made by God, Athanasius followed the Creed in its use of the Father-Son analogy. To be a Father is to beget a child, so they reasoned, thus as a Son, Jesus is begotten. This is certainly supported by several passages (Heb 1:5; 5:5) and it is one possible interpretation of the Greek word μονογενής (*monogenes*; "one and only" or "only begotten," cf. John 3:16).[21] However, because Jesus is also God and eternal, without beginning or end, the sort of begetting characterising their relationship must be of an eternal sort, thus Jesus is "eternally begotten from the Father." Furthermore, this begetting must not be understood in a corporeal way—like the way a human father begets a child (e.g. *De Synodis* 51). Because the Father has always been a Father, "He is always generative by nature," as he also is always good.[22] Reasoning from the Father-Son

---

[21] The meaning of μονογενής is a point of great debate in the contemporary literature, but not much rests on one's conclusion either way.

[22] *Contra Arianos* III.66, trans in NPNF 2.4. The use of "nature" here, especially with the predicate "good," is problematic, for if the Father is "generative" in nature and one in nature with the Son, then the Son would likewise be "generative." It is

analogy, Athanasius assumes that like begets like, that a son is identical in nature to his father, thus, in a similar manner, the Son of God the Father will be what the Father is in essence, namely, God. However, acknowledging that God the Father and God the Son were alike in essence raised a more serious problem.

If both were alike in essence, two individuals of the same kind, then they would be ἀδελφά (*adelpha*), that is, ontologically collateral. This would lead to two devastating conclusions. On the one hand, there would now be two "gods," for both are ontologically co-ordinate; on the other hand, there would be another substance (on a platonic ontology) that was itself the true God. That is, if they are co-ordinate, what is it by which they both are qualified as God? An easy answer would the transcendent form "Godhead" individuated by both of them.[23] However, this would make the Form itself God, not the persons of the Trinity. The Son and the Father would be "god" in some sense, but there would be two "gods" submitted to a more real being, the Form of Godhead. Therefore, Athanasius rejected the claim that they were collaterals.[24] Instead, the father-son analogy offered a different account of ontology that fit comfortably in the Neoplatonic milieu of the 4th century and seemed to meet all the needs of the debate.[25]

In the Trinity, as with humanity, there is an identity of essence through derivation: the Son has divinity because his Father has divinity. However, it is not as if divinity is apportioned to one and the other, or as if there were two separate divinities possessed by each. Nor is there a "Divinity" that stands behind them, by which they are both divine. No, the Father himself is the Godhead, the very God and being of Divinity, from which the Son proceeds like a river flowing from its head, a vine extending branches, or the

---

better to understand nature here as loose term for what the Father is (essence plus individual properties) rather than "essence," as the term is usually used.

[23] Basil's *Ep. 361-362* (*Basil to Apollinaris* and *Apollinaris to Basil*) in Prestige, *St Basil the Great and Apollinaris of Laodicea*.

[24] Synods 51.1, in Opitz, p. 275 lns. 4-11.

[25] On similar ontologies, see Johannes Zachhuber, "Derivative Genera in Apollinarius of Laodicea," in *Apollinaris Und Die Folgen*, Studien und Texte zu Antike und Christentum 93 (Tübingen: Mohr Siebeck, 2015), 93–114.

radiance of the Sun beaming forth.[26] In this way, the Son receives his Godhood from the Father but is not separated from the Father. In fact, he shares in the being of the Father. The Father is the One God and the Son has existence and essence by partaking of the Father's being and essence through unbroken, organic derivation. This derivation is eternal and perfect, so the Son is "true God from true God," "Light from Light," "eternally begotten but not made," as the Creed puts it. There was never a time when the Son was not. Because there is one being or substance of God encompassing Father and Son (and Spirit), there is only one God. Because the Father is the fount from which the Son and Spirit flow, he is himself the one God; they are, however, rightly called "God" because of this relationship.

In Athanasius and the others, this ontology was identical for God and for humanity; it is justified on analogy with the way humanity relates to humans. This is most evident in Apollinaris dialogue with Basil. As with humanity, so with God; there is one human, Adam, from whom we all have humanity and thus are humans, though he is the true "human" and the substance from which we derive.[27] This is exactly what ὁμοούσιος (*homoousios*; "consubstantial") means, then, the true identity and unbroken connection between the first in a series, as between Adam and humanity and the Father and Son, even (on a lower ontological level) between David and his house.

C. Basil, Nazianzus, and Constantinople

In Basil and Gregory of Nazianzus, we are met with the same ontology as it played out in different battles. As Christopher Beeley has argued, in Nazianzus there is an emphasis on the monarchy of the Father, or the Father as the first in this ontological series. There are times where the logical account of the Son's essential identity with the Father is stated, or where ὁμοούσιος is found, but throughout his orations, the idea of derivation from Father to

---

[26] *Sent.* 10.3; *Syn.* 42, 48, 51-52. A similar position is found in *Expositio Fidei* 2, but this text is considered spurious by many contemporary scholars, so references to it should be taken with a grain of salt.

[27] See Epistle 362 in Prestige, *St Basil the Great and Apollinaris of Laodicea*. Cf. Apollinaris, *Kata Meros Pistis* in Hans Lietzmann, ed., *Apollinaris von Laodicea und seine Schule: Texte und Untersuchungen* (J. C. B. Mohr (Paul Siebeck), 1904), 173.17–26, accessed April 22, 2020, http://archive.org/details/apollinarisvonl01apolgoog.

Son and Spirit is clear.[28] In Basil, the derivative aspect of ontology is clear, but in his interaction with Eunomius, there is a concern to explain how we know God and how Father and Son are identical in essence.[29] Basil dismisses mere collaterality between the Father and the Son, as did Athanasius; ὁμοούσιος (*homoousios;* "consubstantial") is intended to reject this very thing, he writes in Epistle 52.[30] Instead, "Whenever both the cause [τὸ αἶτον; *to aiton*] and the thing which has its origin from the cause [ἐκ τοῦ αἰτίου; *ek tou aitiou*] are of the same nature [τῆς αὐτῆς ὑπάρχῃ φύσεως; *tes autes huparche phuseos*], these are said to be the same substance [ὁμοούσια; *homoousia*]."[31] In *Against Eunomius*, he draws on Hebrews 1:3 to identifying order in the Father-Son relationship; the Son is the radiance and representation of the Father. There is order which follows "from the sequence that is inherent in them according to nature."[32]

At Constantinople, the Nicene Creed is expanded to address the concerns of those who "make war with the Spirit," as they are identified at Chalcedon and elsewhere. Because ὁμοούσιος was interpreted specifically in terms of the Father-Son relationship (though it was occasionally applied to

---

[28] Christopher A. Beeley, *Gregory of Nazianzus on the Trinity and the Knowledge of God: In Your Light We Shall See Light*, Oxford Studies in Historical Theology (Oxford: Oxford University Press, 2008), 194, 214, 221–222. Cf. Christopher A. Beeley, "Divine Causality and the Monarchy of God the Father in Gregory of Nazianzus," *Harvard Theological Review* 100, no. 2 (April 2007): 199–214; Verna E. F. Harrison, "Illumined from All Sides by the Trinity," in *Re-Reading Gregory of Nazianzus: Essays on History, Theology, and Culture*, ed. Christopher A. Beeley, CUA studies in early Christianity (Washington, D.C: Catholic University of America Press, 2012), 13–30; Gregory Nazianzus, *Faith Gives Fullness to Reasoning: The Five Theological Orations of Gregory Nazianzen*, trans. Frederick W. Norris, Supplements to Vigiliae Christianae v. 13 (Leiden ; New York: Brill, 1990).

[29] Zachhuber, *The Rise of Christian Theology and the End of Ancient Metaphysics*, 40. Zachhuber overstates this point in the above work and Johannes Zachhuber, "Basil and the Three-Hypostases Tradition: Reconsidering the Origins of Cappadocian Theology," *Zeitschrift für antikes Christentum* 5, no. 1 (2001): 65–85.

[30] Cf. Behr, *The Nicene Faith: Vol 2 of Formation of Christian Theology*, 303.

[31] Ep 52.2, quoted in Ibid.

[32] Eun. 1.20.

the Spirit [e.g. Athanasius, *Ad Serap.* 1.27]), a different term was employed at Constantinople. The Spirit "proceeds" from the Father. However, the similar idea of "derivation" or ordered causality is implied in that term, and the account of Athanasius, Basil, and Gregory of Nazianzus is clear that as in the case of the Son, the Spirit is "God" because he partakes of the Father's being and, therefore, has the same essence.

This interpretation was the dominant one, that the Father, Son, and Spirit shared the same being and that the Son and Spirit were identical in essence with the Father because of their derivation from Him. The Father himself was the One God. In this way, 4th-century Christians sought to refute the charge of tritheism and maintain the claims that the Father was the one God and that the Son and Spirit were fully and truly God. Though championed by Athanasius, Basil, and Gregory, this was not the only solution present in the 4th century. Gregory of Nyssa developed a similar though not identical account of God's oneness and plurality, as did Augustine.

J. Alexander Rutherford

4ᵀᴴ CENTURY TRINITARIANISM – PART 2

In this chapter, we will look at two other Trinitarian doctrines among those who are today recognised as Orthodox, those who are "conciliar," who upheld the Nicaean Creed or stood in the tradition descending from it. In Gregory of Nyssa's *Ad Ablabium: That There Are not Three Gods*, derivation from the Father appears to be replaced by true collaterality. In Augustine's *De Trinitate* and elsewhere, the unity of the Godhead is treated in a different manner than it is in the Greek Fathers we have considered; it is not a 4ᵗʰ thing, yet neither is it the Father. God is one in a similar but not identical manner to the way he is three. We will look first at Nyssa and then Augustine.

A. Gregory of Nyssa's *That there Are not Three Gods*

Gregory of Nyssa has received significant attention in recent years. There has been significant debate over his view of universals,[1] and he has been

---

[1] Alden A Mosshammer, "Gregory of Nyssa and Christian Hellenism," in *Studia Patristica*, ed. Elizabeth A. Livingstone, 32 vols. (Leuven: Peeters, 1997), 170–195; Johannes Zachhuber, *Human Nature in Gregory of Nyssa: Philosophical Background and Theological Significance* (Brill, 1999); Richard Cross, "Gregory of Nyssa on Universals," *Vigiliae Christianae* 56, no. 4 (2002): 372–410; Johannes Zachhuber, "Once Again: Gregory of Nyssa on Universals," *The Journal of Theological Studies* 56, no. 1 (April 2005): 75–98; Kevin Corrigan, "Οὐσία and Ὑπόσταις in the Trinitarian Theology of

championed as a proponent of a person or individual-centred ontology.[2] However, a close reading of his work shows that he is much closer to his brother Basil and to Gregory of Nazianzus than these 20th-century readings would suggest.[3] However, though similar, there are notes of difference between his account of the Trinitarian relations and those of Basil and Gregory, this is seen especially in his letter *That There Are not Three Gods*.[4]

Zachhuber argues that in his work on human nature, Gregory presents a view of the universal as a real thing that only has existence in the particulars yet is what truly matters about them. The universal or form of Humanity is not more than particular humans, yet particular humans are not more than humanity. Instead, the particulars exist solely as realisations of Humanity, which is itself the really existing thing.[5] Cross responds to this account, yet so far as the Trinity goes, this ontology appears to be an apt reading of Nyssa's letter *Ad Ablabium*, or *That There Are not Three Gods*.[6]

In this letter, Nyssa unpacks the provocative claim that it is improper but acceptable to speak of "humans," despite the fact that there is properly only one "human," and by analogy it is improper to speak of "Gods" and theologically problematic to do so. Lewis Ayres describes this letter as "short but surprisingly complex."[7] The letter is a response to Ablabius, a Bishop according to Nyssa's *Epistle 6*; Ablabius has enquired concerning the proper response to an argument which Nyssa recounts in the letter. In essence, the argument of the first part (with which we are concerned) is this: we enumerate "Peter, James, and John" as "three" men though they are "in one

---

the Cappadocian Fathers: Basil and Gregory of Nyssa," *Zeitschrift für Antikes Christentum* 12, no. 1 (January 2008): 114–134.

[2] Jean Zizioulas, *Being as Communion: Studies in Personhood and the Church* (London: Darton Longman & Todd, 2004).

[3] For an overview of 20th-century readings of Nyssa and response to them, see Sarah Coakley, ed., *Rethinking Gregory of Nyssa* (Malden, Mass: Blackwell, 2003).

[4] Translations from NPNF 2.5.

[5] Zachhuber, *The Rise of Christian Theology and the End of Ancient Metaphysics*, 10. Cf. Zachhuber, *Human Nature in Gregory of Nyssa*, 104; Zachhuber, "Once Again."

[6] Cross, "Gregory of Nyssa on Universals."

[7] Ayres, *Nicaea and Its Legacy*, 47.

nature," why then are we "at variance with our confession" to enumerate the "three persons" acknowledged with "no difference of nature between them" as "three Gods"? Acknowledging the difficulty of the matter, Nyssa begins by accepting the initial premise that three men are "in one nature." Going further, he argues that, properly speaking, there is only "one nature" or "one human" and that it is only colloquially ("a customary abuse of language") that we speak of three "humans," the plural name derived from the one nature. Separation is permitted by the non-essential attributes of each individual; the nature itself is indivisible. His logic is as follows: "the term 'man' does not belong to the nature of the individual as such, but to that which is common. For Luke is a man, or Stephen is a man; but it does not follow that if any one is a man he is therefore Luke or Stephen." That is, logically speaking, if "Luke" or "Stephen" were predicates of the nature itself, then it anything that "is a man" would also be "Luke" or "Stephen." That these names are not interchangeable with the nature suggests that they denominate something other than the nature, namely, "the peculiar attributes considered in each severally." Thus, "according to the more accurate expression, 'man' would be said to be one, even though those who are exhibited to us in the same nature make up a plurality." Thus, Nyssa does not resolve the argument by introducing disanalogy between the Trinitarian persons and humans; instead, he presses the analogy further. Humanity is properly one, though frequently spoken of as "three." Similarly, the Trinity is properly one in the same way, according to nature. Thus, instead of transferring the "erroneous habit" of our speech concerning humans to God, we ought to instead forgo the habit in its entirety. Given the difficulty of this, we may continue with the habit as it regards "the lower nature" but as it regards "the Divine nature," "the various use of terms is no longer free from danger." In the rest of the letter, Nyssa will argue that θεός (theos, "God") does not refer to God's "nature," yet the ontology that is employed in this first part of the letter is that of collaterality.

In this account, there is an emphasis on the primacy of the Divine nature, but the Godhead is not identified with the Father. Moreover, here, the persons of the Trinity seem to be truly co-ordinate or collateral, as Athanasius and Basil denied. Nyssa may hit on different themes elsewhere in his corpus, as Behr argues, but the account given here is of collaterality.[8] Given the differences between this account and that of Athanasius, Basil, and Gregory, it seems appropriate to speak of 4th century Trinitarian *theologies*, even among the conciliar parties who supported Nicaea. Moving Westward, Augustine's doctrine of the Trinity is significantly different than what we have seen thus far.

B. Augustine

A full account of Augustine's trinitarian doctrine would require a book length treatment, looking not only at his *De Trinitate* but also his many commentaries and other works. There has been far ranging discussion concerning Augustine in the 20th and 21st centuries, and he has not often fared well. Ayres and others have attempted to show how Augustine is more in line with the Eastern, Greek speaking theologians we have discussed, and has offered a helpful corrective in many ways.[9] However, as Behr has argued, there remain claims throughout Augustine's corpus that stand at odds with the Eastern Fathers we have considered.[10] For the Fathers of the East, the one true God is God the Father, the "monarchy of the Father" for the Eastern Fathers is "the monarchy of the one God as Father."[11] In Augustine,

---

[8] Cf. John Behr, "'One God Father Almighty,'" *Modern Theology* 34, no. 3 (July 2018): 320–330.

[9] In addition to Ayres' *Legacy*, see also *Augustine and the Trinity* and "The Fundamental Grammar." Lewis Ayres, "The Fundamental Grammar of Augustine's Trinitarian Theology," in *Augustine and His Critics: Essays in Honour of Gerald Bonner*, ed. Gerald Bonner and George Lawless (London; New York: Routledge, 2000), 51–76; Ayres, *Nicaea and Its Legacy*; Lewis. Ayres, *Augustine and the Trinity* (Cambridge, UK; Cambridge University Press, 2010). Cf. Michel René Barnes, "Augustine in Contemporary Trinitarian Theology," *Theological Studies* 56, no. 2 (June 1995): 237–250; Michel René Barnes, "De Régnon Reconsidered," *Augustinian Studies* 26, no. 2 (1995): 51–79; David Bentley Hart, "The Mirror of the Infinite: Gregory of Nyssa on the Vestigia Trinitatis," in *Rethinking Gregory of Nyssa*, ed. Sarah Coakley (Malden, Mass: Blackwell, 2003), 111–132; Keith E. Johnson, "Appendix: Reclaiming Augustine on the Trinity," in *Rethinking the Trinity & Religious Pluralism: An Augustinian Assessment*, Strategic Initiatives in Evangelical Theology (Downers Grove: IVP Academic, 2011), 220–257.

[10] Behr, "Calling upon God as Father: Augustine and the Legacy of Nicaea."

[11] Ibid., 162.

we find similar language of the Father as the first principle, of the Son and Spirit deriving from the Father, yet we also find something unique (in comparison to the Eastern Fathers we have considered).[12] Augustine uses the term "God" and considers the one God in passages such as Deuteronomy 6:4, and in phrases such as "the Spirit of God" and "the Son of God," to refer to the *one God the Trinity*. Consider, for example,

> The Trinity is one God, not that the Father is the same as the Son and the Spirit, but that the Father is Father, the Son is Son, and the Holy Spirit is the Holy Spirit, and this Trinity is one God, as it is written: "Hear, O Israel, the Lord your God is one [God]" (Deut 6.4).[13]

Writing from an Eastern perspective, Behr says of this use, "Augustine, on the other hand, does not seem to be aware that he is using the term 'God' of the Trinity in a radically new manner, one that is not only different but also problematic."[14]

Augustine is able to speak of the three persons and the derivation of the Son and the Spirit, yet the use of "God" for the Trinity itself has its closest parallel only in Nyssa's *Ad Ablabium*. However, elsewhere in Nyssa's corpus, he uses the language of Athanasius and Basil, that God the Father is the one God. The language of *Ad Ablabium* may be interpreted in light of that, which would make Augustine language unique. Moreover, for Nyssa, the use of

---

[12] In *De Doctrina Christiana*, Augustine will say, "in the Father there is unity." Augustine, *On Christian Teaching*, trans. R. P. H. Green, Oxford World's Classics (Oxford; New York: Oxford University Press, 2008), 10, Book I, Sec. 12.

[13] *De fide et symb.* 9.16. Translated in Behr, "Calling upon God as Father: Augustine and the Legacy of Nicaea," 160. Behr has "is one Lord." The discussion at this point presupposes it reads "one God," and the Latin text in Corpus Scriptorum Ecclesiasticorum Latinorum, Vol. XXXXI (Sect. V Pars III) has "*Deus unus est*." Cf. "Faith and the Creed," translated by Michael G. Campbell. However, in *De Trin.* the same text is given as "*Dominus unus est*" and the following discussion refers to "one Lord our God." On either reading, the text could also be translated "the Lord/God is one," which could, perhaps, in light of Augustine's discussion, reflect similar exegesis as we have presented above. Augustine, "Faith and the Creed," in *The Works of Saint Augustine: A Translation for the 21st Century*, ed. Boniface Ramsey, trans. Michael G. Campbell (Brooklyn: New City Press, 1990).

[14] Behr, "Calling upon God as Father: Augustine and the Legacy of Nicaea," 161.

God for the substance in all three persons is an impersonal use, denoting the essence or the reality. The unique idiom of Augustine continues, for he speaks of the One God, the Trinity, in personal language, as acting and revealing himself. The prevalence of this idiom along with the use of the One God for the Trinity supports Behr's claim that in Augustine we find something "radically new" (again, in comparison with the East). Augustine speaks of the Trinity, "Who is God."[15] This Trinity is the "one God."[16] In his exposition on the Psalms, he asks, "whether we should understand the Father, or the Son, or the Holy Spirit, or the Trinity, 'to have stood among the congregation of the gods, and in the midst to distinguish the gods;' because Each One is God, and the Trinity itself is One God."[17] In *De Trinitate*, Augustine is able to say, "Neither does anything forbid us, not only to understand those words spoken to Adam as spoken by the Trinity, but also to take them as manifesting the person of that Trinity."[18] In this and the following paragraph, he entertains this thought at length. He speaks of the unity of God as a "person," as speaking and revealing. Unlike Athanasius, Basil, and Gregory, when Augustine speaks of the one God, he intends a personal unity that does not resolve into one of the three: he is One God the Trinity, not One God the Father. This pattern of speech continues throughout the treatise, and appears throughout Augustine's corpus. In *De Doctrina Christiana* Augustine will say "perhaps the Trinity is better called the one God from whom, through whom, and in whom everything is [Rom 11:36]. There is the Father and the Son and the Holy Spirit—each one of these is God, and all of them together are one God."[19] For Augustine, the unity of the Godhead is personal, speaking and revealing.[20]

Though he does not put it this way, it is hard to escape the conclusion that for Augustine, God is fundamentally personal, one Person in three

---

[15] *Trin*, 1.4.7

[16] Ibid.

[17] Psalm 82.2, cf. 59.12, 37.3.

[18] 2.10.18 in NPNF, Cf. 2.11.20.

[19] *De Doct.* I.10-11 [Green, 10].

[20] Cf. Herman Bavinck, *Reformed Dogmatics Volume 2: God and Creation* (Baker Books, 2004), 303–304.

Persons. In recent times, Cornelius Van Til has articulated the Trinity along similar lines. As Behr addresses, this is a radically different Trinitarian doctrine than Athanasius, Basil, and Gregory. There is not, therefore, one "doctrine of the Trinity," not even in the 4th century. There is, however, a tension recognised by all these theologians, and they all seek to resolve this tension that they find in the Bible with the tools they have at hand, doing so in the context of serious challenges raised by their theological and ecclesiastical opponents. In each of these answers, we see shades of the biblical teaching, yet in light of each other and the biblical witness we have considered, we are beginning to gain clarity on what exactly the biblical doctrine of the Trinity is.

18

BIBLICAL TRINITARIANISM?

Hear, O Israel, YHWH our Gods, YHWH is one.
– Deuteronomy 6:4

Our examination of the biblical data and 4th-century Trinitarian thought leaves us in an uncomfortable place. We witnessed Christians and their opponents in the 4th century wrestling with the Trinitarian tension in Scripture, and we need to commend the conciliar tradition for recognising the full divinity of the Son. Many of those rejected by the various 4th-century councils and by the key theologians we have considered abandoned one or the other side of the tension, often for reasons external to Scripture. With great boldness, the bishops of the 4th-century upheld the Bible's claim that Jesus is God as the Father is God. However, when we begin to examine the way they did so, problems emerge. This is where discomfort arises. We have been confronted by stark differences between Augustine and Athanasius; thus, even before weighing the biblical testimony, we are already faced with a choice, who is correct? Having to evaluate the theology of these men is further necessitated by what we have seen in Scripture.

It is clear that these theologians were drawing on philosophical tools available to them at their time, tools that did not yet exist in the 1st century, yet that does not necessarily mean they were wrong—we do this all the time! I have argued elsewhere that the ontology that undergirds their solution is not consistent with the Bible, yet we have not argued this here.[1] However, our investigation suggests that by using the philosophical tools available to them, they arrived at a solution that does not line up with what we have seen in Scripture. For the Eastern theologians, the one God was God the Father. Though one reading of 1 Corinthians 8:5-6 supports this claim, a broader reading of Scripture, especially the use of the proper name "Yahweh," indicates that the one God of the Christian Scriptures is not any one person of the Trinity, yet he is all three persons. In this way, the biblical testimony lines up rather with Augustine's position; the one God is Yahweh, who is Father, Son, and the Spirit. The word "Trinity" is not a biblical Word, yet as a title for Yahweh, it accurately captures the fact that this one being—the Shema's "one (God)"—is simultaneously three.

A. The Bible and 4th-Century Trinitarianism

At this point, the favourite analogy of the 4th-century fathers breaks down. For the Athanasius, Basil, Gregory of Nazianzus, and Gregory of Nyssa, along with Hilary of Poitiers and (to a lesser extent) Augustine, the Trinitarian tension lined up almost naturally with the philosophical problem of "the one and the many," or the relationship between things and what unites them. With few (though significant) exceptions, philosophers identified the "one" as the fundamental reality and equated it with an abstract definition of a thing, its "whatness" or quiddity. That is, though there are many humans, they have "Humanity" in common. "Humanity" is not merely a word or even an idea, but it is the fundamental reality that unifies and is expressed in each individual human we meet. Humanity can be summarised in a tight logical definition, such as that attributed to Aristotle, "the rational animal," but Humanity is more than just a definition. The many were instantiations or particular instances of that one universal reality. The relationship between the one and the many was a notoriously difficult issue, yet it was clear that the One really existed and the many existed in lesser way, only as expressions or realisations of the One. This is tantalisingly similar to the problem of the Trinity, where we are confronted with God who is one and three. Thus, the philosophically astute theologians of the 4th century (and, of course, in the centuries before and after) seized on this parallel.

---

[1] Rutherford, *The Gift of Knowledge.*

The language of the one and the many interacted with the Trinitarian tension in the Bible and resulted in their response. Unlike Arius, these theologians did not abandon the true deity of the Son or the Spirit in favour of God's oneness, nor did they abandon the real distinction between the Father, Son, and Spirit, as Sabellius and others did. However, by using the analogy of the one and the many, they did prioritise the One. They made ontological realism (the view that the One or that thing shared by multiple like things, e.g. the Treeness of trees, was real and extramental) an essential component of Christian theology. They treated the predicate "God" shared by each of the persons as a signifier of substance, such that there was single reality shared by the persons that was an abstract "Godhead" or Divinity, which was, in theory, definable (an "essence") yet inaccessible to humanity.[2] The latter claim had an immense influence on the doctrine of God's incomprehensibility and how the knowledge of God was and continues to be conceived.[3]

However, Augustine's thought pushed against these assumptions, presenting on occasion the Trinitarian unity or oneness as *personal*. This line of thought has been taken up again in recent years by Cornelius Van Til, who has contended that the Christian God is fundamentally personal, both on the level of the one and the many.[4] For Van Til, unity and plurality, the one and

---

[2] On the priority of the one, see Zachhuber, *The Rise of Christian Theology and the End of Ancient Metaphysics*. On the priority of the one and ontological realism, see Rutherford, *The Gift of Knowledge*.

[3] Cf. Andrew Radde-Gallwitz, *Basil of Caesarea, Gregory of Nyssa, and the Transformation of Divine Simplicity*, Oxford early Christian studies (Oxford; New York: Oxford University Press, 2009); Basil of Caesarea, *Against Eunomius*, trans. Mark DelCogliano and Andrew Radde-Gallwitz, The fathers of the church v. 122 (Washington, D.C: Catholic University of America Press, 2011); Dragoş-Andrei Giulea, "The Divine Essence, That Inaccessible Kabod Enthroned in Heaven: Nazianzen's Oratio 28,3 and the Tradition of Apophatic Theology from Symbols to Philosophical Concepts," *Numen* 57, no. 1 (2010): 1–29; Russel P Moroziuk, "Heathen Philosophers and Christian Theologians: Apophaticism and Nicene Orthodoxy at Nicaea," *The Patristic and Byzantine Review* 12, no. 1–3 (1993): 55–63; Gary R Poe, "Light to Darkness: From Gnosis to Agape in the Apophatic Imagery of Gregory of Nyssa," *Baptist History and Heritage* 53, no. 1 (September 2018): 57–67; Williams, "The Nicene Heritage."

[4] Van Til, *An Introduction to Systematic Theology*, chap. 17. Cf. A.A. Hodge, "But for aught we can know, in the depths of this infinite Being there may be a common consciousness which includes the whole Godhead, a common personality"; Herman

the many, are equally ultimate: neither resolves into nor has priority over the other. For Van Til, this *solved* the problem of the one and the many.

Instead, as John Frame suggests, the Trinity fundamentally redefines and re-orients the problem. I explore this claim at length in my book *The Gift of Knowledge*.[5] For now, it is important to observe that in none of the biblical passages concerning the oneness of God, God's unity is conceived of as abstract or typical (that is, corresponding to a philosophical type, a genus or species).

To the contrary, the unity of God is, as Augustine and Van Til contended, a *personal* or (to use the philosophical terminology) an *individual* unity. The one God is Yahweh, the creator and sustainer of all things. This one God acts and is acted upon, speaks and makes himself known. The "one" in the Trinitarian tension is not the universal of the philosophers but the personal covenanting God of Scripture. Yet this one individual thing is also three individual things, the Father, the Son, and the Spirit. The Father is Yahweh, the Son is Yahweh, the Spirit is Yahweh. Each is God. Though the Bible does not use the terminology, and there are reasons 4th-century Christians avoided it, there is a genuine sense in which the Christian God is three Gods, the God(s), אֱלֹהִים (*'elohim*) as the Hebrew Scriptures have it. However, in contemporary thought as in ancient thought, the assertion of plurality is often in contrast with oneness; there is an army of many or an army of one, alone or in company, one apple or three. Thus, to speak of "three Gods" suggest polytheism, where the three are "collateral," of the same genus but with nothing but an abstract unity or a unity that is itself the true God (the "One" of the philosophers). Christians throughout the ages have rightfully denied these consequences and so have denied the claim that the Christian God is three Gods. However, in doing so, they have met the

---

Bavinck, "there is in God but one eternal, omnipotent, and omniscient being, having on mind, one will, and one power." A. A. Hodge, *Evangelical Theology: Lectures on Doctrine* (Carlisle, Penn.: Banner of Truth Trust, 1990), 102–103; Herman Bavinck, *Reformed Dogmatics Volume 2: God and Creation* (Baker Books, 2004), 302; quoted in, Lane G. Tipton, *The Trinitarian Theology of Cornelius Van Til* (Libertyville, Ill.: Reformed Forum, 2022), 71, 75.

[5] *God's Gifts for the Christian Life – Part 1: The Gift of Knowledge* (Campbell River, BC; Teleioteti, 2021).

ridicule of polytheists, monotheists, and atheists alike, for only on the most obtuse logic did the plurality exist without the corresponding claim "three Gods." Nyssa relegated this phrase to the common, vulgar tongue, but that is the problem; to deny that God is in some sense "three Gods" is to deny the common way language works. So, our God is three Gods, yet as soon as we admit this, we must simultaneously proclaim the necessary complement to this, that this God who is three is also one. There are three Gods who are one God; Yahweh is the Father, the Son, and the Spirit, each are truly God and truly Yahweh. As we will explore below, the logic behind "Yahweh" is a touch different, for there is one Yahweh, the true God over all things, but not a corresponding sense that there are three "Yahweh"s. However, even here, nothing is lost if my logic of names is denied (whereby I grant three Gods on the biblical warrant but deny three "Yahweh"s), so long as the affirmation of three "Yahweh"s does not deny the claim the one true God is Yahweh.[6] The atheist, monotheist, and agnostic alike will respond that such talk is nonsense, a contradiction surely!

B. The Trinity and Logic

However, there is nothing that is logically contradictory about these claims, and they are coherent with the teaching of Scripture. Now, I am not saying we should adopt the phrases "three Gods" in our liturgy and theology—by no means! I am only saying that we do not need to go through logical gymnastics to show why these phrases are impermissible. They are permissible, yet they have the danger of denying the unity of God that is so important to the Bible, so they should not be used willy-nilly. However, by admitting the validity of the phrases in some sense, do we commit ourselves to a different form of mental gymnastics, to show that the claims "God is one God and three Gods" or "God is one individual and three individuals"—

---

[6] Among other things, I deny the claim that there are three "Yahweh"s because the Bible doesn't make such a claim, though it does seem to permit if not articulate three "gods." I think there is a grammar of names/terms behind this, which I will unpack below, but I do not think this is the only grammar one could adopt; within a different grammar, the claim three "Yahweh"s may not be problematic. This is similar to my claims concerning one God and three Gods; I have given biblical warrant for permitting such a claim and a rational for why it is not a problem, yet in many contexts throughout the ages, a different grammar is in use and within that grammar, this same claim is highly problematic!

or "God is one person" and "God is three persons"—are not logical contradictions? I do not believe we do. A contradiction ensues when we violate the law of non-contradiction, that something is A and Not-A at the same time and in the same way. "A" here stands for any predicate (e.g. James is *a man*). A contradiction only ensues when contrary (incompatible predicates, "here or there," of which only one can be true but both may be false) or complementary (opposing predicates, black and not-black, one must be false) predicates are asserted at the exact same time, for a laptop may be blue now and black later, or at home now and at work later. "In the same way" means that to be contradictory, the predicates must have the same sense in both claims: "at home" and "at work" must refer to two different places for the claims "the laptop is at home" and "the laptop is at work" to be contradictory. So, is our doctrine of the Trinity a contradiction? Not clearly.

a. The Compatibility of "one person" and "three persons"

Think about it, are the claims "three persons" and "one person" necessarily incompatible? We are speaking of the same subject; "God" is the subject of both predicate clauses, "is one" and "is three." And "person" is used in the same sense in both clauses, a subjective, responding, active thing. Yet it is not clear to me that "one" and "three" contradict each other. There are clearly cases where something may be three and one: a triangle has three angles but is one thing, a Trapezoid can be considered one shape or three shapes and yet is one thing. A person with a personality disorder can be one person from his perspective and three from the psychologist's. Now, none of these are parallels to the Trinity, and we can think of contradictory claims. If we have one and only one apple, there are not three apples, though if we have three apples, we have one apple. Yet with apples, the one is a part of the three or the one is exclusive of the three. Finally, if there is only one person in a room, there are not three persons in the room. None of these are exact parallels to the Trinity, yet logically, they help us elucidate the supposed contradiction. When we speak of "one person" and "three persons," we are not envisaging a parts-whole relationship, like a trapezoid divided into three. Nor are we considering a modal relationship like the disordered man who is one person now and one person then. However, in each of these cases, we have seen that "one" and "three" are not necessarily exclusive; what makes them exclusive is our understanding of the noun they modify. So, the question we need to ask is this: is it impossible to have one "person" who is three "persons"? That is, does "one person" in the claim "God is one person" mean "one and only one"? I see no reason why this must be the case. There is no logic of "personhood" that says someone who is one person cannot be three. We may respond that we cannot envisage what it would be like to simultaneously enjoy the subjective perception of unity—being one—and being three distinct subjectivities (which is an implication of our definition of "person), yet we cannot say this is impossible even if we cannot imagine it. I cannot imagine what it would be like to be aware of every single thing in the entire universe simultaneously and act on each of them in the same moment, yet this is what God's governance, knowledge, and omnipresence imply. There is nothing contradictory about these attributes. Thus, there is no reason to think that "one person" means "one and only one." Moreover, we have the biblical testimony that it does not.

What about "God is three?" Does the claim "God is three" exclude true, personal unity, as in the case of the apples (where "three apples" implies "one apple," yet that one apple is only one of three not all of them). Though I cannot think of a created analogy where oneness exists on same level as plurality, the sort of limitations that make this impossible in the case of apples or the disordered man do not exist with God. For there to be three apples implies three discreet, physical objects: they cannot be simultaneously discreet apples—with independent skin, stem, flesh, and seeds—and one apple—with one skin, stem, flesh, and seeds. However, "person" in our case does not mean discreet physical object; the ability to act and have subjectivity would suffice. A person can act one way with one arm and another with the other, so a multiplicity of action is not restricted by a unity of person.[7] Again, we return to the subjectivity question. In the case of the disordered man, he cannot be this person and that at the same time; there are physical limitations pertaining to the shared body and mind. I think that in this case, even if such limitations were removed, there is a fundamental unity that does not permit

---

[7] There is extensive literature concerning the bizarre scenarios where a person is capable of contradictory actions or intentions, usually resulting from some sort of disruption to the physical brain. Cf. Iain McGilchrist, *The Master and His Emissary: The Divided Brain and the Making of the Western World*, New expanded edition. (New Haven: Yale University Press, 2019).

both "persons" to present themselves, yet I do not share this intuition concerning God. I see no reason why God could not have one subjectivity that three independent subjectivities within that. The same elements that make "three apples" and "one apple" contradictory do not seem to apply here. For these reasons—and the lack of an argument to the contrary—I see no reason to believe that "one God" and "three Gods" or "one person" and "three persons" are contradictory. "Person" or "God" in these clauses do not appear to be the types of things that excludes unity and plurality on the same level. Moreover, we have the biblical testimony that this is indeed the case, that these are not contradictory claims. Surely we can trust the God whose stability upholds logic and who created all things that these are not mutually exclusive claims.[8] On what basis are we to call foul—because we have no adequate analogy? That will not withstand much scrutiny when we stand before the bar at final judgment.

b. Predication and the Names of God

There is another angle from which we need to approach the question of Trinitarian logic before wrapping up this chapter, addressing the relationship between our account of God's Triune nature and the role of names in grammar and predication. In our discussion above, I teased the need for such an account with the phrases "inclusive" and "exclusive terms" and "non-exhaustive references." These are ways I am attempting to describe the biblical phenomena concerning the naming of God, phenomena that emerge from the uniquely triune nature of God. Thus, though I find these phenomena in the Scriptures themselves, I have yet to identify a meaningful parallel in the Western / English linguistic context (though perhaps one may be found in another language / linguistic context). I have argued that the Bible doesn't begin to be Trinitarian in the New Testament—and that the Trinity did not emerge from post-biblical theological reflection—instead, God has revealed himself in Trinitarian parameters throughout Scripture. Thus, we have found no evidence for a monarchy of the Father where "God" refers to "God the Father" unless otherwise clarified. There are certainly moments where "God" *does* refer exclusively to God the Father, but these moments (in the New Testament) are always qualified: "my Father and your

---

[8] On God upholding logic, see Poythress, *Logic*.

Father, to *my* God and your *God*" (John 20:17; cf. John 1:18). This what I will call an exclusive use of a biblical term for God, where "God" is used for one and only one of the persons of the Trinity: {"My God" → The Father (YHWH, Not Son, Not Spirit)}, where "→" indicates reference (that ontological reality which the linguistic sign signifies).[9] However, when we turn to the Old Testament—which undoubtedly gave the New Testament authors their basic theological grammar for thinking and speaking about God—we find that God is nearly always used *inclusively*, without differentiation among the persons of the Godhead (I say *nearly* to cover myself, but I do not have any specific instances of an exclusive use in mind; an example may, perhaps, be Isaiah 53:4, but this could be a case of non-exhaustive reference, which we will shortly discuss). A term is used *inclusively* when it refers to the One God without differentiation, and therefore all three persons at once: {"God" → Yahweh (Father, Son, and Spirit)}. For example, in Genesis 1:26-31 we get a glimpse of the intra-Trinitarian participation in creation (see Ch. 6.A.): here, all three persons are implicated in the "God" who speaks, and we are given no qualification to indicate that the term is being used exclusively or even for one person in particular but not exclusively (non-exhaustive reference). This is common for the use of the terms "God" and Yahweh" throughout the Old Testament: we discussed significant instances where these terms are qualified in Chapters 7-9, yet these are the exceptions not the rule. There are other areas were a qualification only becomes evident in light of the New Testament's progressive revelation, such as the association of "our Father" with God the Father in particular (e.g Deut 32:6; Isa 63:16, 64:8; Jer 31:9; see C. below). However, for the most part, these terms are unqualified. Though it is often assumed that, by default, "God" refers to the Father, there is simply no biblical testimony to this assumption. To the contrary, we have seen that the Bible presents God as one person and three persons: our exegesis has led as towards the assumption that unless qualified, terms such as "God" and "Yahweh," to which we can add "Lord" (אֲדֹנָי, *'adonay*; κυρίος, *kurios*) and the various permutations of these terms (e.g. YHWH of hosts; YHWH our healer; the Lord YHWH, etc.), refer to the undifferentiated Godhead, the One, true God. This is supported by our discussion of Deuteronomy 6:4, where we identified the terms אֱלֹהִים

---

[9] "Reference" also encompasses inter-textual reference, but in this section, I use "reference" solely for extra linguistic reference ("*that sofa*, over there").

('*elohim*) and יהוה (YHWH) as referring to the Godhead, yet they did so in different ways: YHWH is God's covenantal name (cf. Ch. 7.A.), "God" describes YHWH in relation to creation, creator and its authority (cf. Ch. 4), אֱלֹהִים also indicates YHWH's plurality. This conclusion is also confirmed by the fact the biblical authors do frequently qualify "God" and "YHWH" to specify the individual persons, e.g., "The Angel YHWH," "the Spirit YHWH," "God the Father," "The Lord Jesus Christ," etc. That is, in addition to particular phrases that function as exclusive titles ("our Father," "my Father," "Jesus," "Christ," "The Holy Spirit"), the inclusive terms are sometimes specified to become exclusive terms or instances of non-exhaustive reference, where one person is referred to but not to the exclusion of the others, {"YHWH" → Son (Yahweh, Spirit, Father)}. Thus, given an extensive range of options to specify the persons, and the personal reality of the One God, it follows that the use of YHWH, God, Lord, and similar terms referring to God refer to the undifferentiated Godhead unless accompanied by such qualifications. Thus, the Spirit and Son are not called "God" only here or there—when they are specified—but they are called God along with the Father wherever qualification is absent. Before we draw out the logic of these naming conventions, it is important to consider the New Testament in light of what we have seen in the Old Testament.

It is commonly presumed that unless otherwise qualified, κυρίος (*kurios*) refers to God the Son and θεός (*theos*) to God the Father in the New Testament. However, this assumption has serious theological ramifications, for the Spirit is barely alluded to as God (Acts 5:1-6), the Son is called God a mere handful of times (e.g. Rom 9:5), and God the Father is apparently called the only God (1 Tim 1:17). Reading in this way, the few references to Jesus and the Spirit as God almost appear accidental![10] Yet, when read against the Old Testament background, a different picture emerges. The three persons are not occasionally called "God," but are identified with Yahweh, the One God, one every page of Scripture, occasionally—as necessary—being named by an exclusive use of these regularly inclusive terms or an instance of non-

---

[10] Eg. Walter Dulière argues that it is the ambiguity of κυρίος as a Christological or secular title and its use for "YHWH" that led the early church to deify Christ. Walter L Dulière, "Theos--Dieu et Adonai—Kurios," *Zeitschrift für Religions- und Geistesgeschichte* 21, no. 3 (1969): 193–203.

exhaustive reference. Moreover, we have no warrant for this sudden change in the pattern of the biblical grammar for speaking of God—and it is certainly a significant change! If the New Testament authors are truly shaped by the Old Testament—which they undoubtedly are—then we would expect them to follow its grammar concerning the doctrine of God (especially given that the Old Testament is as Trinitarian as the New). If we assume that this is indeed the case, then we find the same pattern: κύριος (*kurios*), "Lord," (being the Greek translation of both יהוה [YHWH] and אֲדֹנָי [*Adonay*]) and θεός (*theos*), "God," are used without qualification inclusively or for non-exhaustive reference, and the biblical authors frequently qualify these terms and other titles throughout the New Testament to refer to the individual persons. Indeed, this is where we find a significant element of progression in the New Testament Trinitarian grammar. The New Testament does not eclipse the inclusive use of θεός and κύριος, no, but it does enrich our understanding of the One God by favouring the qualification of these terms and the particular titles for the individual persons (and more frequent use of non-exhaustive reference): we are thus given greater insight into the relationship among our Trinitarian God and the economy of their interactions with the creation. We will consider this element of progression in the following section. Before we do so, we will briefly unpack these three categories with regard to Trinitarian names and titles, namely, inclusive terms, exclusive terms, and non-exhaustive reference in logical terms, according to the implications these categories have for Trinitarian predication (which is certainly not the only way they can be considered; thus far, I have tended to describe them merely as grammatical phenomena, of signs as they refer to extra-textual realities, in this case, the complex ontological reality of our Triune God).

What I am calling "inclusive terms" (IT) can be parsed as, for example, {"God" → Yahweh (Father, Son, and Spirit)}. In this analysis, the word on the left side indicates the textual sign, here "God," the arrow symbol (→) indicates referential function, and the term or phrase on the right indicates an extra-textual referent. For example, in a sentence where "this computer" refers to the computer here on my desk (lets abbreviate it, CD), "This computer is terrible!," we can parse the reference function of "This computer" as {"This Computer" → CD}. In the sentence, "God created the heavens and the earth" (Gen 1:1), I have argued that "God" here is an inclusive term, thus its reference function can be diagrammed as I have above, {"God" → Yahweh (Father, Son, and Spirit)}. We can unfold this parsing in terms of predication as follows: in the case where an action is performed by "God" used as an IT, then the following four propositions are implied,

1)"Yahweh created the heavens and the earth"
2)"the Father created the heavens and the earth"
3)"the Son created the heavens and the earth"
4) "the Spirit created the Heavens and the earth."

This is the case so long as in propositions 2-4, "**A** created" is not taken to mean, "**A** and **A** alone created," as in the claim, "God created the heavens and the earth, therefore Baal did not create the heavens and the earth." If proposition 2 means "the Father alone created the heavens and the earth," then this would make propositions 3 and 4 false. Thus, in the case of inclusive terms, the resulting propositions are not exclusive propositions, where "**A** created" is the equivalent of "**A** alone created." Furthermore, in the resulting proposition, "Yahweh" denominates Yahweh as one, yet anything said of the one God Yahweh without qualification is true of each of the persons. According to our discussion thus far, we can conclude that so far as predication is concerned, everything that a particular person does can be attributed to the one God, Yahweh, but everything that is predicated of the one God, Yahweh, is not true of each person. We will offer a diagram to illustrate this momentarily and explain in what way things can be said of Yahweh as one that are not true for each person, but first, having explained the predicational logic of what I am calling an inclusive term, we will turn to exclusive terms and non-exhaustive reference.

In contrast with an IT, an exclusive term (ET) is used for one of the Trinitarian persons apart from the others, thus I have parsed this category as, {"my God" → The Father (Yahweh [Not Son, Not Spirit])}. When an ET is used, that action attributed to God is predictable only of the Unitary person of God and one person, in this case, the Father, not either of the other persons. Thus, if we take the sentence uttered by Jesus, "to your God and my God," we can analysis the term "my God" in this way. In doing so, we can formulate two propositions from this sentence,

1) God the Father is the God of the Son

2) Yahweh is, as Father, God of the Son.

The first proposition is obvious, but the second may take some unpacking. Because all of the persons are Yahweh, the one God, then anything true of them is true of Yahweh.[11] However, predications made from a person to the one person cannot be attributed to Yahweh simpliciter, according to the logic of the ITs treated above, otherwise such predications would also be true of the other two persons. Therefore, we need to qualify either the use of "Yahweh" as the subject of the proposition or add an adverbial determiner, as we have. Because on our ontology explained above, we are talking about God as a personal unity, not merely one of the persons, we cannot modify the subject of the proposition: we are not speaking of God the Father merely but Yahweh, the one true God. Therefore, the phrase "as Father" indicates the way in which the predicate phrase, "God of the Son," is made of the subject, God. To use another example, it was our Lord Jesus Christ, the divine Son, not God the Father or God the Spirit who was crucified on the Cross. Therefore, if we take Peter's words, "this Jesus whom you crucified," and substitute the ET "God the Son," we can conclude that "God the Son was crucified," therefore "Yahweh, as God the Son, was crucified," but not "God the Father was crucified" or "Yahweh was crucified," the simpliciter proposition which would imply, "God the Son was crucified," "God the Father was crucified," and "God the Spirit was crucified." Now, an ET does not imply the contrary proposition concerning the other persons, which I have indicated by putting "not the Spirit" in square brackets. "Not" in the formula for an ET indicates that the corresponding proposition cannot derived for this or that person, not that the corresponding proposition is false concerning that person. Our final category to parse is the use of non-exhaustive reference.

What I have in mind when I speak of "non-exhaustive reference" (NER) are instances where the biblical text refers primarily to one person of the Trinity yet is not excluding the others. I have parsed this above in this way, {"YHWH" → Son (Yahweh, Spirit, Father)}. In such cases, the logical implications are the same as that of an IT, where what is said of God is true

---

[11] Traditional Christology has offered an alternate interpretation of this terminology, but I find that account unpersuasive. This is the topic of my PhD thesis, "Rightly Defining the Son of God."

of God as one and each of the persons. However, unlike in the case of an IT, here the text is particularly referring to one person. The logic remains the same for predication: in an instance of NER, any predicate made of the primary referent is true of Yahweh simpliciter and of the other persons. For instance, since no one person of the Trinity is Yahweh himself, but Yahweh is the name of Israel's true God, and since everything that is true of God simpliciter is true of each of the persons, therefore the Son is Yahweh, the Spirit is Yahweh, and the Father is Yahweh. However, in each case, the predicate "Yahweh" includes the other two persons, so we do not have three "Yahweh"s. No, God is one and he is Yahweh; the God who is Yahweh is three, therefore, each is identified with Yahweh but no one person is the whole of Yahweh. Thus, in every instance where one speaks of "Yahweh," it is an instance of non-exhaustive reference or an IT. Thus, I can use the name of our God, Yahweh, or the Greek equivalent, Kurios, to name Jesus in particular, but doing so is never exclusive of the other persons.

We could introduce the classical concept of "perichoresis" or inter-penetration at this point: because our one God is the three persons and these three persons are not parts such that God is part Father, part Son, and part Spirit but the Father is entirely God, the Son is entirely God, and the Spirit is entirely God, therefore, when we speak of God, we are speaking of Father, Son, and Spirit: They are present with and in one another without separation or division. When we speak of each person, we are drawn back to the others because they there is no Father without the Son and Spirit, Son without Father and Spirit, and Spirit without Father and Son. This does not mean we cannot speak in particular about the Father, Son, and Spirit, yet in doing so, we are never far from the others, for they are intimately involved in all the other does. There is distinction in the acts of the persons revealed especially in the New Testament, as we will discuss shortly, and therefore a distinction in predicates, yet even these are caught up in the unity of God, for all that is true of one person and not the other is true of God whom they constitute. I am thus using "non-exhaustive reference" to describe the textual and logical phenomena of this ontological reality. Textually, there are instances where "Yahweh" in a particular context refers to the Father, the Son, or the Spirit, yet the doctrine of perichoresis as we have discussed it means that such reference is not to the exclusion of the others. Thus, though something may be attribute to "Yahweh, the Son," such would also be true of Yahweh the Spirit and Yahweh the Father unless we have reason to believe that it is being used exclusively (as we discussed above under ETs). That is, for this or that reason, biblical authors may want to speak of the Father, Son, or Spirit while not asserting that what they are saying concerns merely the Father, Son, or Spirit (as would be the case with an ET). For example, in John 12:38-40, John quotes from Isaiah 53 and Isaiah 6, where Yahweh is exalted upon his throne; in 12:41, he says that the prophet said what he said because he saw "his glory," where "his" refers to Jesus. John is making a point about Jesus' ministry, so he applies Isaiah 6 to Jesus: it was Jesus' glory which Isaiah saw. However, in doing so, he is not saying that this glory was not that of the Father or the Spirit: nothing in the context of Isaiah 6 makes it clear that this is God the Son, and John's use of this passage does no require this to be the case. Instead, he refers specifically to the Son without excluding the others, {"YHWH" → Son (Yahweh, Spirit, Father)}. We can summarise these three categories of divine naming with the figure below, which visualises the logic involved, not ontology (i.e. by illustrating the Father, Son, and Spirit as individual circles within a larger circle, I am not intimating that they are parts of a whole).

The Logic of Trinitarian Naming

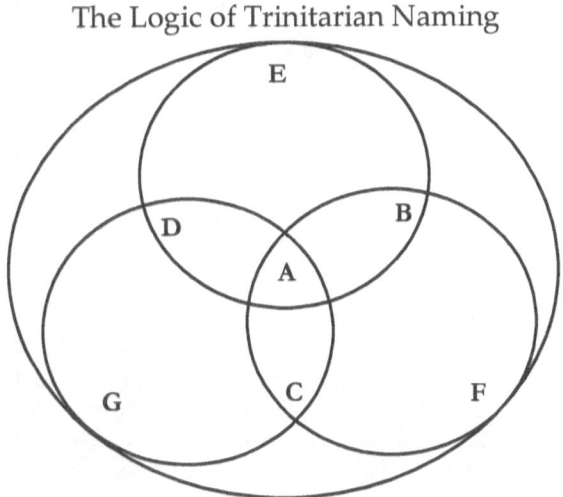

In this diagram, I have laid out each possible type of signifier discussed above spatially, represented with a letter from **A – G**. Any signifier that is equivalent to **A** is logically equivalent to {"God" → Yahweh (Father, Son, and Spirit)}, that is, an IT. A signifier equivalent to A may also be the logically equivalent but semantically different NER, such that {"YHWH" → Son (Yahweh, Spirit, Father)}. Thus, in a proposition where the subject term, e.g. Yahweh, is an IT or NER, we can place the predicate in the space designated A in the diagram. Everything that is located at A is simultaneously within the circles representing God as One (the whole) and each person. Therefore, a predicate located at A is true (the spatial diagram representing what can be predicated as true of the subjects it represents) of Yahweh, Father, Son, and Spirit.[12] For example, if we place the predicate "omniscient" at A, then the following propositions are true:

1) Yahweh is omniscient.
2) The Father is omniscient.
3) The Son is omniscient.
4) The Spirit is omniscient.

As will become clear, only what can be placed in space A is said of Yahweh simpliciter (without a "as Father," "as Son," or "as the Spirit" qualification). The areas marked **C-D** represent partial ETs or NERs, such that what is said is true of two persons but not the other. Let us suppose that only the Father and Spirit did an act **A1** (representing any possible action performed by Father and Spirit but not the Son). We could locate **A1** at Point **D** (Presuming the Top and Left inner circles represent the Father and Spirit, respectively), and the following propositions would be true:

1) The Father did **A1**.
2) The Spirit did **A1**.
3) Yahweh as Father and Spirit did **A1**.

---

[12] Vern Poythress uses Venn Diagram's similarly in his book *Logic* to spatially represent set theory. We could use his more technical language to describe what I am doing here. In Logic and Math, a set is (roughly) "a collection, and its members are whatever individuals belong to that collection." In our diagram, each section of the diagram represents a set of true predicates pertaining to a subject. **E** represents a set of all true predicates pertaining to God the Spirit, **F** represents a set of all true predicates pertaining to God the Son, and **G** represents a set of all true predicates pertaining to God the Spirit. **B** represents the intersection ($\cap$) of sets E and F ($E \cap F$), which is the equivalent of all predicates which are members of both sets E and F ($x \in A \cap B$ if and only if $x \in A$ and $x \in B$, where $x \in A$ means "x is a member of A") (Poythress 262). If E was the set $\{1, 2\}$ and F $\{2, 3\}$ then B would be the set $\{2\}$. **A** would then represent the intersection of all sets, $A \cap B, C, D$ such that $x \in A$ if and only if $x \in B$, $x \in C$, and $x \in D$. Conversely if $x \in A$, then $x \in B, C, D$. Cf. Poythress, *Logic*, 256–265.

The area marked by **E-G** represents full ETs. If we place a predicate in one of these areas, two propositions result. Christ was crucified, so we can put "was crucified" in area **F**, and the following two propositions would result:

1) The Son was crucified.
2) Yahweh as the Son was crucified.

There is another set of predicates that don't fit into this diagram but can be superimposed as the prime of each area, e.g. **A'**, **B'**, etc. In these cases, something is true because of the persons, etc. For example, we could put the predicate "Trinity" or "three" at **A'** because God is Triune or threefold because of the three Persons. It should be observed that a visual representation such as this is inadequate, for in reality, there is nothing said of the One God that is not said of the persons, so the space between the individuals and the whole implies an impossible reality, a predicate true of God without being true of or because of the Divine persons (even "one" is true of each of them by virtue of their identity as YHWH, the one God). However, we could draw a similar diagram for predications concerning a human person, providing an analogy for our discussion (though as we have qualified, a human has parts, whereas the Father, Son, and Spirit are not *parts* of the One God). I can say "I am typing," yet this predicate is not true of every part of me. Instead, it is true *because* of my fingers, thus, "I am typing *with my hands*" prevents extending the proposition to every other part of the body. "I" simpliciter would be area "A" with every part of a person moving outward.

Concluding our discussion of the grammar and logic of the Trinitarian unity-in-plurality, it is clear that we can follow the biblical testimony in proclaiming one God who is three, one person who is three persons, without abandoning rationality in the process—though the biblical account of rationality we adopt, where God is ground and measure of reason and he has spoken clearly in his word, will not be acceptable to many who do not themselves believe.[13] This is the biblical teaching we have seen. One person, Yahweh, the True God, is three persons, the Father, Son, and Spirit. It is

---

[13] Cf. Cornelius Van Til, *A Christian Theory of Knowledge* (Philadelphia: Presbyterian and Reformed Pub Co., 1969); Cornelius Van Til, *The Defense of the Faith*, ed. K. Scott Oliphint, 4th ed. (Phillipsburg: P & R Pub, 2008); Frame, *The Doctrine of the Knowledge*.

important to observe what this does to our perception of the Trinitarian "tension" in Scripture. The Bible upholds these claims without perceiving them to be in tension, yet it intentionally rules out misinterpretations of the relationship between God's oneness and threeness. Thus, I am led to the conclusion that the "tension" in the "Trinitarian tension" we have discussed in this book is the result of something we bring to the table. In a polytheistic context, threeness seems to exclude oneness. In a philosophical context of absolute monotheism, oneness seems to exclude threeness. Thus, being biblical about the Trinity is not about living with tension but seeing how the biblical teaching removes the tension. The Bible's doctrine of the Trinity is that Yahweh the One God is three, each of whom are Yahweh and God. We have followed the Bible in interpreting these as "individual" terms, referring to things, and in identifying them as things of the sort that can be called a "person." There is no need in this doctrine of the Trinity to provide a metaphysic resolving a tension in the doctrine, for when we follow the Bible's lead, we have no reason to believe that a "person" is the sort of thing that cannot be (at least in the case of God) one and three simultaneously. Thus, the extensive testimony to God's plurality and unity found in both Testaments constitutes the Bible's doctrine of the Trinity. The New Testament authors didn't need to resolve the tension between these claims because, within the biblical frame of reference, there is no tension.

Excursus: Properties, Predication, and Divine Simplicity

There are significant issues I have chosen not to address in this book. Though we have touched on issues of ontology, logic, and epistemology, I have attempted to keep such discussions to the minimum. I have addressed these issues elsewhere at length, but I have chosen not to make them a focus of this volume.[14] However, because the traditional doctrine of the Trinity as formulated in the 4th century and by later theologians such as Thomas Aquinas is thoroughly metaphysical, our discussion thus far cannot help but tread on some toes. I want to briefly address what I think will be the most problematic issue raised thus far, namely, divine simplicity. A traditional understanding of propositions is that their truth value rests on an actual correspondence between what is said and the reality that it signifies such that

---

[14] See *The Gift of Knowledge*.

if it is true that "God is omniscient," then God possess some ontological reality that corresponds to "omniscience," making the proposition true. However, this is problematic in reference to God, for if omniscience is something God possesses, then it is something other than God and God depends on that reality to be who he is: he would, therefore, be dependent on some other reality and less than God. The usual response—which we do not have space to explore here—is to say that God himself, full stop, is the reality to which predicates such as "omniscience" correspond. Now, I think this solution has significant problems, which I address elsewhere, but the problems for our position thus far are more significant, if this account of truth (ontological correspondence) is accepted.

That is, I have suggested that things can be predicated of one Person independent of the others; this would, on the classic model, mean that person was ontologically different than others—possessing an ontological reality corresponding to "omniscience," which we saw was problematic, or being himself ontologically different than the others such that a property is true corresponding to one Person but not the others. (The examples I have used also suggest that God can gain properties, which challenges the traditional understanding of immutability, but I direct the reader to my *The Gift of Seeing* in *The Gift of Knowledge* for that problem.) In several of my works, I offer a conceptualist account of knowledge that accounts for the diversity in our knowledge of God (that is, that "wise" and "omnipotent" say different things about God) without implying that God is dependent on something other than himself. However, this solution does not allow us to escape the fact that on our model, the persons of the Trinity are ontologically differentiated: there are differences in their "character," as I have elsewhere called that interior reality that determinatively corresponds to a person's unique engagement with others, that produces different actions and, therefore, different properties true of this person and not the others. Now, I do not think so-called "Classical Theism" is free from problems here—indeed, I think this is one of the areas where it fails most severely—however, our job is to give an account of what we have said, not what others have said.

Though this ontological differentiation is an implication of our argument thus far, it is an implication firmly rooted in the biblical testimony. That is, we have biblical attestation to differences in our God's interior activity: the Son is uniquely the Son of the Father. Moreover, we have biblical attestation for the diversity of their activity towards the creation (which we will consider shortly): the Son goes forth as the suffering servant and is active for God's people as the Angel YHWH; the Spirit uniquely inhabits the Temple and God's people as temples; the Father uniquely sets forth the pattern his Son follows; the Spirit has a unique role in regeneration not attributed to the others, etc. If we deny that these distinctions are arbitrary, then we are forced to say they correspond to the character of each person in a way that they do not to the others. Thus, we acknowledge, on a firm biblical basis, ontological differentiation among the persons of the Trinity. However, we have also affirmed on an equally firm biblical basis that God is truly one: so this differentiation cannot be permitted to threaten God's unity—nor his aseity, as the traditional doctrine has rightly guarded. However, I do not see how the differentiation we have introduced, between person and person, necessarily threatens God's unity or aseity. That is, if the distinctions thus drawn imply that each person is a *part* of the One God such that God is *part* Father, *part* Son, *part* Spirit, then God is dependent on something other than himself, the distinguishable "parts." However, this is not what we are claiming. The ontological distinction we are drawing do not imply that the persons are themselves composed of parts (because of a conceptualist account of truth), furthermore, we have maintained the each one is fully the True God, and the True God is fully the Son, Spirit, and Father—what the church Fathers called "*perichoresis*."

I do not intend to pretend that I know how this works, but we have arrived at the conclusion from the Bible that God is one person and three persons, that they work in perfect harmony yet have distinct activity within themselves and towards the creation. Above, we saw that this is not logically objectionable; similarly, though I cannot positively explain how God is one and three and the three are not parts of a whole but are perfectly united as a genuinely singular person, I can affirm that we have no reason to deny this reality. "Simplicity" is thus not an apt description of our God, not even ontologically, yet each person and their one person are mutually interdependent but do not depend on anything outside of themselves for anything. What we have argued thus far, therefore, neither precludes God's unity nor aseity, provided that "unity" and "aseity" are interpreted within a biblical, trinitarian framework.

C. The Progression of Trinitarian Revelation

In recent centuries, the Trinity has been treated as a progressively revealed doctrine, concealed or perhaps absent in the Old Testament but revealed in some manner in the New. We have argued against this conclusion throughout this book: the Bible is thoroughly Trinitarian, we have contended. However, by arguing that the Trinity has not been progressively revealed is not to deny either progressive revelation entirely nor its particular relevance to the Trinity. The Bible clearly reveals new things or old things with greater detail across its scope: for instance, what appeared in the Old Testament as a single event—the eschatological salvific work of God (a new Exodus) and the final judgment, both summarised as "the Day of the Lord"—is shown in the New Testament to be a two-part event, initiated at Christ's first coming and awaiting its consummation at his return. When we read the Old Testament afresh, with New Testament eyes, we see the consistency of these pictures, yet the Old Testament itself does not clearly reveal this two-stage eschatology. Similarly, when we consider the Old Testament testimony to the Trinity, we find unity and differentiation, One God and several beings who are the One God. However, the distinctions do not appear as clear as they do in the New Testament, nor is the interrelationship of the Trinity and their diverse works outward as clearly laid forth as they are in the New Testament.[15]

In the Old Testament, for example, God is identified as the Father of his people, Israel (e.g. Isaiah 63:16): in the New Testament, we find this role of Father particularly identified with God the Father, with we as his adopted children. In this way, we become coheirs with Christ, who is God's eternal Son. To the best of my knowledge, we do not find a Trinitarian Father-Son relationship elucidated in the Old Testament. Though God is described as a Father to the Messiah, this fits with theme of the earthly king representing

---

[15] In line with our considerations in Part 1, the progressive revelation as we are discussing is literary, not necessarily historical. I am describing a shift between the Testaments, but the Old Testament is not the whole picture concerning ancient Israel's self-understanding and perception of their God, so it is possible that the portrait of God we find reading the Old and New together was possessed by some who encountered God through the writings we now call the Old Testament along with other prophecies and the ritual participation in the religious life of Israel.

the Divine King, and thus doesn't necessarily point to the Father-Son dynamic the New Testament reveals. Thus, the eternal Father-Son relationship within the Trinity, which is central to the New Testament teaching of the incarnation, appears to a be an element of progressive revelation—an element which sheds immense light on the Old Testament when viewed in hindsight (such as the sacrifice of Isaac). In addition, in the Gospel of John and elsewhere, there is a pattern of the Father ordaining and accomplishing something through the Son and the Spirit. God the Father created through the Son in the power of the Spirit, and the Father gives to the Son certain people whom the Spirit fills and draws to Christ. God the Father gives the Son what he is to say and do, and the Father and the Son pour out the Spirit empowering his people to obey Christ. Even the rule of God is dynamic, with God on the throne, the Son at his right hand, and the Spirit before the throne ready to act (Rev 4:1-11, 5:1-8). This appear to be genuinely progressive insights, from the Old to the New, in the revelation of our God.

D. Conclusion

Our conclusions concerning the Trinity elucidated in this chapter have significant implications. Against the abstractions of the philosophers, where unity is impersonal and universal, not personal and individual, we have discovered that universality and the impersonal are not fundamental aspects of reality. The Creator is one concrete thing and three concrete things, one person and three persons. We should not, therefore, expect abstract unity to obtain in the created world; we have no reason to believe in impersonal "forms," nor ontological realism. Moreover, "god" is not the sort of term where "one and only" means that the term cannot be rightly attributed to others. That is, it is not abstract or essential, as philosophers have claimed. Instead, "god" is a relative term, denoting the relationship between individual objects. The Bible's claim that there is one God means there is only one creator and sustainer of all things; all other "gods" are only thus so far as they are (pale) imitations of this one true individual, Yahweh. This suggests that an essentialist metaphysic and interpretation of language are off the table.[16]

---

[16] Poythress, *Symphonic Theology: The Validity of Multiple Perspectives in Theology*; Rutherford, *The Gift of Knowledge*.

Perhaps most significantly for our Modern age and contemporary theology, this understanding of the Trinity leaves us in an uncomfortable place.

If God is fundamentally personal and individual, why do we tend to seek impersonal and universal explanations for everything? That is, in the physical sciences (physics, medicine, geography, chemistry, etc.), there is a search for the fundamental explanations of everything; we break things down into laws and furnish other laws that explain those laws. In fundamentally personal universe, I do not see how we can escape the conclusion that these laws are themselves personal, expressions of God's consistency.[17] However, if the laws explain God's consistent action, the only immutability they enjoy is God's faithfulness. Yet God has not promised to only ever act in this way and no other, so we must accept our science for what it is, an explanation of the regular ways God works. However, we know from the Bible that God works in extraordinary ways—as do angels and demons: the possibility of God's personal action in the world, and that of innumerable powerful, personal beings should caution our hubris about the past and the future. That we know how God regularly works does not mean we know how he has and will work in the future: miracles happen, the creation happened, a global flood happened, illness does not always have a mechanistic cause, etc. Laws are helpful, therefore, but they will not explain everything in our experience; we need to continually pay attention to the details, to the individuals and individual things we experience. The whole human life, in all its dimensions, must, therefore, be attentive to the details without recourse to universalising explanations.

This effort to reduce things to laws is common in all dimensions of human behaviour. We do this not only in the physical sciences but in the so-called "social sciences," in the study of the human mind and subjectivity, in history, etc. Most significant for us theologians, theology has often been performed along this plane. John Webster explained theological knowledge as "universal, necessary truths."[18] T. F. Torrance drew on Polanyi's multileveled ontology of scientific knowledge to explain theology.[19] In both

---

[17] Cf. Vern S. Poythress, *Redeeming Science: A God-Centered Approach* (Wheaton: Crossway Books, 2006).

[18] Webster, "What Makes Theology Theological?," 221.

[19] Thomas F. Torrance, "The Trinitarian Mind," in *The Christian Doctrine of God*,

cases, theology is the search for the universal, necessary realities that stand behind the contingency of our experience. However, our investigation has revealed something all together unsettling. Behind the contingencies of our experience is something individual, neither necessary in the cold logical sense nor universal. We cannot reduce God or his activities to a box of this or that definition or this or that explanation; he will always be fundamentally personal. "Personal" does not mean unpredictable, for God covenants and is faithful, yet it does mean that we cannot anticipate all that God will do or come up with a logical explanation for all of God's actions. This is simultaneously terrifying yet reassuring. Terrifying, because I cannot anticipate exactly what God's faithfulness looks like today or tomorrow. Yet, it is also reassuring, because unlike the God of the philosophers, the Christian God is a person, and we know from everyday experience that we can know persons. We know that our knowledge of this or that person—my knowledge of Nicole, my wife—will never be exhaustive, yet not knowing everything does not mean I know nothing. Instead, relationship is ever growing into the knowledge of the other person and at each step, I know enough to step out in trust, simultaneously knowing what to expect, that Nicole will act as the Nicole I know, yet being confronted with the unexpected: I know Nicole will be faithful and love me, but what that looks like today or tomorrow is unknown to me. This is what we will take up in the next chapter, how the doctrine of the Trinity we have arrived at help us understanding our knowledge of God.

Before we do so, it worth making one more observation. Given all that we have seen thus far, the most appropriate summary of the Bible's doctrine of the Trinity is that which Moses gave us, "Hear, oh Israel, YHWH your Gods, YHWH is One." Where "Gods" is interpreted as referring to the one creator God who is revealed in multiplicity, as Father, Son, and Spirit, each acting subjects, and "One" is interpreted as referring to "one (God)" in the same sense, an acting subject, the polarity of the biblical doctrine of the Trinity is secured. God is a plurality of persons, each with equal and co-extensive authority and power, without beginning or end, and this plurality is no less than the one acting, personal creator God, who is the God and Father of us all. To him be the glory throughout the ages, forever and ever, amen.

One Being Three Persons, Paperback ed. (London: T&T Clark, 2001), 73–111.

19

PRACTICAL KNOWLEDGE OF THE TRINITY

[18]For the wrath of God is revealed from heaven upon all the ungodliness and righteousness of humans, who hold the truth unrighteously. [19]For the knowledge of God is evident among them; for God has made it evident among them. [20]For his invisible attributes have been mentally comprehended from the creation of the world by created things, both his eternal power and his divinity, in order that they would be without excuse. [21]For although they knew God, they did not glorify him as God or give thanks, but they became foolish in their reasoning, and their foolish hearts became dark. [22]Claiming themselves to be wise, they became foolish [23]and exchanged the glory of the incorruptible God for images in the likeness of corruptible humans, birds, quadrupeds, and reptiles.

– Romans 1:18-23

A significant issue throughout the history of Christian theology, an issue particularly pertinent in the 4th-century debates, has been God's incomprehensibility. Christians throughout the ages have attempted to hold together two claims that appear to stand in tension with each other, that God is known to his people and that he transcends us and is not comprehended by us. Add to this the claim of Paul in Romans 1, that God is known to everyone—even though most people would disavow such knowledge—and you have a recipe for chaos. What does it mean to know God at all, let alone for everyone to know him? However, by bringing this last claim into interaction with the tension of the first two, remarkable light is shed on the topic. This intersects with our discussion thus far in two ways: first, the claim of God's incomprehensibility in history is closely tied to the ontology that was used in the 4th century to explain God's unity; second, the knowledge of God is usually treated as the necessary and universal sort that can be best captured in a proposition, the sort of knowledge that unbelievers disavow concerning God and some Christians may not be able to confess concerning the Trinity.

A. The Ancient Paradigm of Knowing God

In a world where the primary object of knowledge was a thing's essence, knowing something is in a significant sense, quite easy. What matters about Joe is not his ethnicity, appearance, history, personality, or any such things. No, what really matters so far as knowledge is concerned is the definition that describes what is most enduring about him, his humanity—which will endure long after he is gone. Once I know the "account of his being," I know what needs to be known. However, if I do not know this, what do I know after all? All we would have is what Plato called "opinion," the knowledge of contingent reality, those things that might not have been—Joe's actions, character, personality, family, ethnicity, history, etc. However, if God is pure necessity, with no shadow of change (on a strong reading of divine immutability, with no "accidence," namely, any of the things mentioned about Joe), then all there is to know is the essence of God. Either God is wholly known or wholly unknown. In the 4th century, Eunomius claimed that God's essence was "unbegottenness"; Basil of Caesarea responded that it is preposterous to claim to know God's essence![1]

However, this was an area of serious contention: how can a wholly transcendent and unknown, unchanging and unmoved God be known to his

---

[1] Eunomius, *The Extant Works*, trans. Richard Paul Vaggione, Oxford Early Christian Texts (Oxford; New York: Clarendon Press; Oxford University Press, 1987); Basil of Caesarea, *Against Eunomius*.

creatures? Arius himself wrestled with this question, wanting to uphold Jesus' unique place as the mediator of the knowledge of God yet being driven by his philosophy to acknowledge that as a creature, Jesus could not know God's essence; how then was he to mediate the knowledge of God?[2] This was a problem faced by the Nicene and anti-Nicene Theologians alike. They all refused to give up completely on the knowledge of God, for this was essential to the Christian faith, yet they wrestled extensively with the question of how our knowledge about God could be true. Various answers were given, such as knowing God according to his effects, knowing God according to the relationships perceived between himself and the creature, knowing the individuating aspects of each of the persons, knowing that God is not what he is, etc. However, all these positions seem to deny what is treated as common in the Bible, genuine knowledge of God. The Bible does claim that God is above and beyond us—even his thoughts are beyond us, and we cannot exhaust him (Isa 40:13; Isa 55:8; Rom 11:34; 1 Cor 2:16). However, it also claims that even a child can know God and his ways (Deut 6:1-25) and that all humans know God. Indeed, the Bible claims that unbelievers know a lot about God (Rom 1:18-32). A similar problem confronts us with the Trinity.

Though it is not always expressed in propositions, it seems like the great proportion of Christians throughout history and in the Bible, as judged by their prayers, theology, and actions, have believed in the Trinity. However, if asked to articulate the doctrine of the Trinity, most would not be able to express the 4th-century doctrine of the Trinity nor what we have argued is the Bible's doctrine of the Trinity. What do we do with these claims? How do we explain this knowledge? I think our investigation thus far points us in two directions. First, it would lead us to disavow the ontology and epistemology that has proved problematic for many theologians; second, it would lead us to explore the paradigm of the knowledge of persons for our knowledge of God.

B. Against Essentialism

First, we have seen that the God we meet in the Bible, the Trinitarian God, is not an abstract necessity, a universal object, or an analogy with the

---

[2] Cf. Williams, *Arius*.

philosophical One. Instead, the God of the Bible is personal all the way down. He is personal in his unity and personal in his plurality. We have no biblical warrant to believe that he has an "essence" in the abstract philosophical sense, let alone to believe that such a thing is an object (perhaps the ideal object) of our knowledge of God.[3] Though this is not the place to mount the case in this regard, I would also want to argue that the doctrine of immutability mentioned above—the presence of no accidence—is simultaneously contrary to the Bible, which presents God as acting frequently in his creation, and so intimately involved with the ontology rejected by our doctrine of the Trinity that to reject that ontology is to require a revision of the doctrine of immutability and simplicity conceived in terms of essence, metaphysical composition, and accidence or inherent properties. For an exploration of these matters, see my book *God's Gifts for the Christian Life – Part 1: The Gift of Knowledge.* But if that whole paradigm of knowledge is rejected, especially as it regards the doctrine of God, then a new paradigm is needed.

C. Person-Knowledge of God

Second, the paradigm of our knowledge of persons thus enters our purview. In my book *The Gift of Knowledge,* I discuss several dimensions of human knowledge, but the knowledge of persons is one that I think is severely undervalued, especially in its applicability to the question at hand. The knowledge of persons is, very simply, the sort of knowledge we have of other people, even of ourselves. If you think about your knowledge of your best friend, for example, you will very quickly realise that it cannot be fully resolved into propositions (i.e. subject + predicate claim: "James Rutherford was writing"). Now, to say that it does not resolve into proposition does not mean that it has no propositional content: this would be a ludicrous claim. If you knew nothing propositional about your mother, brother, or best friend— if you did not know their names (e.g. "my mother is Carolyn"), anything about their appearance, no facts about them—then any claim you made to know them would be immediately treated as a farse.[4] However, no matter

---

[3] Cf. Rutherford, *The Gift of Knowledge.*

[4] Cf. Ronald H. Nash, *The Word of God and the Mind of Man* (Grand Rapids: Zondervan, 1982).

how many propositions you can name off, none of this is equivalent to your knowledge of your best friend: your knowledge of your best friend includes propositions but is more than propositional.

Indeed, one of the most frustrating things about this knowledge is that it is mostly inexpressible, yet it is involved in all interpersonal interactions. Though my mother-in-law probably knows more propositions about my wife, Nicole, than I do, I know Nicole better than her mother. This knowledge is a product of numerous interactions between Nicole and I, where I have listened and observed what she does, how she responds, and watched her grow in these ways. My knowledge of Nicole includes who she once was but incorporates an element of growth: I do not act towards her as I did when we were first married seven years ago, yet I remember what she was like then. My knowledge of Nicole allows me to anticipate her response to things I say, to anticipate how she will react in certain circumstances. This knowledge allows me to surprise her with gifts and to counsel her amid despair. This ineffable but clearly real knowledge is what I mean by "knowledge of persons." It is knowledge I have gained through observation and through the effects of the Nicole's interiority, her "self," seen in what she does. This knowledge incorporates both interiority, what cannot be seen, and exteriority, her physical presence and features. It is a knowledge gained through effects, yet it is genuine knowledge of the one who affects things. It is knowledge of the visible and of the invisible, of a person's "invisible attributes," to steal Paul's phrase in Romans 1:20.

If God is a person, a subjective self that acts and is acted upon (however much we qualify that latter claim), does not the paradigm of person-knowledge seem to offer a promising avenue through which to consider our knowledge of God? Indeed, the tensions between knowing and being on the edge of the unknown (incomprehensibility) receives vivid content: this is a description of all interpersonal relationships—though magnified to an inestimable degree in the case of God. I truly know Nicole, yet I have not and will not ever stop growing in my knowledge of her. Part of that is because she is constantly changing, but it is more than that. Consider what it would mean to know someone completely. Would it not mean knowing them so thoroughly that we knew everything propositional about them and could anticipate their response to every single circumstance they faced, thus gaining a true and fully orbed portrait of that inner self manifest in their life? Such is knowledge only God has. So, my knowledge of Nicole is simultaneously true and incomplete, perfect in as much as it is true and imperfect in as much as it is limited.

Consider God through this paradigm. God has truly revealed himself in word and deed. We know what we are to expect of him: he will fulfill his promises. We know he desires mercy not sacrifice, that he will freely forgive us through his Son, Jesus Christ. We know that he loved us so much that he sent his Son while we were yet enemies to die for us and to ransom us from our sins. This knowledge is propositional, yet it is more than that. As Martin Kähler once argued, the Bible paints us a portrait of Jesus.[5] Is this not the case for the whole Trinity? We encounter the living God in Scripture and walk away with a portrait of a person, a glimpse of his interiority. We can anticipate how God will act, we can depend on him, and begin to commune with him according to the portrait painted in Scripture. This is much like a long-distance relationship in a bygone age, where correspondence was delayed by distance and performed through writing. Through the exchange of letters, one could gain true knowledge of the other person, though perhaps limited in comparison to interactive and in-person communication. Our knowledge of God is thus genuine and personal. Yet, as with all personal knowledge, it is not exhaustive. I know God is faithful and that I can trust him; I know that he will work all things together for good.

However, despite what I have known of God, I could not have anticipated him taking the life of my unborn son, Asher, in the 28th week of pregnancy. I truly believe that it is the Lord who gives and who takes away, so this was not out of his control; it is my great comfort that God is truly in control. I could not anticipate how his faithfulness and goodness would look in these circumstances, that he would permit such a thing and that he would not give life miraculously back as he once did for Lazarus. However, that I could not anticipate the course of events surrounding Asher's death nor how God would act towards Nicole, Aliyah, and I in the following months did not invalidate my original knowledge of God; it only expanded it. As I clung fast to the personal God in whom I trust, my understanding of his power and goodness was expanded in the midst of grief, as in innumerable ways he acted

---

[5] Martin Kähler, *The So-Called Historical Jesus and the Historic, Biblical Christ* (Vancouver: Regent College Pub., 1998).

to comfort the three of us and to transform, to strengthen, and to sustain us.

I do not know God perfectly and am growing in my knowledge each day, yet there is a stable core to this knowledge. My knowledge of the God I meet in the Bible is ever added to but does not become other than it is. In this way, God is immutable: the same God who acted to send his Son to the Cross for my sake and raise him from the dead is the same God who acts each day in my life. This is the same God, "yesterday, today, and forever" (Heb 11:8). This paradigm makes sense of the tension between knowing and unknowing, between resting in our knowledge of God as we stand on the precipice of the unknown. I know of no other paradigm that succeeds in these regards. In addition, this paradigm allows us to make sense of the knowledge of God Paul talks about in Romans 1:18-32.

D. The Knowledge of God in Romans 1:18-32

Though many Christians, especially of the Reformed persuasion, agree that all unbelievers have knowledge of God, what "knowledge of God" could mean with reference to an unbeliever is a difficult issue. The key text in consideration is Romans 1:18-32. It is clear in this text Paul intends to teach that all people know God, in some sense, and for this reason are liable to judgment. However, it is also clear that unbelievers deny such knowledge: few unbelievers are willing to admit they have any beliefs concerning God except that he may exist or does not exist. What, then, are we to make of this knowledge? To suggest that it is unconscious does not fit any account of "knowledge" well nor of Paul's point.[6] The same can be said of the view that they "suppress" it: to suppress the truth of God implies that they have knowledge of God which is then "suppressed." What is meant by "suppressed" is vague—sometimes taking on Freudian tones of "repression"[7]—but may be best interpreted as "consciously restrained." However, interpreted in this way, what is meant is still not clear. How can you consciously restrain what is unconscious, what is not acknowledged at

---

[6] There are clearly tacit beliefs in a person's worldview, but tacit belief is not what we would usually call "knowledge." Knowledge involves belief but also consciousness of that belief, whether consciousness in the present or in memory. Cf. Polanyi, *The Tacit Dimension.*

[7] Frame makes this observation. Frame, *The Doctrine of the Knowledge,* 52.

all? This is not consistent with the denial of such belief among unbelievers. Instead, unbelievers regularly deny knowing any "God," and many would deny positive knowledge of the Christian God.[8] In what sense, then, do unbelievers know God? Our paradigm of person-knowledge introduced above goes a long way to resolving this problem. I will proceed by making several observations on the text and then drawing a summary.

a. Εν ἀδικια Κατεχοντων (1:18b)

This phrase (en adikia katechonton) is often translated "who by their unrighteousness supress" (ESV), often substantiated with an appeal to the present context and the meaning of κατέχω (katecho) in 2 Thessalonians 2:6-7 and Philemon 13.[9] Yet, once again, what does it mean for the unbeliever to "suppress" the truth? Certainly, they do not allow the truth (whatever "truth" refers to in this context) to shape their lives, but it is not even clear how they possess the truth, so how can they hinder it? Furthermore, there is no clear text in the Bible where this word means "suppress." In Philemon, the word means "hold/possess" as in all other biblical uses, though the context has a specific manner of "holding" in view, namely, keeping Onesimus with him. This is clearly a contextual instance of a sense "keep/hold/possess." The two instances in 2 Thessalonians 2:6-7 are also unclear. Morris suggests "hold back" (with appeal to Phlm 13), with "hold firm" (cf. 1 Thess 5:21) as a plausible option.[10] However, if Philemon 13 does not mean "hold back," then "hold firm" is the default option and fits the context as much as "hold back."[11] Such an idea actually fits well if Paul intends something like the vision of Satan held by chains in Revelation (Rev 20:1-3). This corresponds to the other 13 uses of the verb that mean "hold/possess/keep." Without

[8] That is, they have knowledge *about* the God of Christianity but deny that this knowledge accurately represents the nature of reality.

[9] E.g. Douglas J. Moo, *The Epistle to the Romans*, NICNT (Grand Rapids: Eerdmans, 1996), 103.

[10] Leon Morris, *The First and Second Epistles to the Thessalonians* (Grand Rapids: Eerdmans, 1991), 128.

[11] Now, both senses are nearly identical. However, "hold back" has the added nuance of "restraint" which may be present in an event where someone is "held firm," yet it is not clear that κατέχω is ever used to invoke such connotations.

evidence for even "hold back" in the New Testament—let alone "suppress," which would appear to be an extension of the meaning "hold back"—"hold" or "possess" would be the evident meaning for Romans 1:18, if it fits the context.

This actually makes great sense here, resulting in the translation "who possess the truth in an unrighteous manner" (my translation, cf. KJV). That is, they have the truth but do not have it in a righteous manner. This fits well in the biblical picture of knowledge, for truth brings moral obligation so that knowledge can be unrighteous (disobedient) or righteous (obedient).[12] The unbeliever has the truth but their possession of it is not in accordance with what it is. We still must identify what it means for the unbeliever to "hold truth," yet the problem of explaining how the unbeliever consciously withholds or suppresses the truth without any acknowledgment of positive belief in God is removed.

b. νοούμενα καθορᾶται (1:20a)

This phrase (*noumena kathoratai*) could be translated as "being seen with mental comprehension," "perceived with the understanding." The phrase (lit. "being understood, are seen") employs a relatively rare word for physical perception in the LXX (cf. Exod 10:5; Num 24:2; Deut 26:15), used only here in the New Testament, καθοράω (*kathorao*). This word is used along with a standard word for understanding or comprehension, νοέω (*noeo*), which is used specifically for mental acts. This suggests an interpretation such as BDAG's, "perceived with the mind's eye."[13] It does not denote something seen *in the creation* or (directly) something arrived at by reason, but something perceived mentally. It does not of course preclude an experiential component, but it focuses on the mind. If all people possess this knowledge, this suggests it is not experiential, for many people have significant physical and mental handicaps that may prevent deriving knowledge from experience.

---

[12] Moo, *The Epistle to the Romans*, 102–103; Frame, *The Doctrine of the Knowledge*, 108–109.

[13] Frederick W. Danker, *A Greek-English Lexicon of the New Testament and Other Early Christian Literature*, 3rd ed. (Chicago: University of Chicago Press, 2000), s.v. ποίημα.

It is also not clearly rational, for there is no mention of an active process by which potential knowledge is grasped, and many people are unable to mentally deduce the existence and nature of God from reason.[14] Because the phrase refers to mental comprehension rather than physical perception, I think that "τοῖς ποιήμασιν (*tois poiemasin*)" does not mean "in the created things" but "by the created things." Both are acceptable interpretations of the Greek dative case.

c. Γνόντες τὸν θεὸν (1:21a)

Now we are in a place to consider the meaning of "knowing God" (γνόντες τὸν θεὸν; *gnontes ton theon*) Nowhere in this passage is a content-knowledge statement ("know Person A to be B," "know that Person A did B") unambiguously used. However, personal knowledge statements are used ("know Person A"). The statement in verses 19-20, that God's "invisibles" (ἀόρατα; *aorata*) are clearly perceived (namely, eternal power and divine nature) could imply either direct content-knowledge ("they know that God has eternal power and divinity) or an aspect of personal knowledge ("they know God who has eternal power and divinity). That is, when a knowing verb receives a personal or analogously personal object (i.e. an object or objectified concept: "the way of righteousness," "human heart," "will of the master," "times"), person-knowledge is in view.

In the biblical sense, "to know person A" does not mean to know something specific but to have relation of some familiarity with Person A. Such a relationship could be hostile (e.g. Ps 138:6) or familial, from which the idiom for sexual intercourse emerges. Such a statement does not mean "A knows B about C," though context may specify a content statement (Deut 9:2, Ezek 28:19); it means something more than but not less than propositional knowledge. An example sometimes used is that of a president: a history buff may have much propositional or content knowledge of George

---

[14] Cf. Jeffery D. Johnson, *The Failure of Natural Theology: A Critical Appraisal of the Philosophical Theology of Thomas Aquinas*, New Studies in Theology (Free Grace Press, 2021), 8–32.

Bush Sr. but having not met him, may not know him in the personal sense.[15] ("May not" is an important limitation, for there is a sense in which rigorous study of a subject may yield a certain personal knowledge.) The gardener at the white house, on the other hand, may have little content-knowledge of George Bush Sr. and yet *know him* better than the history buff. It is this later sense of knowledge that I call person-knowledge and is sometimes found in the biblical use of a verb of knowledge with a concrete object or, occasionally, a complex concept ("the way of righteousness"), but it is used especially with a person.

Turning to Romans, γνόντες τὸν θεὸν (*gnontes ton theon*) would seem to be a case of person-knowledge, given that it has a concrete, personal subject, and no specific content-knowledge (even "invisibles" and "eternal power and divinity," though they could be ideas making up content-knowledge, are ambiguous and an aspect of, not identified with, the knowledge of God). It must be emphasized that personal knowledge is not *content-less* but not necessarily *content-explicit*. That is, the gardener never has to cognise the beliefs "George Bush Sr. is the president of the USA," "George Bush Sr. lives at the white house," "George Bush Sr. is kind," etc. to have personal knowledge of George Bush Sr. and know these things implicitly. When asked, he may answer correctly to questions concerning the character of the president without having previously formulated his opinions. As observed above, person-knowledge is not proposition less, but it cannot be resolved into propositions. Moreover, we could distinguish between propositional knowledge as the explicit knowledge of certain things (e.g. "the gas constant R is 8.314") and propositional knowledge as an implication of person-knowledge. In the former case, what is known is a proposition; in the latter, what is known is a person and that knowledge can be expressed in a proposition, such is the case of the gardener who may never have thought "George Bush Sr. is kind" but can say so and affirm its veracity when asked. This contrast, between content-knowledge which involves belief in a certain proposition and person-knowledge which minimally involves implicit content-knowledge, gives us better categories for interpreting what is going on in Romans 1:18-32.

---

[15] I cannot trace the source from which I am borrowing this illustration.

Person-knowledge is such that it can be implicit (I may know, in some limited sense, the bus driver I see daily and talk to occasionally without ever identifying this as knowledge or thinking intentionally about the man) and can be misidentified. This last point is very important. For content-knowledge, misidentification falsifies the knowledge: if George Bush Sr. was president in the 1990s and George W. Bush was president in the 2000s, it would be false to say that "George Bush was president in the 1990s" while referring to George W. Bush. However, we can conceivably have genuine, true personal knowledge that is misidentified—leading to false content-knowledge. For example, if Baby A and Baby B were swapped at birth. The parent of Baby A would acquire personal knowledge of Baby B but misidentify Baby B as Baby A. They may believe that Baby B was born at a certain time, to certain parents, with certain biological origins, certain genetic proclivities, etc. and be wrong about all these things but nevertheless have genuine personal knowledge. Furthermore, if they attribute their personal knowledge of Baby B to Baby A, they are wrong while possessing genuine personal knowledge.[16]

Applying this analysis to unbelieving knowledge of God, we can make sense of the significant statements and implications Paul makes in this passage. Unbelievers know God even if they have no propositional beliefs concerning him—or even a negative belief (i.e. "Yahweh does not exist" or "he is not god"). I explore this to a much greater extent in my *The Gift of Knowledge*, but if we are all born with person-knowledge of God, then we have the sufficient conditions to recognise the creation as his handiwork and give him the glory due his name and to interpret our behaviour in light of him and so make positive or negative moral evaluations. This the content Paul gives to the knowledge of which he speaks in Romans 1. This knowledge is enough to convict us of unbelief and moral failing. This knowledge is expressed in action, yet under the guidance of sin, this knowledge of God is applied to the creation, as in the case of the swapped babies. Though unbelievers know God to be in this or that way (to be eternal, beneficent, powerful, good, etc.) and reflexively interpret the creation and their lives in light of this knowledge

---

[16] Tragically, I have drawn this analogy from real events, e.g. https://www.cbc.ca/radio/ thecurrent/the-current-for-jan-15-2020-1.5427568/it-tore-me-in-pieces-men-switched-at-birth-regret-never-meeting-biological-parents-1.5427574.

(rightly identifying good or bad, assuming the creation to be inherently ordered, etc.), they give glory to created things instead of God, deifying nature as all powerful, good, eternal, etc. Thus, person-knowledge allows us to explain our knowledge of God and its limitations as well as the unbeliever's knowledge of God and its corruption.[17]

d. Implications

Several significant implications may be drawn from this. First, because this epistemological sin involves miss-association, the unbeliever will err in knowledge in two ways. 1) They will fail to associate everything they learn and know with God. 2) They will attribute their knowledge of God to created things—whether idols, demons, creatures, humans, etc.—implying misapplied content-knowledge (e.g. the created order is eternal; fate determines all things). The unbeliever has what they need to make the proper identification but in unrighteousness they make this exchange, leaving them liable.

Second, this epistemological exchange will be pervasive, infecting all areas of human life—for in every area, humans are commanded to submit to God and further his glory. We can expect a mixture of error and truth in all human thought, for there is the knowledge of God (truth) misapplied to the creature (falsehood). God will be tamed into a creature, such as when Feuerbach proclaimed "god" to be the idealisation of all that humanity is and could be.[18] Nature itself might be made into god, as Carl Sagan exemplified: "In its encounter with Nature, science invariably elicits a sense of reverence and awe. The very act of understanding is a celebration of joining, merging, even if on a very modest scale, with the magnificence of the Cosmos."[19] In intellectual effort, attributes of God will be attributed to the creature, such as when Aristotle made matter to be eternal.

---

[17] See *God's Gifts for the Christian Life – Part 1: The Gift of Knowledge*.

[18] Ludwig Feuerbach, *The Essence of Christianity*, trans. George Eliot (Amherst, New York: Prometheus Books, 2010).

[19] Carl Sagan, *The Demon-Haunted World: Science as a Candle in the Dark*, 1st Ed. (New York: Ballantine Books, 1997).

E. Conclusion

In the introduction to this book, we raised the problem of the relationship between the doctrine of the Trinity and our knowledge of God. If God is fundamentally triune, it is hard to conceive how someone could truly know God without knowing he is a Trinity. However, most Christians cannot articulate the 4th-century doctrine of the Trinity, and some have argued that they are ill-equipped to do so, for example, "the decline in the study of Greek philosophy by theologians also renders them unable to comprehend what the fourth-century debates were all about," and so to be unable to talk about God in an orthodox fashion.[20] However, our discussion in the last two chapters allows us to draw a radically different conclusion. Many mature Christians can articulate biblical teaching that God is one person and three persons. Even when they cannot articulate this, this knowledge is evident in Christian praxis across ages, denominations, and cultures. When people acknowledge in prayer, liturgy, praise, and life that the Father, the Son, and the Spirit are God, whether explicitly or implicitly (such as treating the Spirit as possessing God's power and presence and as a person), it would seem that their knowledge of God is shaped in trinitarian terms. Moreover, in many cases, these same people will address God as one, flowing between the persons and not making proper distinction theologians would like to make; this suggests, on the other hand, that their knowledge of God is shaped in the trinitarian terms of personal unity as well. I have no trouble affirming that the person-knowledge possessed by unbelievers is itself trinitarian, perhaps this is why there is swing in non-Christian religion from absolute Unitarianism towards extreme polytheism, or between abstract unity and concrete plurality in philosophy. If the creation is mis-identified in terms of a Trinitarian God, such confusion would appear to be natural.

---

[20] Carter, *Contemplating God*, 29, 296.

STANDING ON THE SHOULDERS OF GIANTS: DOCTRINE AND TRADITION

> We are like dwarfs sitting on the shoulders of giants so that we are able to see more and further than they, not indeed by the sharpness of our own vision or the height of our bodies, but because we are lifted up on high and raised aloft by the greatness of giants. – Bernard of Chartres[1]

> We must take heed of men's traditions, especially since the Lord saith, "In vain do they worship me, teaching doctrines the precepts of men." So that now the surest way is, to cleave to the word of the Lord left to us in the scriptures, which teacheth abundantly all things that belong to true godliness.[2] – Henry Bullinger

There are many lies in the modern world, of which theologians are particularly susceptible to two. On the one hand, there is what C.S. Lewis called "chronological snobbery"; this is the view that the past has nothing to say to the present and that thought is ever upwards and onwards, without the

---

[1] Given in Jean de Salisbury, *Metalogicon*, ed. John Barrie Hall and Julian Haseldine, Corpus Christianorum in translation 12 (Turnhout: Brepols, 2013), 257.

[2] Bullinger, *The Decades of Henry Bullinger: Volume 1*, 64.

need to look to its past.[3] This is exemplified by many streams of 19th through 21st-century theology. On the other hand, there has been the glorification of the "premodern," where the ancient world is thought to have the answers to today's problems. Not only can we learn from the past, but we need to go back to the past if we are to recover from the chaos of the present.[4] The church fathers are particularly treasured by those who would idolise pre-modernism.

In this book, I have hoped to avoid both temptations. If we are to look to the past and learn from those who have come before, it must be with humility that recognises they have something to say to us today. However, if we are to look to the past and avoid the same errors our forefathers fell into, we must do so critically, measuring them against standards other than their own writings. Augustine encourages us in this very regard, writing,

> As I say to the former [pious reader], Do not be willing to yield to my writings as to the canonical Scriptures; but in these, when thou hast discovered even what thou didst not previously believe, believe it unhesitatingly; while in those, unless thou hast understood with certainty what thou didst not before hold as certain, be unwilling to hold it fast: so I say to the latter [the corrector], Do not be willing to amend my writings by thine own opinion or disputation, but from the divine text, or by unanswerable reason.[5]

Our conclusions in this book raise several significant questions concerning our relationship with those who came before us. First, many today want to attribute creeds and confessions with an important role in the life of the church, even with authority, but if they are fallible and imperfect, what is this

---

[3] This phrase is used in his account of his conversion, *Surprised by Joy*, but see his introduction to Athanasius' *On the Incarnation*, "On the Reading of Old Books."

[4] E.g. David C. Steinmetz, "The Superiority of Precritical Exegesis," in *A Guide to Contemporary Hermeneutics: Major Trends in Biblical Interpretation*, ed. Donald K. McKim (Grand Rapids: Eerdmans, 1986); Hans Boersma, *Nouvelle Théologie and Sacramental Ontology: A Return to Mystery* (Oxford; New York: Oxford University Press, 2009); Hans Boersma, *Heavenly Participation: The Weaving of a Sacramental Tapestry* (Grand Rapids: Eerdmans, 2011); Matthew Barrett, *None Greater: The Undomesticated Attributes of God* (Grand Rapids: Baker Books, 2019); Carter, *Contemplating God*.

[5] *De Trinitate* in NPNF 1.3, B. III, preface par. 2.

role?[6] Second, if ancient documents do not give us a set orthodoxy by which we can determine who is in and who is out (and implication of the fallibility of these documents), we need to ask, what does it mean to be "orthodox"? Third, how do we engage with those who have come before us in a humble, careful, and critical manner?

A. Creeds and Confessions

> Whenever the decree of a council is produced, the first thing I would wish to be done is, to examine at what time it was held, on what occasion, with what intention, and who were present at it; next I would bring the subject discussed to the standard of Scripture. And this I would do in such a way that the decision of the council should have its weight, and be regarded in the light of a prior judgment, yet not so as to prevent the application of the test which I have mentioned. – John Calvin

In previous works, especially my series "God's Gifts for the Christian Life," I have argued that Christians need tradition. We do not need tradition as another source for theology but as a starting point, the received framework within which we begin the hermeneutical spiral, interpreting and being interpreted by Scripture. Tradition describes the received faith that is taught in the local church from Scripture; it also describes the faith taught in the church from Scripture across the ages. We need tradition in this second sense to escape the blinders of our culture; it is all too easy to blindly follow our culture's assumptions until we are confronted by someone outside those assumptions, showing us in what ways our assumptions align with Scripture and in which ways they diverge. We will discuss this process in the third part of this chapter, but our question here is different. If this is the role of tradition, what is the role of creeds and confessions?

If tradition is the sum total of human reflection on and application of

---

[6] Cf. Carl R. Trueman, *The Creedal Imperative* (Wheaton: Crossway, 2012); J. V. Fesko, *The Need for Creeds Today: Confessional Faith in a Faithless Age* (Grand Rapids: Baker Academic, 2020); Carter, *Contemplating God*.

Scripture to life and thought throughout the ages, in what way do creeds and confessions differ from other parts of this tradition? Moevover, if Scripture is our authority, what authority do such documents have? This is especially pertinent when we have reason to believe that a creed has errors in it. For example, in this book, I have argued that the Nicene Creed fits within Eastern 4th-century thought, which itself is imperfect, and that it had critical ambiguities in its original context. My PhD research has focused on the council of Chalcedon, at which time the incarnation of Christ received a thorough "definition" (or application of the Nicaean Creed as the council saw it). Following several authors, I have argued that there is a conceptual tension in that Definition, one that calls into question the compatibility of the Nicaean Creed, along with the tradition of its interpretation, and the incarnation.[7] Elements of that argument have emerged in this work, and I have argued the point from a different angle in my book *The Gift of Knowledge*. Thus, there are several lines of evidence that suggest that the Nicene Creed and Definition of Chalcedon are not only theoretically fallible but, when interpreted in their historical context, actually fallible. Craig Carter suggests that the burden of proof is too high to make such a claim: who are we to disagree with the vast majority of the church?[8] However, as we have argued, it is not evident that the vast majority of the church is in agreement on the meaning of the Nicene Creed (see Chs. 16-19), and the fallout from Chalcedon shows that Nicaea and Chalcedon sat in uneasy tension that raises questions concerning their compatibility.[9] So, this is an actual problem, yet a

---

[7] Cf. Jean-Yves Lacoste, "Homoousios et Homoousios: La Substance Entre Théologie et Philosophie," *Recherches de science religieuse* 98, no. 1 (January 2010): 85–100; Zachhuber, *The Rise of Christian Theology and the End of Ancient Metaphysics*. Bruce McCormack also identifies a problem (or, *aporia*) in the Definition, but I disagree with his identification of the problem. Zachhuber is closest, I argue in my thesis, to identifying what is going on. McCormack, *The Humility of the Eternal Son*.

[8] Carter, *Contemplating God*, loc 1225. Cf. Trueman, *The Creedal Imperative*, 128–129.

[9] On the various and divergent ways Nicaea was received, see (in addition to the chapters above) Smith, Gray, and Grauman. On the fallout of Chalcedon, see Zachhuber, and for its reception, Grillmeier and Leuenberger-Wenger. Smith, *The Idea*; Patrick T. R. Gray, "Covering the Nakedness of Noah: Reconstruction and Denial in the Age of Justinian," *Byzantinische Forschungen* 24 (1997): 193–205; Thomas Graumann, "Orthodoxy, Authority and the (Re-) Construction of the Past in Church Councils," in *Invention, Rewriting, Usurpation: Discursive Fights over Religious Traditions in*

theoretical problem remains: what right do we have to insist on certain teachings of men, admittedly arrived at on reflection of Scripture not immediately taught therein (on which, see Carter)?[10] How is this not "teaching as doctrines the commandments of men" (Matt 15:9), for which Jesus condemned the Pharisees? In his book *The Need for Creeds Today*, J.V. Fesko argues that there are biblical passages mandating the creation of creeds, yet in each instance, his arguments fail for a want of biblical evidence.[11] There is simply no biblical warrant for producing statements of doctrine that synthesize Scripture and declaring them to be the standard of orthodoxy across the ages. Carl Trueman articulates the view that Creeds are "normed norms," having authority derived from and therefore submitted to Scripture. However, if a creed is synthetic in the above sense and it has authority to demarcate orthodoxy, then this I believe is a significant error. The value of creeds and confessions within denominational structure is an important discussion to be had, but it is different from the matter at hand.[12] It is arguable that articulating a synthetic orthodoxy (i.e. a universal measure of

---

Antiquity, ed. Jörg Ulrich, Anders-Christian Jacobsen, and David Brakke, Early Christianity in the context of antiquity v. 11 (Frankfurt am Main: Lang, 2012); Sandra Leuenberger-Wenger, *Das Konzil von Chalcedon und die Kirche: Konflikte und Normierungsprozesse im 5. und 6. Jahrhundert* (Leiden: Brill, 2019); Aloys Grillmeier, *Christ in Christian Tradition Vol. 2, Part 1: From the Council of Chalcedon to Justinian I*, trans. Pauline Allen and John Cawte (London: Mowbrays, 1987); Aloys Grillmeier and Theresia Hainthaler, *Christ in Christian Tradition Vol. 2, Part 2: The Church of Constantinople in the Sixth Century*, trans. Pauline Allen and John Cawte (London: Mowbrays, 1995); Aloys Grillmeier and Theresia Hainthaler, *Christ in Christian Tradition Vol. 2, Part 3: The Churches of Jerusalem and Antioch from 451 to 600*, trans. Marianne Ehrhardt, vol. 2 (Oxford: Oxford University Press, 2013); Aloys Grillmeier and Theresia Hainthaler, *Christ in Christian Tradition Vol. 2, Part 4: The Church of Alexandria with Nubia and Ethiopia after 451*, trans. O.C. Dean Jr. (London; Louisville: Wobray; Westminster John Knox Press, 1996).

[10] Carter describes the orthodoxy with which he is dealing as a second-exegesis or a second-order reflection on the testimony of Scripture. Carter, *Contemplating God*. Cf. Rhyne R. Putman, *When Doctrine Divides the People of God: An Evangelical Approach to Theological Diversity* (Wheaton: Crossway, 2020), 104–105.

[11] Fesko, *The Need for Creeds*, chap. 1. Cf. Trueman, *The Creedal Imperative*, chap. 2.

[12] Though I would not say "confessions are a bad idea," the considerations below in "B. Orthodoxy" suggest that confessions can be a danger when they function apart from considerations of character and a broader understanding of knowledge.

Christian belief that is synthesised from Scripture) is not what the fathers at Nicaea intended to do, yet by the end of the 5th century, this is what had become of the Creed: it was the final word, authoritative and sufficient.[13] Consider the way the Definition of Chalcedon describes the Nicaean Creed,

> We therefore decree—we ourselves upholding the order and all the decrees of the faith of the holy synod formerly taking place at Ephesus, over which presided the most holy in memory Celestine of Rome and Cyril of Alexandria—on the one hand, that the exposition of the right and spotless faith by the 318 holy and blessed fathers at Nicaea, gathered together by the pious in memory Constantine who was then Emperor, shines forth preeminent and, on the other hand, that the decrees of the 150 holy fathers in Constantinople give support for the uprooting of heresies that then sprung up and the confirmation of the same universal and apostolic faith which is ours.
>
> … Thus this wise and saving Creed of divine grace was sufficient for complete knowledge of and confirmation of godliness; for it both thoroughly teaches the complete matter concerning the Father, the Son, and the Holy Spirit, and it also presents the Lord's *enanthropation* [i.e. "becoming human"] to those who receive it faithfully.
>
> … this now present holy, great, and ecumenical synod, teaching thoroughly the immovability of the proclamation previously given, sets forth firstly that the faith of the 318 holy fathers is to remain inviolate. Because of those who made war against the Holy Spirit, [the council] confirms [the teaching of Constantinople vis-à-vis the Spirit]." (ACO V.31, 34; 2.1.2, 127 lns 1-8; 128 lns 15-18; 128, ln 24 – 129, ln 6)[14]

Carl Trueman draws on 2 Timothy 1:13 to support the making of creeds, but his argument is severally strained.[15] In 2 Timothy 1:13, we read "Follow the pattern [ὑποτύπωσις; *hupotuposis*] of the sound words that you have heard

---

[13] See *The Definition of Chalcedon* in Session V of the Acts of Chalcedon; cf. Smith, *The Idea.*

[14] ACO = *Acta Conciliorum Oecumenicorum*. This is my translation, from my PhD thesis (in progress).

[15] Trueman, *The Creedal Imperative*, chap. 2.

from me, in the faith and love that are in Christ Jesus." Trueman contends that "what Paul is saying here is: Timothy, make sure that your teaching is sound by using the standard [i.e. ὑποτύπωσις] of teaching you see in my ministry as the basic rule."[16] Trueman stresses Paul's use of ὑποτύπωσις as "form," not just content. As applied to the question of creeds, this means, for Trueman, that Paul is commending the development of "a special vocabulary" along with the teaching of the right use and meaning of that vocabulary. This is a commendation of the formation of a technical, creedal vocabulary, a "normative form of sounds words." Therefore, "Anyone who claims to take the Bible seriously must take the words of Paul to Timothy on this matter seriously. The Bible itself seems to demand that we have forms of sounds words, and that is what creeds are."[17] The problem with Trueman's argument is that this is, simply, not what Paul is saying. For one, the word Trueman takes to mean "form" is better understood as a "pattern" or "example" (ὑποτύπωσις), such as in 1 Timothy 1:16 when Paul identifies himself as "as an example to those who were to believe in [Jesus]" (ESV). So, Paul is not commending Timothy and following generations to develop a technical vocabulary and a creedal orthodoxy; no, he is instructing Timothy to imitate Paul's sound, or healthy, words. This sounds like paying close attention to and imitating what Timothy finds in Paul's letters and sermons— i.e., for us today, in Scripture—rather than drafting new, technical forms of words. Paul's words certainly do not deny the validity of creeds, but that is because Paul's words have nothing to do with creeds (understood as something other than the biblical teaching). Notice that Paul does not command Timothy to craft new "forms of sound words"—if Trueman was right on the meaning of that word—but to follow that pattern he received from Paul.

The closest thing the Bible gives us to a creedal mandate is the Jerusalem council, yet here we do not find a mandate for producing universally binding statements. Instead, we find an appropriate model for the sort of conciliar decisions we find in the Early Church councils. In Acts 15, we read of a council in Jerusalem that consisted of the apostles and elders in Jerusalem

---

[16] Ibid.

[17] Ibid.

along with "Paul and Barnabas and some others" (Acts 15:2). The debate at hand was the concern of "some believers from the party of the Pharisees" that the Gentile converts were not being circumcised and not being instructed to keep the law of Moses (Acts 15:5). After agreeing from Scripture that Gentiles were not bound to do these things, the council did give specific instructions, "to abstain from the things polluted by idols, and from sexual immorality, and from what has been strangled, and from blood" (Acts 15:20). This is then written in a formal letter (Acts 15:23-29). Notice the reason given in Acts 15:21 for these commands, "For from ancient generations Moses has had in every city those who proclaim him, for he is read every Sabbath in the synagogues" (Acts 15:21). The reason for these commands is the presence of Jewish believers throughout the cities of these Gentiles. These instructions have every pretence of being circumstantial, not universally binding. That is, sexual immorality may refer to a particular pattern of behaviour, yet it is clear from the New Testament that all sexual immorality is prohibited for Christians; the emphasis here appears to lie on the potential for this behaviour among new converts and the effect it would have on their Jewish neighbours.[18] None of the other commands are presented in Scripture as universally binding for Christians. Acts 10:9-23 and Galatians suggest that all the food restrictions of the Old Testament are inapplicable to Christians, which indicates that these commands from the council are meant to be circumstantial restrictions, defining how the new Gentile converts can live with their Jewish neighbours. This is supported by the reference to "things polluted by idols," for in a different context, Paul indicates that food itself isn't a problem (1 Cor 10:14-33), though eating in an idol's temple is (1 Cor 8:1-13).

Interpreted this way, the Jerusalem council and its decree is not a model for future conciliar activity in the manner which Nicaea, Constantinople, and Chalcedon came to be interpreted. However, it does give a model for understanding these later councils as part of the tradition within which we stand. At each of these councils, a crisis confronted the church, and the church responded in light of its contemporary ecclesiology. Because of their understanding of the universal church and a newly developing understanding

---

[18] Cf. Richard N. Longnecker, "Acts," in *The Expositors Bible Commentary: Luke-Acts*, ed. Tremper Longman and David E. Garland, Revised ed. (Grand Rapids: Zondervan, 2007).

of Christendom, Christians at this time saw the decision of the global church as the tool for addressing the error perceived in Arius and others. They used the ecclesiological, political, theological, and philosophical tools at hand to address Arius' error. This is very much the sort of contextualised theology of the Jerusalem council.

Creeds and confessions understood along these lines are not universal, necessary summaries of Christian belief or snippets of a larger dogmatic system. Instead, they are localised, contextualised articulations of biblical faith against the challenges and questions of their age. They are an example on a corporate or global level of theology as John Frame defines it, "The application of the Word of God by persons to all areas of life."[19] Reflecting on the impermanence of the Jerusalem council, Luther wrote in his *On the Councils and the Church*, "If we wish to be conciliar, we will have to keep this council [Jerusalem] above all others. If not, we need not keep any of the other councils either, and thus we are rid of all councils."[20]

Nothing about the councils, whether they were actually or artificially ecumenical (e.g. Chalcedon) or merely home synods (e.g. Constantinople 449), supports the view that their canons, definitions, or creeds have a special, normative role for the Christian faith or defining Christian orthodoxy across the ages.[21] However, as the gathered wisdom of God's people in the presence

---

[19] Frame, *The Doctrine of the Knowledge*, 81.

[20] Paul W. Robinson, *The Annotated Luther, Volume 3: Church and Sacraments* (Fortress Press, 2016), 344–345.

[21] On "ecumenical," Chalcedon, for example, was held in the Eastern Empire under the auspices of the central Eastern Church, Constantinople; it was attended predominantly by Eastern Bishops; and in many ways, it had a distinctly Eastern emphasis (such as redefining the centre of the Christian world as "Constantinople, the New Rome"). Tommaso Mari, "The Latin Translations of the Acts of the Council of Chalcedon," *Greek, Roman & Byzantine Studies* 58, no. 1 (March 2018): 126–155; Tommaso Mari, "Greek, Latin, and More: Multilingualism at the Ecumenical Council of Chalcedon," *Journal of Latin Linguistics* 19, no. 1 (July 2020): 59–87; Gaddis and Price, *The Acts of the Council of Chalcedon*, Vol. 1 p. 80; Vol. 3 202-203; Ernest Honigmann, "The Original Lists of the Members of the Council of Nicaea, The Robber-Synod and the Council of Chalcedon," *Byzantion* 16, no. 1 (1942): 20–80; Richard Price, "Truth, Omission, and Fiction in the Acts of Chalcedon," in *Chalcedon in Context: Church Councils 400-700*, ed. Richard Price and Mary Whitby (Oxford: Oxford University Press, 2011), 92–106.

of error, we ought to listen carefully to what is said and not dismiss it flippantly. Denying that anyone has the right to disregard the councils as they please, Calvin counsels,

> whenever the decree of a council is produced, the first thing I would wish to be done is, to examine at what time it was held, on what occasion, with what intention, and who were present at it; next I would bring the subject discussed to the standard of Scripture. And this I would do in such a way that the decision of the council should have its weight, and be regarded in the light of a prior judgment, yet not so as to prevent the application of the test which I have mentioned.[22]

The prior judgment of the church to the value of the council and its words should be granted, yet not in such a way as to excuse it from the test of Scripture. Nor is it the name "council" that immediately justifies what is said by it, for the occasion, time, intention, and attendance need also be weighed. I think Calvin is wise in this. As with the writing of any ancient or modern author, we need to read the Councils with humility yet critically in light of Scripture. Christians who recognize that they are part of a global, catholic, universal church—united with all of God's people across the ages—will not be quick to cast off the wisdom of the past but will do so only after careful deliberation with others, brothers and sisters alive today and from the past, and with the prayerful reading of Scripture. However, any authority possessed by the councils is that of the minister of the word of God, a derivative authority that is present when the word of God is rightly taught and absent when it is not.

B. Orthodoxy

This people honors me with their lips,
    but their heart is far from me;
in vain do they worship me,
    teaching as doctrines the commandments of men. –

---

[22] Calvin, *Institutes of the Christian Religion*, IV.ix.8.

Matthew 15:8-9 (ESV)

You shall not add to the word that I command you, nor take from it, that you may keep the commandments of the LORD your God that I command you. – Deuteronomy 4:2 (ESV)

For some, the Christianity of the ecumenical creeds or their brightest interpreters is "orthodoxy"; to diverge from the creeds or even their interpreters is to be less than orthodox.[23] On a lesser level, creeds and confessions serve as the gatekeepers for participation in many Protestant denominations. On the opposite extreme, there are many who decry the creeds and tradition as unchristian, accommodation to paganism and Hellenistic philosophy.[24] Others call for a "generous orthodoxy," which looks past many of the traditional lines that divide the Christian from the non-Christian or theologically Liberal and Conservative.[25] None of these approaches seems adequate. On the one hand, the Bible (as we will see) forbids us from exalting human doctrines to the status of God's word, namely, from giving human doctrine the role of declaring who is in and who is out. On the other hand, to sever ourselves from Christians who have gone before us, often in the name of contemporary values, is simultaneously to disregard the work of God's Spirit and word in and through his people across the ages and to surrender ourselves to the blindness of our own little slice of history. It also represents a shallow reading of history and contemporary theology; in both cases, we find men and women wrestling with the word of God amid and often with the help of contemporary culture, in doing so, they succeeded in some things and made mistakes in others. Reading the early church theologians and pastors, we are confronted both by their use of

---

[23] Cf. James E. Dolezal, *God without Parts: Divine Simplicity and the Metaphysics of God's Absoluteness* (Eugene, OR: Pickwick Publications, 2011); James E. Dolezal, *All That Is in God: Evangelical Theology and the Challenge of Classical Christian Theism* (Grand Rapids, Mic: Reformation Heritage Books, 2017); Barrett, *None Greater*; Carter, *Contemplating God*.

[24] E.g. Deuble, *Christ before Creeds: Rediscovering the Jesus of History*.

[25] E.g. Brian D. McLaren, *A Generous Orthodoxy: By Celebrating Strengths of Many Traditions in the Church (and beyond), This Book Will Seek to Communicate a "Generous Orthodoxy."* (Zondervan, 2009).

contemporary philosophy in ways that we find highly disagreeable, yet we are also confronted by their willingness to reject, twist, and re-invent that philosophy when they are aware of conflict between their philosophy and God's word. I would argue that there are cases where they miss the conflict, but it is not for a lack of desire to be submitted to Scripture.

Scripture also insists on excluding false teachers and maintaining "healthy doctrine" (e.g. 1 Tim 1:3-11). This perhaps gets at the nub of the issue; Protestants have traditionally presented Scripture and Scripture alone (though perhaps not Scripture by itself) as the standard of right or wrong faith, of orthodoxy.[26] However, the fragmentation of Protestantism after the Reformation has led many to turn back towards the tradition or ecclesiological structures of the Catholic or Eastern Church. Many are asking, how can *sola scriptura* be an adequate principle of orthodoxy when this is what has resulted?[27]

In this section, I want to make four points in response to these questions and in light of our discussion throughout this book: 1) God forbids us from elevating human doctrine, even if it is the product of biblical reflection, to the role of doctrinal standard (demarcating Christian from non-Christian); 2) the Bible is intentionally broad in its teaching permitting great divergence among local churches (or denominations, if that is more consistent with your ecclesiology); 3) for Scripture to function as the authoritative standard, we need a biblical hermeneutic; 4) Scripture is as concerned with character as belief, so exalting either one or the other undermines Scriptures role as the norm for orthodoxy.

---

[26] Vanhoozer argues that they held to *sola scripture* not *solo scriptura*: Scripture alone is the authority but its authority is that of God expressed through his administration of his work on earth, including the present and past church. Kevin J. Vanhoozer, *Biblical Authority after Babel: Retrieving the Solas in the Spirit of Mere Protestant Christianity* (Grand Rapids: Brazos, 2016).

[27] E.g. Boersma, *Heavenly Participation*.

a. We Must Not Elevate Human Doctrine

Here is a significant tension within Christian life and the Church. Firstly, God's Word alone is the perfect and sufficient guide for life and godliness (2 Pet 1:3); secondly, the application of God's Word by his people is authoritative (e.g. Heb 13:17). That is, though God's Word is sufficient so that all we do may be pleasing before God and it alone is ultimately authoritative, the Bible does not balk at assigning a mediating authority to God's people.[28] Yet, thirdly, God's people are barred, I will argue, from setting up any human teaching in the place of God's Word, as a standard of or necessary component of godliness. The tension between these three things may not be immediately evident, yet it emerges when we think about it a bit more closely.

We have seen that the Bible teaches the Trinity, yet the Bible does not explicitly state that it is wrong to believe that the Son is "god" in a different sense than the Father is "god," such as Arius taught. Our immediate intuition is that it does speak to Arius' error, yet it does not explicitly address the terminology, framework, or specific propositions he developed. So, our extension of the biblical teaching of the Trinity to refute Arius' error seems to be justified, yet if we declare this error to be unchristian and a dangerous false teaching, are we violating the biblical prohibition on adding anything to the Word of God? Yet, in favour of this sort of judgment, the Bible in numerous places instructs pastors and teachers to speak authoritatively to God's people from his Word and to make judgments on situations beyond what the Scriptures directly address (e.g. Deut 17:8-13, 18:19; 1 Tim 4:11, 5:7, 6:2; Heb 13:17). Thus, the application of the Word of God by the people of God shares in the authority of God's very words; to disobey those who speak God's word rightly is to disobey God. Therefore, there is a sort of extension of God's word that receives God's approval, that is not the invention of human doctrines, yet there is another sort that is wrong, the elevation of human teaching to the place of God's word. We will first look at what is prohibited, and then consider what is permitted, finding "orthodoxy" in that latter category of the biblical teaching and the justified extensions of that

---

[28] On the Bible's sufficiency and authority, seem my books *The Gift of Knowledge* and *The Gift of Revelation*.

teaching.

i.   _Matthew 15:8-9_

> This people honors me with their lips,
>> but their heart is far from me;
> in vain do they worship me,
>> teaching as doctrines the commandments of men.
>> (ESV)

In Matthew 15, Jesus confronts the teachers of Israel over their treatment of God's Law. They ask him why his disciples do not follow the traditions of the elders; he responds with a criticism of their traditions as a whole and particularly the way their tradition was used to justify their violation of God's law. It is important to observe that Jesus does not condemn only the error these teachers were making, namely, abrogating God's Law with human tradition, but he addresses the more general error of elevating human commands to the status of doctrine.

The particular teaching with which Jesus is concerned is the use of religious giving to override God's command to honour mother and father (Exod 20:12). Instead of honouring their parents, the pharisees and scribes were taking that which would have been given to their parents and giving it to God, telling their parents, "What you would have gained from me is given to God" (Matt 15:5, ESV). This giving was not commanded in Scripture, it was a human tradition, yet in fulfilling this tradition, they violated God's very commands. Against this use of tradition, Jesus cites Isaiah's condemnation of the false worshipper, whose lips "honour me, but his heart is far from me" (Isa 29:13). Their particular error, in Isaiah's day as in Jesus' time, was to build right living and right thinking not on the word of God but on the teachings of human beings.

"Doctrine" is perhaps not the best translation of διδασκαλία (_didaskalia_) in this context. "Doctrine" is often used in terms of not only right-thinking but a certain type of right-thinking; it is often used for the abstract, universal truths of philosophy and theology. That Jesus rose from the dead is not so much "doctrine" these days as is the significance of the resurrection. If that is what comes to mind when the word is used, then "doctrine" is not the best word to use in this context. In Isaiah, the phrase is "their fear of me" (יִרְאָתָם אֹתִי; *yir'atam 'oti*) The fear of the Lord in the Old Testament encompasses both right thinking and right doing in relation to God; it is the proper posture of love, submission, and right knowledge of God accompanied by the appropriate actions. Διδασκαλία (*didaskalia*) generically means a "teaching"; in the New Testament, it is used for what we believe about God and his actions in the world and our proper response to them (e.g. Col 2:22; 1 Tim 1:10, 4:1-6). The problem is that the Jewish teachers in Jesus' day and their predecessors in Isaiah's day were filling in "the fear of the Lord" with human teaching, not with the teaching of the Bible. However, God cares about how we think about him and act in response to him; he cares enough to give us sufficient teaching concerning life and godliness (2 Pet 1:3), a sufficient word so that "the person who follows God [ὁ τοῦ θεοῦ ἄνθρωπος; *ho tou theou anthropos*] may be adequate [ἄρτιος; *artios*], equipped for every good work" (1 Tim 3:17, my translation).[29] We deny the sufficiency of God's Word and the wisdom of his commands when we feel the need to supplement what God has said with our own inventions. If the Bible is sufficient for the fear of the Lord, how then would God take our efforts to hedge in the biblical teaching with added material? When we claim that you need to do this or that or believe this or that to be a Christian, to follow God rightly and truly—to fear the Lord—and the content we are claiming is not taught by the Bible, this is the sort of innovation condemned by God. If our "orthodoxy" involves such additions, then we would hear from God these same words, "in vain do you worship me!" However, if this is the case, what do we do with the rightful extension of God's word that we find attested to throughout Scripture? What is the line between human invention and rightful biblical application?

ii. *The Application of the Word of God*

There is a line here, for the Bible was written for us through the circumstances of others. It does not address what to do in the contemporary

---

[29] Alternatively, "the man of God," referring to a male specially appointed for ministry, such as an elder, apostle, or prophet; however, I think "the person of God" is more appropriate for the context. "Of God" could have many connotations, I chose "follow" because it is similarly broad in its connotations and "person of God" sounds too ambiguous and unnatural to my ear.

world in direct terms, yet it says enough that we may live rightly before God today as Christians were able to in the 1st century. If we identify orthodoxy as solely the words of Scripture, then no application beyond the narrow situations condemned in the Bible would be justified—not even the translation of the Scriptures in English. So when we identify "orthodoxy" or right belief with God's word, we are not saying with the bare letter but with the application of the word. This is a pattern we find throughout Scripture: in the Old Testament, for example, the exceedingly broad Ten Commandments are complemented by the casuistry, or case-laws, which give concrete circumstances where this or that law applies. Between these two, the abstract command "you shall not kill unlawfully" (Exod 20:13)[30] and the concrete examples, e.g. if a man falls off your roof through negligence you are guilty of that commandment (Deut 22:8), innumerable circumstances are caught.[31]

The Bible is sufficient for all human life, that we may live godly and obedient lives before our God. The Bible's sufficiency is expressed not only in the words on the page but the innumerable applications it has to our lives. It is through this extension, through right application, that we understand the Old Testament to have been written for Christians throughout the ages (1 Cor 10:11). Right belief is then encompassed by all that Scripture says and all that it rightly applies to. One implication of this, I believe, is that we need to guard against making applications of applications, or "second-order" reflection, a standard of "orthodoxy." That is, we can distinguish different ways the Bible applies.

Though there are innumerable points between them, we can juxtapose two sorts of applications, those that are directly connected to Scripture and those that are distant from it. For example, the Bible does not directly teach that killing someone with a car while driving drunk is a violation of the commandment "you shall not kill unlawfully," yet we have good reason to apply the text in this case. Though there are some acts of killing that are not unlawful according to this command (e.g. various cases in war), in this case, the driver has both violated civil law (which God has commanded us to obey,

---

[30] My translation: "kill" is too broad, "murder" too narrow for what is intended.

[31] See my *The Gift of Reading – Part 1* (2021), *The Gift of Reading – Part 2* (2021) (both in *The Gift of Knowledge*), and *The Gift of Revelation* (2022).

e.g. Rom 13:1-7) and committed negligence as in the case of the one who does not fence in their roof. From the case laws in Scripture, we adduce that "kill" in this command encompasses death via negligence; through common sense and contemporary law, we conclude that drunk driving is a case of negligence. This is "direct" in the sense that the application made falls within the scope of that command as interpreted within the analogies Scripture provides. It is tangibly different from the sort of application that involves a mediating principle to fill the gap of Scriptural analogies.

Take our doctrine of God, for example. The Bible teaches that God is unchanging, perfect, and different from us. No example of these qualities in Scripture states explicitly that God does not experience substantial change (in his "essence"), subjective change (in his "experience"), change in states of knowledge (from knowing it will be to knowing it has been), or changes in non-substantial predicates (e.g. he did this or that). Now, if we assume that essentialism is correct, that everything including God has an essence, then being perfect and unchanging must mean that God's essence does not change (he can never become not-God). If we assume that subjective experience is undesirable, then God's perfection must exclude such experience. If change in non-substantial predicates (e.g. colour, size, activity) indicates imperfection and creatureliness, then God as the perfect Creator cannot undergo such change. However, Scripture does not identify the change or imperfection involved in each of these cases as something inappropriate to God. In each case, there is some mediating principle involved that moves from the Bible's teaching to the conclusion. If every principle were itself taught in the Bible, I believe that such a conclusion would be warranted as orthodox, yet in all these cases, the principles involved are not derived from the Bible. They involve the application of the Bible to a question or problem produced through reasonable reflection upon the world. Such reflection is good and right and ought to be done in interaction with the Bible, yet the applications derived therefrom are separated by several orders from Scripture.

The Bible does not regard such reflection as "doctrine" in the sense of the right fear of the Lord. This, again, does not make such thinking bad, but it should caution us against making it the standard of who is in or who is out, what is false teaching or not. In addition to the argument from silence (i.e. that Bible does not warrant this), we can also point to the positive teaching that the Bible is sufficient for us to live right before God and worship him properly. That *we* are to live and think rightly encompasses the application of the Bible to our circumstances, yet it does not warrant us to extend beyond that. The Bible cautions us from elevating human doctrine to the status of the fear of the Lord. Finally, the Bible teaches us that we are all fallen and sinful and that this extends to our thinking as much as our doing. We not only act wrongly but we think wrongly because of sin. Thus, we ought to be cautious in assuming that our second-order conclusions and the non-biblical assumptions that we use to arrive at them are sufficiently secure to declare such conclusions the measure of orthodoxy.

This leaves us in an uncomfortable place, for the Bible leaves many things unsaid. If we accept that the Bible and the justified application thereof is sufficient for orthodoxy, we open ourselves to great diversity in the Christian faith. Especially at the level of second-order thinking, we are going to face much disagreement—and this is not necessarily a bad thing. There may be great diversity in the way we think about the Bible's application to the bigger themes of philosophy and living.

However, we must avoid the error of pretending that "second-order" thinking is sequestered in its own world and untouched by the Bible's teaching. This is the sort of error that imagines that what we dream up in our philosophies and sciences is unaccountable to the Bible because it is not the study of the Bible, preaching, or theology—those things that ostensibly have Scripture as their primary subject matter. This is an error because the Bible has immediate application across innumerable areas of life, some that we may wish could be separated as "second-order." Integrating the Bible doctrine of immutability and perfection with Aristotelian physics and metaphysics has led some Christians to conclude that God is not actually active in the World: he is distant, unmoved, timeless, and unaffected by anything in the created world. However, this stands at odds with the biblical testimony to a God who is perfect and whose perfect plan unfolds without flaw, yet who engages with his creatures, talks with them, loves them, commits himself to them, and acts on their behalf.[32] The direct application of Scripture in this regard is that our philosophy is wrong if it postulates that God cannot do such things. Also, if our science arrives at a conclusion that invalidates the biblical teaching concerning miracles, a historical Adam, a global flood, or God's personal involvement in creation, here also the Bible has something say. In such cases,

---

[32] See my *The Gift of Seeing*, in *The Gift of Knowledge*.

principles drawn from outside of the Bible are often used to cast doubt on the Bible's teaching or explain why it cannot affect our conclusion. Brothers and sisters, we cannot let this be our approach to such matters. The Bible does speak to many of these things.

If we are to take the Bible itself as our standard of orthodoxy, we need to introduce several more principles to help us. We need to accept that the Bible is broad in its application, that it applies in many areas and is able to speak into diverse circumstances, and that this is God's good purpose. We also need to have an approach to interpretation that is itself rooted in the Bible, lest orthodoxy is tossed around by the interpretative mood of the day. Finally, we cannot elevate right thinking, or orthodoxy, over right practice and character. We will consider each of these in turn.

b. The Bible Is Intentionally Indifferent in Many Areas

If God wants his people to be united, as is evident throughout Scripture (consider John 17 and Ephesians 2-3, for example), then why is the Bible ambiguous on so many things? For example, why does not it give us an answer to the "worship wars"—telling us what sorts of songs and instruments are acceptable? It does not command us to use certain buildings and not others, to have two leaders in the church or ten (yet it does tell us to have more than one), or to have the Lord's supper every week or monthly. The Bible is specific about many other things that we wish it were not specific about, yet there are a good many practical issues about which the Bible is silent. This, I believe, serves an important purpose.

The Bible fosters a healthy diversity, a unity that is based not on external conformity but right faith and right worship. The Christian church is made up of male and female, the Greek world and everyone else, Jews and the nations. God in his word has laid out many things that confront our cultures and challenge us to change our views of what it means to be men and women, how we are to live as spouses, parents, and children—ways that will fit comfortably in some cultures and stand out boldly in others—yet in as many ways as it confronts and affirms our culture, it also gives space for us to express our faith in different ways. The adiaphora or "things indifferent" are many, and this makes us uncomfortable.

We would often like God to tell us that praising him with an organ alone is ungodly or that drums are of the Devil, yet he does not do so. He does not tell us exactly how he relates to time, how and to what extent he allows himself to be affected by creatures and to what extent he transcends us: there are some things said clearly on these matters, but other things are left silent. There is much room for us to engage in second-order reflection on God and his ways, and there is much room for us to embody the Gospel in different ways in Canada, Australia, Uganda, or Thailand. We have the freedom to translate the Bible in different ways and are not told that only this or that translation principle is perfect. We are not given one model of preaching or teaching, the appropriate length of a sermon, what a minister should wear when they lead a worship service, how often we should meet together in a week or month and how many times missing a corporate gathering is sinful—though we are told that churches should gather (Heb 10:24-25). We are not actually told that God's people must gather on the Lord's Day, on Sunday, though that is certainly appropriate and has been regular Christian practice from the 1st century until today. Yet, if we live in a country where God's people are best able to gather on Friday instead, we have no biblical teaching that would say that is ungodly and wrong (though perhaps it would strike us as irregular).

The Bible speaks to a great many things, and we tread a dangerous line when we use the Bible's ambiguities in some areas to ignore God's teaching in others. Yet in pursuit of right beliefs, we cannot stretch "orthodoxy" to encompass the grey area where God has granted us freedom. 5th-century Christology is an area that I believe attests to this danger, of making our second order reflections normative. The Bible tells us that God came as a man, Jesus Christ our Lord. It teaches us many things about what it means for Jesus to be God and to be human. Yet the Bible does not fill in much more than this. It does not tell us the logic of the compatibility of humanity or deity or the ontology (the real-world makeup of humanity and divinity) that justifies the claim that one person is God and is human. In the 5th century, this became an area of significant debate.

Christians who agreed on the essential claims that Jesus is truly God and like the Father in every way except for that he is the Father and Jesus is the Son, who agreed that Jesus was like us in every way except that he was also God in every way and born of a virgin, Christians who agreed on these two claims disagreed in dozens of ways on how these claims could be reconciled.

A particular difficulty emerged because the interpretation of the Trinity in the 4th-century didn't quite work with the facts of the incarnation; trying to reconcile the 4th-century solution to the Trinity with the incarnation led to solutions that were inadequate in various ways.

There are layers to this conflict that we cannot explore here, including the character of those involved, yet as measured by the Bible, all those who we call "heretics" in this century, namely, Nestorius and Eutyches, agreed on the same points of the biblical teaching as the "orthodox," Cyril and Leo among others. On this point, there is no biblical reason to say one or the other was not a true follower of Jesus. However, the fallout of different sides branding the others a heretic continues to this day; though the Western churches (namely, Protestants and Roman Catholics) are largely in agreement with each other, the Eastern churches are divided along the same lines as the they were in the 5th-century, with the Orthodox, Miaphysite, and Nestorian traditions continuing independently today. If we are to take the Bible as our sole standard of orthodoxy, we must be ready to live with an uncomfortable level of diversity. We may analyse, reflect upon, and formulate ideas and philosophies from the biblical testimony, but we cannot make these ideas and philosophies the measure of right and wrong faith, of being a Christian or an unbeliever.

c. To Be Our Ultimate Norm, Scripture Needs to Interpret Itself

A problem that has plagued Protestants since the Reformation comes up at this point. Many Protestants would agree that Scripture alone is our authority and has the ultimate say on who is a Christian and who is not, and the Reformers often understood and articulated the reality of the grey area of Christian freedom, yet disagreements quickly emerged over whose interpretation was correct. On small issues, these disagreements merely led to divisions between local churches. A disagreement over the meaning of baptism might mean that one church or group of churches would need to gather and run services differently than another.

However, what happens when we have disagreements on bigger issues? If Scripture is to be our authority and standard of orthodoxy, it needs to be clear. This was also evident in the teaching of Reformation, though it is often ignored today. If Scripture is clear, then it needs to be the authority not only on our lives, but on its own interpretation: it must contain sufficient tools within itself so that faithful, humble believers can work out their differences on major issues from Scripture itself, without appeals to some principle outside of the Bible. I argue that the Bible gives us such tools in my series *God's Gifts for the Christian Life*, but for now, all we must say is that the Bible needs to be clear in this sense if it is to function as our standard of orthodoxy. In addition to my series, the first decade of sermons in Henry Bullinger's *The Decades* and Augustine's *On Christian Teaching (De Doctrina Christiana)* both unpack how Scripture is read in this way, as its own interpreter. If Scripture is not its own interpreter in this sense, then it is hard to distinguish between first and second-order applications as we have above. If Scripture is not its own interpreter, then all applications involve external interpretive principles upon which Christians may disagree (being something not taught by Scripture) and thus all applications will be subject to each interpreter's framework. However, there is ample evidence that the Bible declares itself to be self-interpreting and practically leads us in this. See my series *God's Gifts for the Christian Life* in addition to Augustine and Bullinger for a more thorough treatment of this claim.

d. Orthodoxy and Character Are Equally Necessary

Finally, at each point that we have discussed so far, character enters as an essential ingredient. It is there that we will now turn. We can define character as a person's posture towards God and his word, as the habits displayed in behaviour that reveal a pattern of conduct towards God, his word, and his world. The Bible is seriously concerned with right character, as much as it is concerned with right belief. Jesus uses the image of tree to describe his followers: someone who follows Christ and loves God will produce good fruit demonstrating a right heart, that is, they will have a true or good character (the heart with its concomitant manifestations) (Matt 17:15-23). This is obviously a key theme in the Psalms and Proverbs (e.g. Psalm 1, 19). In the New Testament epistles, the primary qualifications for pastoral ministry are character qualifications, such as sobriety, purity, truthfulness, humility, faithfulness, etc. (1 Tim 3:1-7; Titus 1:6-9; 1 Pet 5:1-5). When false teachers are discussed—which is often—their character is as much evidence of their error and danger as their doctrine (2 Pet 2:1-22; Jude 3-16). 2 Peter makes the particular connection between bad character and the distortion of Scripture, speaking of Paul's letters,

> There are some things in them that are hard to understand, which the ignorant and unstable twist to their own destruction, as they do the other Scriptures. You therefore, beloved, knowing this beforehand, take care that you are not carried away with the error of lawless people and lose your own stability. (2 Pet 3:16-17, ESV)

It is because these people are already unstable and immoral ("lawless") that they twist Scripture to their destruction. Bad character has implications for doctrine, and the reverse is certainly true. We can imagine two extremes that show the necessity of both right doctrine and good character. Someone may have impeccable character but not believe a word of the Bible; they are not a Christian (1 John 2:18-25). Someone may have impeccable doctrine and yet reprehensible character, they are once again not a Christian (Matt 17:15-23). Thus, right belief and right character are both markers of who is in and who is out, of "orthodoxy." An uncomfortable implication of this is that no list of doctrines will be sufficient a measure of orthodoxy, for no list can verify character. Only careful attention to an individual in their circumstances, with attention to belief and practice, evidencing character, will suffice to demonstrate orthodoxy or heterodoxy.

C. Learning from the Past

> As to all other writings, in reading them, however great the superiority of the authors to myself in sanctity and learning, I do not accept their teaching as true on the mere ground of the opinion being held by them; but only because they have succeeded in convincing my judgment of in truth either by means of these canonical writings themselves, or by arguments addressed to my reason. – St Augustine to Jerome[33]

Neither creeds nor tradition are infallible, yet this does not mean that

---

[33] NPNF 1.1, p. 350.

tradition is useless. On the contrary, reading those who have come before us is often spiritually rewarding and practically relevant. We would be foolish to ignore the past, to ignore nearly 2000 years of reflection on God's word and his world in light of his word. However, our argument thus far leads to the conclusion that we must not read tradition, whether creeds or individual documents, as theological authorities or normative standards for right belief. These are roles reserved for Scripture alone. Nor should we read tradition for answers to today's problems, for if the answers we develop are themselves not biblical, we stand to find ourselves in more trouble soon enough. No, the Bible has the answers to today's problems, yet we often need tradition's help to see God's word clearly, to escape the blindness of our biases to see what God has been saying all along. Thus, the fundamental purpose of reading the Christian tradition is to read the Bible alongside an ancient companion. We read history to see ourselves, our world, and the word of God from the perspective of faithful witnesses in the past. Doing this is richly rewarding, yet it is also incredibly challenging. We need to read history with sympathy, understanding why someone said and did what they did; we need to read history with humility, ready to be corrected; and we need to read history critically, reading everything and weighing everything in light of Scripture.

First, we need to read history with sympathy because it is all too easy to judge. Without the existential threat of invading armies, without the threat of society falling apart, without a theology of the state as God's instrument, it is easy to dismiss the early church as foolish and to impute all sorts of sinful motivations into their use of political power in the 4th and 5th centuries. However, when we put ourselves in the place of Christians coming out of centuries of persecution, seeing Christianity suddenly receive favour from the governing authorities; if we realise that a split in the church in the 4th century could split the secular world into waring religious factions; if we assume for the sake understanding a view of the state as God's chosen instrument to see his gospel spread, then many of the decisions of the Christians in these centuries become understandable—however much we disagree and want to register serious concerns. Reading with sympathy does not mean thinking uncritically; instead, it means that we must first understand not only what was said but why it was said before asking the critical question, is it right?

Second, we need to read history with humility. If God's Spirit was at work throughout church history as God's people read the Bible and reflected on the world, the Spirit will certainly have led them into the truth. Therefore, as much as we may and do find error in the Christian tradition, we will also find much that is edifying, representing the Spirit-led application of Scripture to God's people. Tradition has something to teach us because God speaks through his word and the Spirit guarantees the efficacy of that speaking. We ourselves are imperfect and as subject to the prejudices and errors of our day as were those who came before us. Thus, not only does tradition have something true to say, but we also have much to learn. Therefore, we need to read history as those with much to learn and as if listening to people with much to say.

Third, we need to read history critically. As we have seen, good character matters as much as right belief, so we must pay attention to both as we seek guidance from the tradition. Scripture alone is our authority, so we must seek in the tradition those who are explicitly following Scripture, for this is where we will learn the most. We read critically by measuring all that the tradition says by Scripture, accepting what is true to the Bible and rejecting what is not. We also think critically about second-order thinking in church history, not only investigating the biblical principles and passages used in this reflection but also the non-biblical principles employed.

Thus, the fundamental posture we as Christians adopt in reading history is that of reading Scripture alongside our ancient peers. We read Scripture alongside of our brothers and sisters in order to understand them better, to understand ourselves and our world better, and to understand Scripture itself better. In doing so, we stand to profit greatly.

J. Alexander Rutherford

CONCLUSION

We started with an important question, what is the biblical teaching of the Trinity? We came to the conclusion that the Bible must teach the Trinity, and that the Old Testament is where we should start looking. So this is what we did. After laying forth the method for our investigation in Part 1 (Chapters 1-3), the particular task of arguing for something that modern scholarship tells us cannot be there, we began investigating the contours of the doctrine of God in the Old Testament. After establishing that אֱלֹהִים (*'elohim*) is not a generic term in a rigorous philosophical sense in Chapter 4, that it can both refer to many diverse beings and yet be the exclusive title of Yahweh, the one true God, we then considered the Great Shema, Deuteronomy 6:4 (Chapter 5). In this passage we found the most basic and simultaneously clear statement of the Trinity in the Bible,

Hear, oh Israel, the Lord our God(s), the Lord is one (God).

We saw that the plurality of אֱלֹהִים had not disappeared in the biblical literature and that it actually caused great confusion. However, the use of a plural term for a single being, Yahweh, was exceedingly appropriate for the God who reveals himself as the one, unique God and the three Gods, three persons who are rightfully God and Yahweh. "Our Gods" declared God's plurality but this is immediately balanced by the declaration that Yahweh is indeed "One God," as we interpreted אֶחָד (*'echad*). Turning our eyes to the rest of the Old Testament, we saw in Chapter 6 that God was identified as

271

plurality from the beginning of the Bible and that none of the texts concerning God's exclusive deity or uniqueness rule out this personal unity in personal plurality. Confirming that plurality was not an innovation we had brought to these texts, we saw in Chapters 7-9 extensive evidence for Yahweh's plurality, as the Angel of Yahweh, Isaiah's eschatological messiah, and the Spirit of Yahweh. In this way, we saw that the Trinity was neither an idiosyncratic teaching of this or that text, nor a subtext discerned only with a careful and perhaps creative eye, but a key theme woven throughout God's revelation in the Old Testament. Turning to the New Testament in Part 3, we saw how this revelation of God in the Old is connected with his revelation in the New.

After surveying various contemporary approaches to Christ's deity in the New Testament (Chapter 10), Chapters 11-13 explored several aspects of Jesus' identity in the New Testament. Chapter 11 showed the agreement between the exegesis of the author of Hebrews and our own exegesis of Isaiah. Chapter 12 explored the Old Testament texts about Yahweh applied to Jesus in the New Testament. Then, in Chapter 13, we looked at texts that explicitly identified Jesus as God and yet differentiated him from the Father. In Chapter 14, we then considered the Holy Spirit and, in particular, Paul's identification of the Spirit with Yahweh in 2 Corinthians 3:17-18. We ended our engagement with the Bible (Parts 2-3) in Chapter 15 by considering the oneness of God in the New Testament, concluding that God the Father is not declared to be the one true God. In Part 4, we turned to reflect on the implications of the biblical testimony. In Chapters 16-17, we looked at various Trinitarian theologies from the 4th century, then in Chapter 18, we summarised what we had found in Part 2-3 and evaluated 4th-century Trinitarianism in light of the biblical testimony. We discovered that Augustine was very close to the Bible when he spoke of the unity of the Godhead as personal, of the one true God, the Trinity. We then drew forth various implications from this "biblical Trinitarianism." Chapter 19 applied the insights of Chapter 18 to the question of our knowledge of God, arguing for a paradigm of person-knowledge. In the final chapter, we then considered the implications of our argument for our understanding of tradition and creedalism. Though creeds have their place, we judged them insufficient as a standard of orthodoxy, and we concluded that second-order reflection should not be set up as a measure of Christian fidelity. We then concluded with a reflection on learning from our forefathers, concluding that we must read them with sympathy and humility but also engage with them critically.

In answer to our initial enquiry, we have shown that there is indeed a biblical doctrine of the Trinity, that God's unity and plurality is the uniform testimony of the Bible. There are many lines of further investigation that are touched upon by our topic yet that stand outside of the scope of this work. There are clear implications of our thesis for the "traditional" understanding of God's attributes, namely, for incomprehensibility, simplicity, and immutability. By rejecting an ontology of abstract essence or substantial being for one of ultimate personhood, many of the justifications for the traditional interpretations of these doctrines is put on shaky ground. Furthermore, there are significant implications for the debate concerning the eternal generation and so-called eternal functional subordination of the Son. Finally, our conclusions touch upon the methodology of biblical Studies and show, I believe, the danger of reading as an atheist, one who does not presuppose the true nature of reality as we read a text that ostensibly speaks about that reality.

For now, I pray that this book has enriched your understanding of our Triune God, has challenged you in your interpretation of Scripture, and strengthened your confidence in the integrity of God's word. To the one true God, creator and sustainer of all things, king and benevolent father to all; to Christ our saviour and redeemer, to the Spirit the giver of life and our comforter, and to the Father of our Saviour and us who believe, to him be the glory forever and ever, Amen.

INDEX

BIBLIOGRAPHY

Abernethy, Andrew T. *The Book of Isaiah and God's Kingdom: A Thematic Theological Approach*. New Studies in Biblical Theology 40. Downers Grove: IVP, 2016.

Abernethy, Andrew T., and Greg Goswell. *God's Messiah in the Old Testament: Expectations of a Coming King*. Grand Rapids: Baker Academic, 2020.

Andersen, Francis I. *The Hebrew Verbless Clause in the Pentateuch*. Journal of Biblical literature 14. Nashville: Abingdon Press, 1970.

Augustine. "Faith and the Creed." In *The Works of Saint Augustine: A Translation for the 21st Century*, edited by Boniface Ramsey, translated by Michael G. Campbell. Brooklyn: New City Press, 1990.

———. *On Christian Teaching*. Translated by R. P. H. Green. Oxford World's Classics. Oxford; New York: Oxford University Press, 2008.

Ayres, Lewis. *Augustine and the Trinity*. Cambridge, UK ; Cambridge University Press, 2010.

Ayres, Lewis. *Nicaea and Its Legacy: An Approach to Fourth-Century Trinitarian Theology*. 1st ed. Oxford: Oxford University Press, 2004.

———. "The Fundamental Grammar of Augustine's Trinitarian Theology." In *Augustine and His Critics: Essays in Honour of Gerald Bonner*, edited by Gerald Bonner and George Lawless, 51–76.

London; New York: Routledge, 2000.

Barnes, Michel René. "Augustine in Contemporary Trinitarian Theology." *Theological Studies* 56, no. 2 (June 1995): 237–250.

———. "De Régnon Reconsidered." *Augustinian Studies* 26, no. 2 (1995): 51–79.

Barr, James. *Biblical Words for Time*. London: SCM Press, 2005.

———. *The Concept of Biblical Theology: An Old Testament Perspective*. London: SCM Press, 1999.

———. *The Semantics of Biblical Language*. Oxford: Oxford University Press, 1961.

Barrett, Matthew. *None Greater: The Undomesticated Attributes of God*. Grand Rapids: Baker Books, 2019.

Basil of Caesarea. *Against Eunomius*. Translated by Mark DelCogliano and Andrew Radde-Gallwitz. The fathers of the church v. 122. Washington, D.C: Catholic University of America Press, 2011.

Bates, Matthew W. *The Hermeneutics of the Apostolic Proclamation: The Center of Paul's Method of Scriptural Interpretation*. Waco, Tex: Baylor University Press, 2012.

Bauckham, Richard. *Jesus and the God of Israel: "God Crucified" and Other Studies on the New Testament's Christology of Divine Identity*. Milton Keynes: Paternoster; Eerdmans, 2008.

Baugh, S. M. *Ephesians: Evangelical Exegetical Commentary*. Edited by Wayne H. House, Hall W. Harris III, and Andrew W. Pitts. Bellingham, WA: Lexham Press, 2015.

Bavinck, Herman. *Reformed Dogmatics Volume 2: God and Creation*. Baker Books, 2004.

Beale, G. K., ed. *The Right Doctrine from the Wrong Texts? Essays on the Use of the Old Testament in the New*. Grand Rapids: Baker Books, 1994.

———. *The Temple and the Church's Mission: A Biblical Theology of the Dwelling Place of God*. New Studies in Biblical Theology 17. Downers Grove:

IVP, 2004.

Bediako, Daniel Kwame. "A Note on Rûaḥ 'Spirit/Wind' in Genesis 1:2." *Valley View University Journal of Theology* 4 (2017): 78–84.

Beeley, Christopher A. "Divine Causality and the Monarchy of God the Father in Gregory of Nazianzus." *Harvard Theological Review* 100, no. 2 (April 2007): 199–214.

———. *Gregory of Nazianzus on the Trinity and the Knowledge of God: In Your Light We Shall See Light.* Oxford Studies in Historical Theology. Oxford: Oxford University Press, 2008.

Behr, John. "Calling upon God as Father: Augustine and the Legacy of Nicaea." In *Orthodox Readings of Augustine*, edited by A. Papanikolaos and Dema Copoulos, 153–165. Crestwood, N.Y.: St Vladimir's Seminary Press, 2008.

———. "'One God Father Almighty.'" *Modern Theology* 34, no. 3 (July 2018): 320–330.

———. "Response to Ayres: The Legacies of Nicaea, East and West." *Harvard Theological Review* 100, no. 2 (April 2007): 145–152.

———. *The Nicene Faith: Vol 2 of Formation of Christian Theology.* Crestwood, N.Y.: St Vladimir's Seminary Press, 2004.

———. *The Way to Nicaea.* The formation of Christian theology v. 1. Crestwood, N.Y.: St. Vladimir's Seminary Press, 2001.

Bekken, P. J. *The Word Is Near You: A Study of Deuteronomy 30:12-14 in Paul's Letter to the Romans in a Jewish Context.* Beihefte zur Zeitschrift für die neutestamentliche Wissenschaft und die Kunde der älteren Kirche 144. Berlin; New York: de Gruyter, 2007.

Berger, Peter L. *The Sacred Canopy: Elements of a Sociological Theory of Religion.* N.Y.: Doubleday, 1967.

Block, Daniel I. "The View from the Top: The Holy Spirit in the Prophets." In *Presence, Power and Promise: The Role of the Spirit of God in the Old Testament*, 175–207. Downers Grove, 2011.

Blomberg, Craig L., and Mariam J. Kamell. *James: Zondevan Exegetical*

Commentary on the New Testament. Zondervan Exegetical Commentary Series on the New Testament v. 16. Grand Rapids: Zondervan, 2008.

Boersma, Hans. *Heavenly Participation: The Weaving of a Sacramental Tapestry*. Grand Rapids: Eerdmans, 2011.

———. *Nouvelle Théologie and Sacramental Ontology: A Return to Mystery*. Oxford ; New York: Oxford University Press, 2009.

Budde, K. "Ps. 82:6 f." *Journal of Biblical Literature* 40, no. 1/2 (1921): 39–42.

Bullinger, Henry. *The Decades of Henry Bullinger: Volume 1*. Grand Rapids: Reformation Heritage Books, 2021.

Burnett, Joel S. *A Reassessment of Biblical Elohim*. Dissertation series / Society of Biblical Literature no. 183. Atlanta, GA: Society of Biblical Literature, 2001.

Calvin, John. *Institutes of the Christian Religion*. Translated by Henry Beveridge. Peabody, Mass: Hendrickson Publishers, 2008.

Cannon, W. W. "Isaiah 61 1—3 an Ebed-Jahweb Poem." *Zeitschrift für die Alttestamentliche Wissenschaft* 47, no. 1 (1929).

Cardozo Mindiola, Cristian. "God the Father, Lord Jesus Christ and Their Interrelationship: 1 Corinthians 8:6 as a Test Case." *Theologica Xaveriana* 69, no. 188 (July 2019): 1–27.

Carpenter, Eugene E. *Exodus*. Evangelical Exegetical Commentary. Bellingham: Lexham Press, 2016.

Carson, D. A. *Divine Sovereignty and Human Responsibility*. Eugene, OR: Wipf and Stock Publishers, 2002.

———. "Genesis 1-3: Not Maximalist, but Seminal." *Trinity Journal* 39, no. 2 (2018): 143–163.

———. "Matthew." In *The Expositor's Bible Commentary: Matthew–Mark (Revised Edition)*, edited by Tremper Longman III and David E. Garland. Vol. 9. Grand Rapids: Zondervan, 2010.

———. *The Gospel According to John*. The Pillar New Testament

Commentary. Leicester; Grand Rapids: IVP; Eerdmans, 1991.

Carter, Craig A. *Contemplating God with the Great Tradition: Recovering Trinitarian Classical Theism.* Grand Rapids: Baker Academic, 2021.

Ciampa, Roy E., and Brian S. Rosner. *The First Letter to the Corinthians.* Eerdmans, 2010.

Coakley, Sarah, ed. *Rethinking Gregory of Nyssa.* Malden, Mass: Blackwell, 2003.

Corrigan, Kevin. "Οὐσία and Ὑπόσταις in the Trinitarian Theology of the Cappadocian Fathers: Basil and Gregory of Nyssa." *Zeitschrift für Antikes Christentum* 12, no. 1 (January 2008): 114–134.

Cross, Richard. "Gregory of Nyssa on Universals." *Vigiliae Christianae* 56, no. 4 (2002): 372–410.

Crossan, John Dominic. *Birth of Christianity.* A&C Black, 1999.

Cullmann, Oscar. *The Christology of the New Testament.* Translated by Shirley C. Guthrie and Charles A. M. Hall. 2nd English Edition. London: SCM Press LTD, 1963.

Dahood, Mitchell. *Psalms II: 51-100.* The Anchor Bible. Garden City: Doubleday, 1968.

Danker, Frederick W. *A Greek-English Lexicon of the New Testament and Other Early Christian Literature.* 3rd ed. Chicago: University of Chicago Press, 2000.

Davies, Graham I. "'God' in Old Testament Theology." In *Congress Volume Leiden 2004*, edited by André Lemaire. Leiden: Brill, 2006.

De Sousa, Rodrigo (Rodrigo Franklin). "The Hermeneutics of the Scriptural Citations in Hebrews 2:12-13." *Biblical Research* 64 (2019): 83–101.

Dekker, Jaap. "The High and Lofty One Dwelling in the Heights and with His Servants: Intertextual Connections of Theological Significance between Isaiah 6, 53 and 57." *Journal for the Study of the Old Testament* 41, no. 4 (2017): 475–491.

Deuble, Jeff. *Christ before Creeds: Rediscovering the Jesus of History.* Living Hope

International Ministries, 2021.

Dolezal, James E. *All That Is in God: Evangelical Theology and the Challenge of Classical Christian Theism*. Grand Rapids, Mic: Reformation Heritage Books, 2017.

———. *God without Parts: Divine Simplicity and the Metaphysics of God's Absoluteness*. Eugene, OR: Pickwick Publications, 2011.

Dozeman, Thomas B. *Commentary on Exodus*. The Eerdmans Critical Commentary. Grand Rapids: Eerdmans, 2009.

Driver, Samuel Rolles. *The Book of Exodus ... With an Introduction and Notes by S.R. Driver*, n.d.

Dulière, Walter L. "Theos--Dieu et Adonai—Kurios." *Zeitschrift für Religions- und Geistesgeschichte* 21, no. 3 (1969): 193–203.

Dunn, James D G. "2 Corinthians 3:17: The Lord Is the Spirit." *The Journal of Theological Studies* 21, no. 2 (October 1970): 309–320.

Ellis, Nicholas J. "Biblical Exegesis and Linguistics: A Prodigal History." In *Linguistics and New Testament Greek: Key Issues in the Current Debate*, edited by David Alan Black and Benjamin L Merkle. Grand Rapids: Baker Publishing Group, 2020.

Eunomius. *The Extant Works*. Translated by Richard Paul Vaggione. Oxford Early Christian Texts. Oxford; New York: Clarendon Press; Oxford University Press, 1987.

Evans, Craig A. *Matthew*. New Cambridge Bible Commentary. New York: Cambridge University Press, 2012.

———. *Word and Glory: On the Exegetical and Theological Background of John's Prologue*. A&C Black, 1993.

Fee, Gordon D. *The First Epistle to the Corinthians*. NICNT. Grand Rapids: Eerdmans, 1987.

Fee, Gordon D., and Mark L. Strauss. *How to Choose a Translation for All Its Worth: A Guide to Understanding and Using Bible Versions*. Grand Rapids: Zondervan, 2007.

Fee, Gordon D., and Douglas K. Stuart. *How to Read the Bible for All Its Worth*. 3rd ed. Grand Rapids: Zondervan, 2003.

Fesko, J. V. *The Need for Creeds Today: Confessional Faith in a Faithless Age*. Grand Rapids: Baker Academic, 2020.

Feuerbach, Ludwig. *The Essence of Christianity*. Translated by George Eliot. Amherst, New York: Prometheus Books, 2010.

Fletcher-Louis, Crispin H. T. *Jesus Monotheism: Volume 1: Christological Origins: The Emerging Consensus and Beyond*. Eugene, Ore: Wipf & Stock, 2015.

Fossum, Jarl E. "Kyrios Jesus as the Angel of the Lord in Jude 5-7." *New Testament Studies* 33, no. 2 (April 1987): 226–243.

Frame, John M. *Cornelius Van Til: An Analysis of His Thought*. Phillipsburg: P&R Publishing, 1995.

———. *Systematic Theology: An Introduction to Christian Belief*. Phillipsburg: P&R Publishing, 2013.

———. *The Doctrine of the Knowledge of God*. A Theology of Lordship. Phillipsburg: P&R Publishing, 1987.

———. *Van Til: The Theologian*. Phillipsburg: Pilgrim Publishing Company, 1976.

France, R. T. "Hebrews." In *The Expositor's Bible Commentary*, edited by Tremper Longman and David E. Garland. Rev. ed. Grand Rapids: Zondervan, 2006.

———. *The Gospel of Mark: A Commentary on the Greek Text*. Grand Rapids: Eerdmans, 2002.

Gaddis, Michael, and Richard Price. *The Acts of the Council of Chalcedon*. 3 vols. Translated Texts for Historians. Liverpool: Liverpool University Press, 2005.

Gathercole, Simon J. *The Preexistent Son: Recovering the Christologies of Matthew, Mark, and Luke*. Grand Rapids: Eerdmans, 2006.

Gentry, Peter J. "A Preliminary Evaluation and Critique of Prosopological

Exegesis." *Southern Baptist Journal of Theology* 23, no. 2 (2019): 105–122.

Gentry, Peter J., and Stephen J. Wellum. *Kingdom through Covenant: A Biblical-Theological Understanding of the Covenants*. 2nd Ed. Wheaton: Crossway, 2018.

Gers-Uphaus, Christian. "Gott Als Wahrer אלהים Und Retter Der Armen: Psalm 82 Im Korpus Der Asafpsalmen." *Biblische Zeitschrift* 63, no. 1 (2019): 30–48.

Gignilliat, Mark S. "The Trinity and the Old Testament." In *The Essential Trinity: New Testament Foundations and Practical Relevance*, edited by Brandon D. Crowe and Carl R. Trueman. London: Apollos, 2016.

Giulea, Dragoş-Andrei. "The Divine Essence, That Inaccessible Kabod Enthroned in Heaven: Nazianzen's Oratio 28,3 and the Tradition of Apophatic Theology from Symbols to Philosophical Concepts." *Numen* 57, no. 1 (2010): 1–29.

Glazier-McDonald, Beth. "Mal'ak Habběrît: The Messenger of the Covenant in Mal 3:1." In *Hebrew Annual Review, Vol 11, 1987: Biblical and Other Studies*, 93–104. Columbus, Ohio, 1987.

Goldingay, John. *A Critical and Exegetical Commentary on Isaiah 56 - 66*. The International Critical Commentary on the Holy Scriptures of the Old and New Testaments. London: Bloomsbury, 2014.

———. *Psalms: Psalms 43-89*. Vol. 2. 2 vols. Baker commentary on the Old Testament wisdom and Psalms. Grand Rapids, Mich.: Baker Academic, 2006.

Gordon, Cyrus H. "His Name Is 'One.'" *Journal of Near Eastern Studies* 29, no. 3 (July 1970): 198–199.

Gordon, Robert P. "Standing in the Council: When Prophets Encounter God." In *The God of Israel*, edited by Robert P. Gordon, 190–204. Cambridge University Press, 2007.

Graham, Wyatt. "Is Jesus the Angel of Lord?" Wyatt Graham, 2021. https://wyattgraham.com/.

Graumann, Thomas. "Orthodoxy, Authority and the (Re-) Construction of the Past in Church Councils." In *Invention, Rewriting, Usurpation: Discursive Fights over Religious Traditions in Antiquity*, edited by Jörg Ulrich, Anders-Christian Jacobsen, and David Brakke. Early Christianity in the context of antiquity v. 11. Frankfurt am Main: Lang, 2012.

Gray, Patrick T. R. "Covering the Nakedness of Noah: Reconstruction and Denial in the Age of Justinian." *Byzantinische Forschungen* 24 (1997): 193–205.

Grillmeier, Aloys. *Christ in Christian Tradition Vol. 2, Part 1: From the Council of Chalcedon to Justinian I*. Translated by Pauline Allen and John Cawte. London: Mowbrays, 1987.

Grillmeier, Aloys, and Theresia Hainthaler. *Christ in Christian Tradition Vol. 2, Part 2: The Church of Constantinople in the Sixth Century*. Translated by Pauline Allen and John Cawte. London: Mowbrays, 1995.

———. *Christ in Christian Tradition Vol. 2, Part 3: The Churches of Jerusalem and Antioch from 451 to 600*. Translated by Marianne Ehrhardt. Vol. 2. Oxford: Oxford University Press, 2013.

———. *Christ in Christian Tradition Vol. 2, Part 4: The Church of Alexandria with Nubia and Ethiopia after 451*. Translated by O.C. Dean Jr. London; Louisville: Wobray; Westminster John Knox Press, 1996.

Grindheim, Sigurd. *God's Equal: What Can We Know about Jesus' Self-Understanding?* Library of New Testament studies 446. London ; New York: T & T Clark, 2011.

Grudem, Wayne A. *Systematic Theology: An Introduction to Biblical Doctrine*. Leicester; Grand Rapids: IVP; Zondervan, 1994.

Gunkel, Herman. *Genesis*. Trans. of the 1910 ed. Macon: Mercer University, 1997.

Guthrie, George H. *2 Corinthians*. Edited by Robert W. Yarbrough and Robert Stein. Grand Rapids: Baker Academic, 2015.

Hamilton, Victor P. *Exodus: An Exegetical Commentary*. Grand Rapids: Baker Academic, 2011.

Hanson, R. P. C. *The Search for the Christian Doctrine of God: The Arian*

Controversy 318-381. Edinburgh: T. & T. Clark, 1988.

Harris, Murray J. *Jesus as God: The New Testament Use of Theos in Reference to Jesus*. Wipf and Stock Publishers, 2008.

Harrison, Verna E. F. "Illumined from All Sides by the Trinity." In *Re-Reading Gregory of Nazianzus: Essays on History, Theology, and Culture*, edited by Christopher A. Beeley, 13–30. CUA studies in early Christianity. Washington, D.C: Catholic University of America Press, 2012.

Hart, David Bentley. "The Mirror of the Infinite: Gregory of Nyssa on the Vestigia Trinitatis." In *Rethinking Gregory of Nyssa*, edited by Sarah Coakley, 111–132. Malden, Mass: Blackwell, 2003.

Hays, Richard B. *Reading Backwards: Figural Christology and the Fourfold Gospel Witness*. Waco, Texas: Baylor University Press, 2014.

Heiser, Michael S. "Monotheism and the Language of Divine Plurality in the Hebrew Bible and the Dead Sea Scrolls." *Tyndale Bulletin* 65, no. 1 (2014): 85–100.

Henrichs-Tarasenkova, Nina. *Luke's Christology of Divine Identity*. Library of New Testament Studies vol. 542. New York: Bloomsbury, 2016.

Heskett, Randall. *Messianism within the Scriptural Scroll of Isaiah*. Library of Hebrew Bible / Old Testament Studies 456. New York: T & T Clark, 2007.

Hodge, A. A. *Evangelical Theology: Lectures on Doctrine*. Carlisle, Penn.: Banner of Truth Trust, 1990.

Hodge, Charles. *Systematic Theology*. Oak Harbor, WA: Logos Research Systems, Inc., 1997.

Honigmann, Ernest. "The Original Lists of the Members of the Council of Nicaea, The Robber-Synod and the Council of Chalcedon." *Byzantion* 16, no. 1 (1942): 20–80.

Hurtado, Larry W. *Lord Jesus Christ: Devotion to Jesus in Earliest Christianity*. Grand Rapids: Eerdmans, 2003.

———. "'Monotheism' in the New Testament." In *The Bible and Early*

Trinitarian Theology, edited by Christopher A. Beeley, 50–68. CUA studies in early Christianity. Washington, D.C: The Catholic University of America Press, 2018.

———. *One God, One Lord: Early Christian Devotion and Ancient Jewish Monotheism*. Third edition. Cornerstones Series. London: Bloomsbury T & T Clark, 2015.

Ito, Akio. "The Written Torah and the Oral Gospel: Romans 10:5-13 in the Dynamic Tension Between Orality and Literacy." *Novum testamentum* 48, no. 3 (2006): 234–260.

Janzen, J. Gerald. "On the Most Important Word in the Shema (Deuteronomy VI 4-5)." *Vetus Testamentum* XXXVII, no. 3 (1987): 280–300.

Jean de Salisbury. *Metalogicon*. Edited by John Barrie Hall and Julian Haseldine. Corpus Christianorum in translation 12. Turnhout: Brepols, 2013.

Johnson, Jeffery D. *The Failure of Natural Theology: A Critical Appraisal of the Philosophical Theology of Thomas Aquinas*. New Studies in Theology. Free Grace Press, 2021.

Johnson, Keith E. "Appendix: Reclaiming Augustine on the Trinity." In *Rethinking the Trinity & Religious Pluralism: An Augustinian Assessment*, 220–257. Strategic initiatives in evangelical theology. Downers Grove: IVP Academic, 2011.

Kähler, Martin. *The So-Called Historical Jesus and the Historic, Biblical Christ*. Vancouver: Regent College Pub., 1998.

Kelly, J. N. D. *Early Christian Doctrines*. London: Adam & Charles Black, 1958.

Kirk, J. R. Daniel. *A Man Attested by God: The Human Jesus of the Synoptic Gospels*. Grand Rapids: Eerdmans, 2016.

Kline, Meredith G. *Images of the Spirit*. Eugene, OR: Wipf and Stock, 1999.

Köstenberger, Andreas J., and Richard Duane Patterson. *Invitation to Biblical Interpretation: Exploring the Hermeneutical Triad of History, Literature, and Theology*. Grand Rapids: Kregel Publications, 2011.

Lacoste, Jean-Yves. "Homoousios et Homoousios: La Substance Entre Théologie et Philosophie." *Recherches de science religieuse* 98, no. 1 (January 2010): 85–100.

Lampe, Peter. *From Paul to Valentinus: Christians at Rome in the First Two Centuries*. Fortress Press, 2003.

Lane, William L. *Hebrews 1-8*. Edited by David A. Hubbard, Glenn W. Barker, and Ralph P. Martin. Vol. 1. Word Biblical Commentary Vol. 47a. Nashville: Word Books, 1991.

Leuenberger-Wenger, Sandra. *Das Konzil von Chalcedon und die Kirche: Konflikte und Normierungsprozesse im 5. und 6. Jahrhundert*. Leiden: Brill, 2019.

Lietzmann, Hans, ed. *Apollinaris von Laodicea und seine Schule: Texte und Untersuchungen*. J. C. B. Mohr (Paul Siebeck), 1904. Accessed April 22, 2020. http://archive.org/details/apollinarisvonl01apolgoog.

Long, V. Philips. *The Art of Biblical History*. Foundations of Contemporary Interpretation v. 5. Grand Rapids: Zondervan, 1994.

Longnecker, Richard N. "Acts." In *The Expositors Bible Commentary: Luke-Acts*, edited by Tremper Longman and David E. Garland. Revised ed. Grand Rapids: Zondervan, 2007.

López, René. "Identifying the 'angel of the Lord' in the Book of Judges: A Model for Reconsidering the Referent in Other Old Testament Loci." *Bulletin for Biblical Research* 20, no. 1 (2010): 1–18.

Lowther, James R. "Paul's Use of Deuteronomy 30:11-14 in Romans 10:5-8 as a Locus Primus on Paul's Understanding of the Law in Romans." Doctoral Dissertation, Southwestern Baptist Theological Seminary, 2001.

Machinist, Peter. "How Gods Die, Biblically and Otherwise: A Problem of Cosmic Restructuring." In *Reconsidering the Concept of Revolutionary Monotheism*, edited by Beate Pongratz-Leisten, 189–240. Winona Lake: Eisenbrauns, 2011.

Mackay, John L. *Exodus*. A Mentor Commentary. Ross-shire: Christian Focus Publications, 2018.

Malone, Andrew S. "Distinguishing the Angel of the Lord." *Bulletin for*

Biblical Research 21, no. 3 (2011): 297–314.

Mari, Tommaso. "Greek, Latin, and More: Multilingualism at the Ecumenical Council of Chalcedon." *Journal of Latin Linguistics* 19, no. 1 (July 2020): 59–87.

———. "The Latin Translations of the Acts of the Council of Chalcedon." *Greek, Roman & Byzantine Studies* 58, no. 1 (March 2018): 126–155.

McBride, Samuel Dean. "Yoke of the Kingdom: An Exposition of Deuteronomy 6:4-5." *Interpretation* 27, no. 3 (July 1973): 273–306.

McCann, J Clinton Jr. "The Single Most Important Text in the Entire Bible: Toward a Theology of the Psalms." In *Soundings in the Theology of Psalms: Perspectives and Methods in Contemporary Scholarship*, 63. Minneapolis, 2011.

McCormack, Bruce Lindley. *The Humility of the Eternal Son: Reformed Kenoticism and the Repair of Chalcedon*. Cambridge University Press, 2021.

McGilchrist, Iain. *The Master and His Emissary: The Divided Brain and the Making of the Western World*. New expanded edition. New Haven: Yale University Press, 2019.

McLaren, Brian D. *A Generous Orthodoxy: By Celebrating Strengths of Many Traditions in the Church (and beyond), This Book Will Seek to Communicate a "Generous Orthodoxy."* Zondervan, 2009.

Miller, Patrick D. "The Most Important Word: The Yoke of the Kingdom." *Iliff Review* (1984): 14.

Moberly, R. W. L. *The God of the Old Testament: Encountering the Divine in Christian Scripture*. Grand Rapids: Baker Academic, 2020.

———. "'Yahweh Is One': On the Translation of the Shema." In *Studies in the Pentateuch*, edited by John Adney Emerton. E. J. Brill, 1990.

Moo, Douglas J. *The Epistle to the Romans*. NICNT. Grand Rapids: Eerdmans, 1996.

Moroziuk, Russel P. "Heathen Philosophers and Christian Theologians: Apophaticism and Nicene Orthodoxy at Nicaea." *The Patristic and*

Byzantine Review 12, no. 1–3 (1993): 55–63.

Morris, Leon. *The First and Second Epistles to the Thessalonians.* Grand Rapids: Eerdmans, 1991.

Mosshammer, Alden A. "Gregory of Nyssa and Christian Hellenism." In *Studia Patristica*, edited by Elizabeth A. Livingstone, 170–195. Leuven: Peeters, 1997.

Motyer, J. Alec. "Stricken for the Trangression of My People." In *From Heaven He Came and Sought Her*, edited by David Gibson and Jonathan Gibson. Wheaton: Crossway Books, 2013.

———. *The Prophecy of Isaiah: An Introduction & Commentary.* Downers Grove: InterVarsity Press, 1993.

Moule, C. F. D. "2 Cor 3,18b." In *Neues Testament Und Geschichte: Historisches Geschehen Und Deutung Im Neuen Testament: Oscar Cullmann Zum 70. Geburtstag*, edited by B. Reicke and H. Baltensweiler, 231–237. Tübingen: Mohr Siebeck, 1972.

Nash, Ronald H. *The Word of God and the Mind of Man.* Grand Rapids: Zondervan, 1982.

Nazianzus, Gregory. *Faith Gives Fullness to Reasoning: The Five Theological Orations of Gregory Nazianzen.* Translated by Frederick W. Norris. Supplements to Vigiliae Christianae v. 13. Leiden ; New York: Brill, 1990.

Nogalski, James D. "The Day(s) of YHWH in the Book of the Twelve." In *Thematic Threads in the Book of the Twelve*, edited by Paul L. Redditt and Aaron Schart, 192–213. Berlin, Germany: Walter de Gruyter GmbH & Co., 2003.

Oliver, Willem. "Romans 10:5-13 Revisited." *Hervormde Teologiese Studies* 71, no. 3 (2015): 1–12.

Opitz, Hans-Georg. *Athanasius Werke - Bd. 2 Die apologien: Leiferung 6-7.* Berlin; Leipzig: Walter de Gruyter & Co., 1940.

Oseka, Matthew. "History of the Jewish Interpretation of Genesis 1:26, 3:5, 3:22 in the Middle Ages." *Scriptura* 117, no. 1 (May 2018).

Oswalt, John. *The Book of Isaiah. Chapters 40-66*. NICOT. Grand Rapids, MI: Eerdmans, 1998.

Pate, Brian. "Who Is Speaking? The Use of Isaiah 8:17-18 in Hebrews 2:13 as a Case Study for Applying the Speech of Key OT Figures to Christ." *Journal of The Evangelical Theological Society* 59, no. 4 (2016): 731–745.

Philostorgius, and Joseph Bidez. *Philostorgius Kirchengeschichte: mit dem Leben des Lucian von Antiochien und den Fragmenten eines Arianischen Historiographen*. Leipzig J.C. Hinrichs, 1913. http://archive.org/details/kirchengeschicht21philuoft.

Pidcock-Lester, Karen. "Romans 10:5-15." *Interpretation* 50, no. 3 (July 1996): 288.

Poe, Gary R. "Light to Darkness: From Gnosis to Agape in the Apophatic Imagery of Gregory of Nyssa." *Baptist History and Heritage* 53, no. 1 (September 2018): 57–67.

Polanyi, Michael. *Personal Knowledge: Towards a Post-Critical Philosophy*. First Harper Torchbook Edition. New York: Harper Torchbook, 1964.

———. *The Tacit Dimension*. Chicago; London: University of Chicago Press, 2009.

Poythress, Vern S. *In the Beginning Was the Word: Language: A God-Centered Approach*. Wheaton: Crossway Books, 2009.

———. *Logic: A God-Centered Approach to the Foundation of Western Thought*. Electronic. Wheaton: Crossway, 2013.

———. *Redeeming Science: A God-Centered Approach*. Wheaton: Crossway Books, 2006.

———. *Symphonic Theology: The Validity of Multiple Perspectives in Theology*. Grand Rapids: Academie Books, 1987.

Prestige, G. L. *God in Patristic Thought*. 2nd ed. London: SPCK, 1952.

———. *St Basil the Great and Apollinaris of Laodicea*. London: SPCK, 1956.

Price, Richard. "Truth, Omission, and Fiction in the Acts of Chalcedon." In

Chalcedon in Context: Church Councils 400-700, edited by Richard Price and Mary Whitby, 92–106. Oxford: Oxford University Press, 2011.

Propp, William Henry, ed. *Exodus 19-40: A New Translation with Introduction and Commentary*. 1st ed. The Anchor Bible v. 2A. New York: Doubleday, 2006.

Provan, Iain W., V. Philips Long, and Tremper Longman. *A Biblical History of Israel*. 2nd ed. Louisville: Westminster John Knox, 2015.

Putman, Rhyne R. *When Doctrine Divides the People of God: An Evangelical Approach to Theological Diversity*. Wheaton: Crossway, 2020.

Radde-Gallwitz, Andrew. *Basil of Caesarea, Gregory of Nyssa, and the Transformation of Divine Simplicity*. Oxford early Christian studies. Oxford; New York: Oxford University Press, 2009.

Robinson, Paul W. *The Annotated Luther, Volume 3: Church and Sacraments*. Fortress Press, 2016.

Robson, James. *Word and Spirit in Ezekiel*. Library of Hebrew Bible/Old Testament studies 447. New York: T & T Clark, 2006.

Rutherford, J. Alexander. *God's Gifts for the Christian Life — Part 1: The Gift of Knowledge*. Airdrie, AB: Teleioteti, 2021.

———. *God's Kingdom through His Priest-King: An Analysis of the Book of Samuel in Light of the Davidic Covenant*. Teleioteti Technical Studies 1. Vancouver: Teleioteti, 2019.

———. *Prevenient Grace: An Investigation into Arminianism*. 2nd Revised Ed. Teleioteti Technical Studies 2. Vancouver: Teleioteti, 2020.

———. *The Book of Habakkuk: An Exegetical-Theological Commentary on the Hebrew Text*. A Teleioteti Old Testament Commentary 1. Vancouver, BC: Teleioteti, 2019.

———. *The Gift of Knowing: A Biblical Perspective on Knowing and Truth*. 2nd Ed. God's Gifts for the Christian Life - Part 1: The Gift of Knowledge I. Airdrie, AB: Teleioteti, 2021.

———. *The Gift of Revelation: A Biblical Perspective on the Bible*. God's Gifts for the Christian Life - Part 2: The Gift of Truth I. Airdrie, AB:

Teleioteti, 2021.

————. *The Gift of Seeing: A Biblical Perspective on Ontology*. God's Gifts for the Christian Life Part 1 - The Gift of Knowledge III. Airdrie, AB: Teleioteti, 2021.

————. *The Gift of Theology*. God's Gifts for the Christian Life - Part 3: The Gift of Wisdom III. Campbell River, BC: Teleioteti, Forthcoming.

Rutherford, James. "Review of God's Messiah in the Old Testament." *Reformed Theological Review* 80, no. 3 (2021).

Ryken, Philip Graham, and R. Kent Hughes. *Exodus: Saved for God's Glory*. Preaching the Word Series. Wheaton: Crossway, 2005.

Sagan, Carl. *The Demon-Haunted World: Science as a Candle in the Dark*. 1st Ed. New York: Ballantine Books, 1997.

Sailhamer, John H. *Introduction to Old Testament Theology: A Canonical Approach*. Grand Rapids: Zondervan, 1995.

Sarna, Nahum M. *Exodus*. Philadelphia: Jewish Publication Society, 1991.

Schultz, Richard. "The King in the Book of Isaiah." In *The Lord's Anointed: Interpretation of Old Testament Messianic Texts*, edited by P. E. Satterthwaite, Richard S. Hess, and Gordon J. Wenham. Tyndale House studies. Carlisle: Paternoster Press, 1995.

Schutzius II, Mark D. *The Hebrew Word for "Sign" and Its Impact on Isaiah 7:14*. Wipf and Stock, 2015.

Seccombe, David. "Luke and Isaiah." In *The Right Doctrine from the Wrong Texts?: Essays on the Use of the Old Testament in the New*, edited by G. K. Beale, 248–256. Grand Rapids: Baker Books, 1994.

Seifrid, Mark. "The Near Word of Christ and the Distant Vision of N. T. Wright." *Journal of the Evangelical Theological Society* 54, no. 2 (June 2011): 279–297.

Silva, Moisés. *Biblical Words and Their Meaning: An Introduction to Lexical Semantics*. Rev. and Expanded ed. Grand Rapids: Zondervan, 1994.

Simmers, Gary. "Who Is 'The Angel of the Lord'?" *Faith and Mission* 17, no.

3 (2000): 3–16.

Ska, Jean Louis. *"Our Fathers Have Told Us": Introduction to the Analysis of Hebrew Narratives.* Subsidia Biblica 13. Roma: Editrice Pontificio Instituto Biblico, 1990.

Slotemaker, John T. *""Fuisse in Forma Hominis"* Belongs to Christ Alone': John Calvin's Trinitarian Hermeneutics in His *Lectures on Ezekiel."* *Scottish Journal of Theology* 68, no. 4 (November 2015): 421–436.

Smith, Mark S. *The Idea of Nicaea in the Early Church Councils, AD 431-451.* Oxford: Oxford University Press, 2018.

———. *The Origins of Biblical Monotheism: Israel's Polytheistic Background and the Ugaritic Texts.* Oxford University Press, USA, 2003.

Stead, George Christopher. *Divine Substance.* Oxford: Clarendon Press, 1977.

Steinmetz, David C. "The Superiority of Precritical Exegesis." In *A Guide to Contemporary Hermeneutics: Major Trends in Biblical Interpretation*, edited by Donald K. McKim. Grand Rapids: Eerdmans, 1986.

Strawn, Brent A. "The Poetics of Psalm 82: Three Critical Notes along with a Plea for the Poetic." *Revue Biblique (1946-)* 121, no. 1 (2014): 21–46.

Stuart, Douglas K. *Exodus.* The New American Commentary v. 2. Nashville: Broadman & Holman Publishers, 2006.

Taylor, Charles. *Modern Social Imaginaries.* Public Planet Books. Durham: Duke University Press, 2004.

Tipton, Lane G. *The Trinitarian Theology of Cornelius Van Til.* Libertyville, Ill.: Reformed Forum, 2022.

Torrance, Thomas F. "The Trinitarian Mind." In *The Christian Doctrine of God, One Being Three Persons*, 73–111. Paperback ed. London: T&T Clark, 2001.

Trotter, James M. "Death of the 'lhym in Psalm 82." *Journal of Biblical Literature* 131 (2012): 221–239.

Trueman, Carl R. *The Creedal Imperative.* Wheaton: Crossway, 2012.

————. *The Rise and Triumph of the Modern Self: Cultural Amnesia, Expressive Individualism, and the Road to Sexual Revolution*. Wheaton: Crossway, 2020.

Truggy, Dale. "On Bauckham's Bargain." *Theology Today* 70, no. 2 (2013): 128–43.

Tsevat, Matitiahu. "God and the Gods in Assembly: An Interpretation of Psalm 82." *Hebrew Union College Annual* 40 (1969): 123–137.

Tsumura, David Toshio. "Vertical Grammar of Parallelism in Hebrew Poetry." *Journal of Biblical Literature* 128, no. 1 (2009): 167–181.

Van Til, Cornelius. *A Christian Theory of Knowledge*. Philadelphia: Presbyterian and Reformed Pub Co., 1969.

————. *An Introduction to Systematic Theology*. In Defense of the Faith V. Presbyterian and Reformed Pub. Co., 1974.

————. *The Defense of the Faith*. Edited by K. Scott Oliphint. 4th ed. Phillipsburg: P & R Pub, 2008.

VanGemeren, Willem. *Psalms*. Edited by Tremper Longman III and David E. Garland. Revised Edition. Vol. 5. The Expositor's Bible Commentary: Grand Rapids: Zondervan, 2008.

Vanhoozer, Kevin J. *Biblical Authority after Babel: Retrieving the Solas in the Spirit of Mere Protestant Christianity*. Grand Rapids: Brazos, 2016.

Vanhoozer, Kevin J., Craig G Bartholomew, Daniel J. Treier, and N. T. Wright, eds. *Dictionary for Theological Interpretation of the Bible*. Baker Academic, 2005.

Vogel, H. "The Angel of the Lord." *Wisconsin Lutheran Quarterly* 73, no. 2 (April 1976): 105–118.

de Vries, Pieter. *The Kābôd of YHWH in the Old Testament: With Particular Reference to the Book of Ezekiel*. Studia Semitica Neerlandica volume 65. Leiden: Brill, 2016.

————. "The Relationship between the Glory of YHWH and the Spirit of YHWH in the Book of Ezekiel Part One." *Journal of Biblical and Pneumatological Research* 5 (2013): 109–127.

Wallace, Daniel B. *Greek Grammar Beyond the Basics: An Exegetical Syntax of the New Testament with Scripture, Subject, and Greek Word Indexes*. Grand Rapids: Zondervan, 1996.

Waltke, Bruce K., and Michael Patrick O'Connor. *An Introduction to Biblical Hebrew Syntax*. Winona Lake, Ind.: Eisenbrauns, 1990.

Waltke, Bruce K., and Charles Yu. *An Old Testament Theology: An Exegetical, Canonical, and Thematic Approach*. 1st ed. Grand Rapids: Zondervan, 2007.

Watts, Rikk E. *Isaiah's New Exodus in Mark*. Biblical studies library. Grand Rapids: Baker Books, 2000.

———. "Mark." In *Commentary on the New Testament Use of the Old Testament*, edited by G. K. Beale and D. A. Carson. Grand Rapids: Baker Academic, 2007.

Webster, John. "What Makes Theology Theological?" In *God Without Measure: Working Papers in Christian Theology*. Vol. I. T&T Clark Theology. London ; New York: Bloomsbury T&T Clark, 2016.

Weeks, Noel. "Problems with the Comparative Method in Old Testament Studies." *Journal of the Evangelical Theological Society* 62, no. 2 (2019): 287–306.

Wellhausen, Julius. *Prolegomena to the History of Israel*. Reprint of the 1885 ed. Atlanta: Scholars Press, 1994.

West, M. L. "The Metre of Arius' 'Thalia.'" *The Journal of Theological Studies* 33, no. 1 (1982): 98–105.

West, M L (Martin Litchfield). "Towards Monotheism." In *Pagan Monotheism in Late Antiquity*, 21–40. Oxford, 1999.

Wilcox, Peter, and David Paton-Williams. "The Servant Songs in Deutero-Isaiah." *Journal for the Study of the Old Testament* 13, no. 42 (October 1988): 79–102.

Wildberger, Hans. *Isaiah: Isaiah 1-12*. Fortress Press, 1991.

Williams, Rowan. *Arius: Heresy and Tradition*. 2. ed. London: SCM, 2001.

————. "The Nicene Heritage." In *The Christian Understanding of God Today: Theological Colloquium on the Occasion of the 400th Anniversary of the Foundation of Trinity College, Dublin*, edited by James M. Byrne, 45–48. Dublin: Columba Press, 1993.

Witherington, Ben. *Matthew*. Smyth & Helwys Bible Commentary. Macon, Ga: Smyth & Helwys Publishing, 2006.

Woods, Edward J. *Deuteronomy: An Introduction and Commentary*. Downers Grove: IVP Academic, 2011.

Wright, Christopher. *Deuteronomy*. NIBC. Peabody: Hendrickson, 1996.

————. *Knowing Jesus Through the Old Testament*. Westmont: InterVarsity Press, 2014.

Young, Edward J. *The Book of Isaiah*. Vol. 1. 3 vols. Grand Rapids: Eerdmans, 1965.

Young, Frances M. *From Nicaea to Chalcedon: A Guide to the Literature and Its Background*. 2nd ed. London: SCM Press, 2010.

Zachhuber, Johannes. "Basil and the Three-Hypostases Tradition: Reconsidering the Origins of Cappadocian Theology." *Zeitschrift für antikes Christentum* 5, no. 1 (2001): 65–85.

————. "Derivative Genera in Apollinarius of Laodicea." In *Apollinaris Und Die Folgen*, 93–114. Studien und Texte zu Antike und Christentum 93. Tübingen: Mohr Siebeck, 2015.

————. *Human Nature in Gregory of Nyssa: Philosophical Background and Theological Significance*. Brill, 1999.

————. "Once Again: Gregory of Nyssa on Universals." *The Journal of Theological Studies* 56, no. 1 (April 2005): 75–98.

————. *The Rise of Christian Theology and the End of Ancient Metaphysics: Patristic Philosophy from the Cappadocian Fathers to John of Damascus*. Oxford University Press, 2020.

Zizioulas, Jean. *Being as Communion: Studies in Personhood and the Church*. London: Darton Longman & Todd, 2004.

J. Alexander Rutherford

ABOUT TELEIOTETI

Teleioteti (Τελειοτητι, te-ley-o-tey-tee)—meaning "unto maturity"—is dedicated to faithful, thoughtful ministry. We create resources for Christian discipleship, resources that address theological and pastoral concerns from a Biblical worldview. Our purpose is to see Christ's Church mature in its understanding of God and His Word. We do this through the production of Gospel-centred materials that connect the Bible with the heads, hearts, and minds of Christians. We hope to enable Christians from all walks of life to better understand and glorify God through service in His Church.

To achieve this purpose, Teleioteti publishes online materials and books researched with academic rigour yet based upon Biblical presuppositions. That is, we are neither academic nor lazy. We use methods, or epistemology, informed by the Bible along with the hard work usually associated with professional research and study. We produce resources directed towards all Christians, but most of our resources are directed towards students, pastors, and theologically inclined lay Christians.

To learn more about us and what we are doing, please visit us at https://teleioteti.ca or contact us at info@teleioteti.ca. If you have found this resource helpful, prayerfully consider supporting us by giving a review on the web (e.g. Amazon, Goodreads, etc.), praying with and for us, or giving financially so that we can produce more resources like this one. For more information on how you can support us, visit us at https://teleioteti.ca/about/partner/ or at our page on Patreon,

Other Books by J. Alexander Rutherford

God's Kingdom through his Priest-King: An Analysis of the Book of Samuel in Light of the Davidic Covenant (Teleioteti, 2019)

Though many studies have probed the significance of the Davidic Covenant (2 Sam 7:1-17) within the biblical canon, few have endeavoured to explore its significance within the narrative of Samuel. This thesis argues that by weaving references to God's promises made to David (collectively known as the Davidic Covenant) throughout his narrative, the author of Samuel reveals God's will to strip away all human pretension by bringing his promises to fulfilment through the lowly David, whose ascension to kingship and endurance therein is owing all to God. In this way, the author fulfils his purpose to demonstrate God's sovereign working in history to establish his kingdom on earth through his chosen priest-king, a descendant of David, in fulfilment of the promises he made beforehand. Engaging in a literary close-reading of the text of Samuel, the author shows how the narrative of Samuel is shaped towards this end.

Endorsements:

In the present environment of high interest in the Book of Samuel, this contribution by James Rutherford is most welcome. Rutherford is well versed in current scholarship on Samuel, but his work moves well beyond this scholarship to contribute fresh insights, not least in respect of the priestly character of King David. And concerning its structure, Rutherford argues that the Book of Samuel as a whole is arranged and narrated so as to draw attention to the centrality of the Davidic Covenant of 2 Samuel 7. Having myself studied 1 and 2 Samuel for decades now, I was nevertheless benefitted at numerous points from Rutherford's creative interpretive suggestions. His is a work well conceived, well written, and worthy of a serious read.

- V. Philips Long, PhD Cambridge
  Professor of Old Testament, Regent College

This thesis argues that by weaving references to God's promises made to King David throughout his narrative, the author of Samuel reveals God's will to strip away all human pretension by bringing his promises to fulfilment through a lowly man whose ascension to kingship and endurance therein is entirely owing to God. In this way, the Samuel author fulfils his purpose of demonstrating God's sovereign working in history to establish his kingdom on earth through his chosen priest-king, a descendant of David. The thesis represents an excellent piece of work that does a great job of bringing together into one coherent argument, focused on the Davidic covenant, much of the best recent narrative-critical research on 1-2 Samuel, and from this point of view represents a distinctive contribution to the field of Samuel studies.

- Iain Provan, PhD Cambridge
  Marshall Sheppard Professor of Biblical Studies, Regent College

Prevenient Grace: An Investigation into Arminianism, 2nd Revised Edition (Teleioteti, 2020)

When a building is built on a poor foundation, the inevitable result is its collapse. But this isn't a book on architecture; foundations are found in thought structures as well as in material structures. In theology, a bad foundation will produce results as catastrophic as a bad foundation in architecture. How we think about God and His work in the world will profoundly affect how we live and work out our Christian faith; is your foundation strong? This book evolved from the conviction that a prominent theological system rests on a fragile foundation.

Endorsements:

This book is a fine piece of scholarship. Rutherford presents his arguments with admirable clarity. His intention is to offer guidance for pastors and teachers who may be faced with questions about whether human beings have the freedom to accept or reject God. The great strength of Rutherford's book is his knowledge of Biblical texts and an appropriate interpretation of them. He successfully shows that the claims of Arminianism with its view that prevenient grace allows an acceptance or rejection of God are not supported by Biblical texts. Nor are they justified by philosophical arguments. They layout of the book and its careful treatment of arguments both for and against prevenient grace is a model of excellent writing. His chapters are supplemented by a Glossary that explains all specific terms and Appendices where detailed theological discussions are given. Most helpful is his Index of Scripture passages discussed.

- Dr. Shirley Sullivan, FRSC (elected), Professor Emeritus of Classics, University of British Columbia

Believe the Unbelievable: A Study in the Book of Habakkuk (Teleioteti, 2018)

What would we do if our prayers for justice, our prayers that God's will be done in our nation, were answered with a vision of desolation, of utter destruction?

When Habakkuk prayed for salvation, a prayer for justice in the midst of chaos, violence, and suffering, that was God's answer. He revealed in a vision the invasion of the vicious armies of Babylon. God's answer contradicted everything Habakkuk thought he knew. Yet in the end, he praised God and trusted him for this horrid salvation.

What do we do when God's actions or words contradict our understanding, contradict what we have believed? The book of Habakkuk answers this question in the face of the Babylonian invasion of Judah. Habakkuk is a book of discipleship, a book written to bring its reader to a deeper faith in Yahweh in the presence of His unthinkable deeds.

Using study questions addressing the text, theology, and application of Habakkuk and explanatory comments on difficult themes, *Believe the Unbelievable* seeks to realize this purpose for the contemporary reader.

Endorsements:

James Rutherford is a capable and creative thinker, well equipped to tackle tough projects, such as the book of Habakkuk. In this study guide, Rutherford has produced a very useful resource for individual or group study. He combines theological acumen and well-honed linguistic and literary skills to discover and then to present, in highly understandable fashion, the riches of this not so "minor" Minor Prophet.

- V. Philips Long, PhD Cambridge
  Professor of Old Testament, Regent College

My good friend, James Rutherford, has given the church a gift. He has taken his love for God's Word and focused it on an Old Testament book that most Christians know very little about. The result is a study in Habakkuk that brings together deep insight and real relevance. Habakkuk is a voice among the Biblical chorus that believers need to hear today. Thank you, James, for helping us to hear it clearly and faithfully.

- Fredrick Eaton
  Pastor

www.ingramcontent.com/pod-product-compliance
Lightning Source LLC
Chambersburg PA
CBHW021703120626
46545CB00004B/1384